The World of
Agha Shahid Ali

The World of Agha Shahid Ali

Edited by

TAPAN KUMAR GHOSH
SISIR KUMAR CHATTERJEE

Original cover design by Debmalya Chatterjee

Published by State University of New York Press, Albany

© 2021 State University of New York

All rights reserved

Printed in the United States of America

No part of this book may be used or reproduced in any manner whatsoever without written permission. No part of this book may be stored in a retrieval system or transmitted in any form or by any means including electronic, electrostatic, magnetic tape, mechanical, photocopying, recording, or otherwise without the prior permission in writing of the publisher.

For information, contact State University of New York Press, Albany, NY
www.sunypress.edu

Library of Congress Cataloging-in-Publication Data

Names: Ghosh, Tapan Kumar, editor | Chatterjee, Sisir Kumar, editor.
Title: The world of Agha Shahid Ali / edited by Tapan Kumar Ghosh and Sisir Kumar Chatterjee.
Description: Albany : State University of New York Press, [2021] | Includes bibliographical references and index.
Identifiers: ISBN 9781438481456 (hardcover : alk. paper) | ISBN 9781438484334 (ebook) | ISBN 9781438481449 (pbk. : alk. paper)
Further information is available at the Library of Congress.

10 9 8 7 6 5 4 3 2 1

Contents

Preface ... ix

Agha Shahid Ali: A Chronology ... xi

Abbreviations ... xv

Introduction ... 1
    Tapan Kumar Ghosh and Sisir Kumar Chatterjee

1. Ghazal for Open Hands ... 31
    Martin Espada

2. Shahid, Some Memories ... 33
    Peter Balakian

3. Somewhere without Me My Life Begins ... 39
    Dara Wier

4. Beloved Witness, Beloved Friend ... 43
    Maureen Nolan

5. Agha Shahid Ali: Notes and Anecdotes on the Growth of the Poet ... 51
    Fatima Noori

6. "Separation's Geography": Agha Shahid Ali's Scholarship of Evanescence ... 71
    Amy Newman

7	Agha Shahid Ali and the Ghazals in English *Sagaree Sengupta*	89
8	"I will open the waves": Examining the Hybrid Forms in Agha Shahid Ali's Poetry *Abin Chakraborty*	99
9	Out of Focus: Agha Shahid Ali's Queer Optics *Gayatri Gopinath*	111
10	Beginnings: A Journey with Micronarratives *Amzed Hossein*	121
11	Braiding Disparate Strands: Tracing the Arcs of Agha Shahid Ali's *The Half-Inch Himalayas* *Jason A. Schneiderman*	133
12	Dialing a Joke: Agha Shahid Ali's Long-Distance Calls to Lands without a Post Office *Vedatrayee Banerjee*	141
13	Archiving Absences: Charting Chronotopes in Agha Shahid Ali's Cartography of Desire *Deeptesh Sen*	149
14	Tradition, Home, and Exile in Agha Shahid Ali's *The Beloved Witness* *Christine Kitano*	161
15	"It Is This": Agha Shahid Ali's Representation of Kashmir in *The Country without a Post Office* *Claire Chambers*	173
16	Epistemology of Mourning: A Reading of *Rooms Are Never Finished* *Sisir Kumar Chatterjee and Sinchan Chatterjee*	187
17	Let Your Mirrored Convexities Multiply: On Agha Shahid Ali's *"Tonight"* *Kazim Ali*	219

18	An Interview with Agha Shahid Ali *Suvir Kaul*	225

Bibliography 237

About the Editors 241

About the Contributors 243

Index 249

Preface

Agha Shahid Ali (1949–2001) holds a place of singular distinction as a poet in the ever-expanding Indian diaspora. Born in Delhi and brought up in Srinagar and Indiana, Shahid spent most of his adult life in the United States, and died there. It is thus not easy to define his nationality. He had a transnational background and multicultural affiliations. Kashmir, Delhi (old and new) and the United States feature prominently in his poetry, and he has drawn the geographic and cultural maps of these places like a nostalgist cartographer. Exile, separation, transience, limitless longing and loss (of home, history, and people one loves) recur in his poems, which weave past and present, tradition and modernity, myth and reality, and various historical, cultural, and religious strands as well as multiple personalities to create his unique identity. A citizen of a "country without a post office," a country torn asunder by hatred and violence, Shahid sought throughout his poetic career to bridge gaps between cultures, languages, ethnicities, and religions. Communication, and the lack of it, between peoples and places were obsessive concerns of Shahid as a Kashmiri-American poet. He experimented with various European poetic forms, but his lasting contribution to poetry in English is the introduction of the oriental genre, *ghazal*—with its intricacies and mysteries—to Western readers. He inherited the "ravishing disunities" of the real ghazals from his literary predecessors in the East, and passed them on to his followers in the West. Beloved of all who knew and read him, Agha Shahid Ali grieved for suffering humanity, and his poetry bore witness to the mutating world in the last quarter of the twentieth century.

The present volume is a pioneering collection of essays that explore the world of this peerless poet. The first nine essays attempt to examine the personality, worldview, and poetic style of Agha Shahid Ali. Four of the contributors were intimate friends of Shahid and had seen him from close quarters. Their observation sheds crucial light on the poet's character and temperament. The others probe little-known aspects of this transgeographic poet and his unique craft. The rest of the volume focuses on Shahid's poetic oeuvre, including essays on individual collections of poems, from *Bone Sculpture* to *Call me Ishmael Tonight*.

This book is the first venture of its kind to critically analyze Agha Shahid Ali's poetry at a close and comprehensive level and to put his hyphenated identity and transnational background into perspective. Most of his well-known poems are interpreted by the contributors, who also specify his roots, influences, and contribution. In sum, this anthology of essays is a useful addition to the growing discussion of Agha Shahid Ali as a poet.

A number of people have helped us bring out this volume. We are grateful to them and to the contributors from India and abroad who have submitted well-researched articles to this collection. We are deeply indebted to Professor Suvir Kaul for permitting us to reprint his interview with Agha Shahid Ali, which was recorded at the Mass Communications Research Center, Jamia Milia Islamia, New Delhi, in August 1997. We acknowledge our special debt to the editors of SUNY Press, especially James Peltz and Christopher Ahn, as well as to Patricia O'Neill, Dara Wier, Gayatri Gopinath, the SUNY Press–commissioned anonymous reviewers of the initial versions of our manuscript, Somnath and Sipra Ghosh, and Krishna Chatterjee and Vedatrayee Banerjee, without whose whole-hearted cooperation this book would never have seen the light of the day or attained its level of quality.

Tapan Kumar Ghosh
Sisir Kumar Chatterjee

Agha Shahid Ali

A Chronology

1949   Agha Shahid Ali was born in New Delhi on February 4 to Agha Ashraf Ali and his wife Sufia. Shahid's father's family was from Srinagar in Kashmir; his mother was from Lucknow in Uttar Pradesh. They were Shia Muslims. Shahid's ancestors had come to Kashmir from Central Asia. They were trained as *hakims* (practitioners of Unani medicine) and appointed as court physicians of Kashmir. His great grandfather was the first Kashmiri Muslim to matriculate, and his grandmother was the Inspector of women's schools. She knew four languages: Urdu, Farsi, Kashmiri, and English.

1961   Agha Ashraf Ali, then the principal of Teachers' College in Srinagar, traveled to the United States with his family to complete a PhD in Comparative Education at Ball State Teachers College in Muncie, Indiana. Shahid was twelve years old. For the next three years he attended school in Indiana.

1964   The family returned to Srinagar. Shahid attended an elite Irish Catholic school.

1968   Shahid earned his BA degree from the University of Kashmir.

1970   He joined Hindu College in Delhi University for studies toward an MA in English literature. He passed with distinction and went on to become a lecturer at the same college. He served this college from 1970 to 1975.

1972	His first collection of poems, *Bone-Sculpture*, was published by professor P. Lal's Writers Workshop in Calcutta.
1976	Shahid returned to the United States.
1979	*In Memory of Begum Akhtar and Other Poems* was published by the Writers Workshop.
1981	Earned his MA in English from Pennsylvania State University.
1982	Received Breadloaf Writers' Conference scholarship.
1983	Won Academy of American Poets prize and Pennsylvania Council on the Arts fellowship.
1983–1985	Served as Communications Editor, JNC Companies, Tucson, Arizona.
1984	Earned a PhD at Pennsylvania State University.
1985	Earned a Masters in Fine Arts in Creative Writing at the University of Arizona.
1987–1993	Taught as Assistant Professor of English and Creative Writing at Hamilton College, New York.
1986	Publication of his PhD thesis, *T. S. Eliot as Editor*.
1987	Publication of *The Half-Inch Himalayas* and *A Walk Through the Yellow Pages*.
1987	Received Ingram Merrill Foundation Fellowship.
1987–1993	Visiting Professor of Creative Writing at State University of New York.
1991	Publication of *A Nostalgist's Map of America*. Shahid wrote the poems in the anthology in the years he began a close friendship with poet James Merrill.
1992	Publication of *The Beloved Witness: Selected Poems* and *The Rebel's Silhouette: Selected Poems of Faiz Ahmed Faiz* (translated by Agha Shahid Ali).
1993	Associate Professor of English, University of Massachusetts, Amherst. Received New York Foundation for the Arts Fellowship.

1994	Recorded *Distinct Traditions, Myths and Voices of the Many Americans* as part of the Poetics Program, SUNY at Buffalo.
1997	Publication of *The Country without a Post Office*.
1998	Shahid's mother died in Amherst and was buried in Srinagar. The journey occasioned some memorable poems published in a later collection.
2000	Publication of *Ravishing DisUnities: Real Ghazals in English*, co-edited by Agha Shahid Ali and Sara Suleri Goodyear.
2001	Publication of *Rooms Are Never Finished*, the last volume of poems to appear before Shahid's death. The book became a finalist for the National Book Award, 2001.
2001	Shahid died on December 8 of brain cancer, the same affliction that had claimed his mother's life three years earlier.
2003	Posthumous publication of *Call Me Ishmael Tonight*, a collection of Shahid's English ghazals.

Abbreviations

BS	*Bone-Sculpture*
BW	*The Beloved Witness: Selected Poems*
CMIT	*Call Me Ishmael Tonight*
CWPO	*The Country without a Post Office*
HIH	*The Half-Inch Himalayas*
IMBA	*In Memory of Begum Akhtar & Other Poems*
NMP	*A Nostalgist's Map of America*
RANF	*Rooms Are Never Finished*
RDRG	*Ravishing DisUnities: Real Ghazals in English*
RS	*The Rebel's Silhouette: Selected Poems*
TSEE	*T. S. Eliot as Editor*
VS	*The Veiled Suite: The Collected Poems*
WTYP	*A Walk Through the Yellow Pages*

Introduction

Shahid and His Life

TAPAN KUMAR GHOSH
SISIR KUMAR CHATTERJEE

> "They ask me to tell them what *Shahid* means—
> Listen: It means 'The Beloved' in Persian, 'witness' in Arabic." ("Ghazal")

Agha Shahid Ali was born in New Delhi on February 4, 1949, eighteen months after India's independence. His father hailed from Srinagar in Kashmir, and his mother from Rudauli in Uttar Pradesh. Shahid's ancestors, who were Shia Muslims, had come to Kashmir from central Asia.[1] They were *hakims,* practitioners of unani medicine, and appointed as court physicians of Kashmir. Shahid's great-grandfather was the first Kashmiri Muslim to matriculate and later to be appointed as an official in the court of the Maharaja of Kashmir.[2] His grandmother was one of the first educated women of Kashmir. She passed the matriculation and took several other degrees and became the Inspector of Women's Schools. She could quote poetry from four languages: Urdu, Farsi, Kashmiri, and English. Shahid's father, Agha Ashraf Ali, carried on the family tradition of public service in education. He taught at Jamia Milia University in New Delhi and later became the principal of the Teachers College in Srinagar. In 1961, when Shahid was twelve years old, Ashraf Ali went to the United States with his family to pursue a PhD degree in comparative education at Ball State Teachers College in Indiana. For the next three years, young Shahid attended school in

Indiana. Later his family returned to Srinagar, where Shahid completed his schooling. What is important about this early exposure to America is that Shahid was able to take the country in his stride when he returned there as a post-graduate student in the mid-1970s. The cultural divide that troubles many a diasporic writer had hardly any effect on Shahid. He felt physically at home in both countries, although psychologically and philosophically he was stuck in a state of perpetual reterritorialization and deterritorialization, to put it in geophilosophical terms.

Shahid started writing poems at the age of nine, and his medium of expression became English. In the introductory essay on his translation of Faiz Ahmed Faiz's Urdu poems, *The Rebel's Silhouette* (1995), he made a clear distinction between his mother tongue, which for him was Urdu, and his first language, which was English. He was, however, aware of the pitfalls of using English as his poetic medium and of the criticism that he would invite from the votaries of nationalism in postcolonial India. In an early poem, "dear editor" (*Bone-Sculpture*), he writes in a justificatory tone:

> call me a poet
>   dear editor
> they call this my alien language
>
> i am a dealer in words
> that mix cultures
> and leave me rootless. (1–6)

Shahid received his BA degree from the University of Kashmir, and in 1968 he joined Hindu College in Delhi to study toward an MA in English literature. He passed with distinction and was soon appointed as a lecturer at the same college. It was during this period that he published his first collection of poems, *Bone-Sculpture* (1972), with professor P. Lal's Writers Workshop in Calcutta. This was followed by *In Memory of Begum Akhtar & Other Poems*, in 1979, also published by the Writers Workshop.

Shahid returned to the United States in 1976 and earned a PhD degree at Pennsylvania State University for his dissertation on T. S. Eliot, which was later published as a book entitled *T. S. Eliot as Editor* (1986). He then went on to earn a Master of Fine Arts (MFA) degree in creative writing at the University of Arizona, which led to his procuring a job of teaching at Hamilton College in New York in 1987. In 1993, he became a professor of English in the MFA program at the University of Massachusetts at Amherst. Shahid was a successful teacher, much admired by his students and colleagues. He was loved by all who came into contact with him and who read his poetry. Through his spirit of hospitality, as well as his culinary skills, he won the hearts of friends and acquaintances alike. After 1976, Shahid lived primarily in the United States. His parents continued to live in Srinagar, and it became his custom to spend the summer months with them every year. "I always move in my sad heart between countries," he told Amitav Ghosh during a conversation.[3] Traveling between two countries, between home and the world, Shahid thus became an intermittent but first-hand witness to the escalating violence that seized Kashmir from the late 1980s onward.

Shahid's sexuality (more specifically, his "gay" identity) has been a subject of great interest to critics. Shahid has been generally categorized as a homosexual or gay poet. But very little is truly known about his sexuality, although he was known to have had a number of intimate relationships with both men and women. Moreover, only one critic, Hoshang Merchant, has highlighted Shahid's gayness.[4] Perhaps the best way to define Shahid's sexuality would be to describe him as a "Queer" poet, although his queerness is related less to his biological orientation and more to his artistic philosophy and poetics. Shahid himself asserted: "Sex is very central to my *way of looking at the world*."[5] In the context of Shahid's sexual orientation, Gayatri Gopinath provides the most significant clue in her essay "Out of Focus: Agha Shahid Ali's Queer Optics" (which is included in this book), where she contends that Shahid was "neither a closeted homosexual nor an explicitly out gay poet; indeed the dichotomy of closet vs. Outness, public vs. Private, are relatively meaningless categories in relation to both his life and work." In Arizona in early 1995, Shahid married a much older woman, Jamie Stanley Taylor, to whom he dedicated *A Nostalgist's Map of America*. Their marriage lasted almost seven years, before Shahid died on December 8, 2001, of brain cancer, an affliction that had claimed his mother's life three years earlier.

A brief account of Shahid's upbringing and sociocultural background evinces that he hailed from a culturally sophisticated and socially enlightened upper-class Muslim family. Three languages—Urdu, Kashmiri, and English—were commonly spoken in the Shahid household. Poems were recited in these languages, and poets and musicians frequently visited their home. It was a culturally rich atmosphere, with no hint of any kind of parochialism in the house. The family's tolerance extended to religious affairs, and Shahid was educated at an Irish Catholic school only because the school was an elite institution in Kashmir. In an interview with Christine Benvenuto,[6] Shahid said, "When I was a kid, I remember telling my parents that I wanted to build a little Hindu temple in my room, and they said sure. And then once I said I wanted to build a Catholic chapel with pictures of Jesus, and they said sure, they brought me statues of Jesus, they brought me statues of Krishna, they said go ahead, build your temple. It was a wonderful atmosphere full of possibilities of self-expression." It is thus no wonder that Shahid's worldview was essentially humanist and absolutely free of insularity or dogmatism. His political views were influenced largely by his father,[5] whose beliefs were akin to those of the most secular, left-leaning Muslim intellectuals of the Nehruvian era. Although respectful of religion, Shahid firmly believed in the separation of politics from religious practice.

Shahid was an exile, albeit a self-exile, as he had not been politically forced into his position. He voluntarily chose to live in the United States for personal and professional purposes. One can identify his voice as "a kind of deeply rooted, and yet cosmopolitan voice with a deep desire for internationalism."[7] His poetry draws materials from three major cultures—Hindu, Muslim and Christian—which formed an inextricable part of his intellectual and emotional make-up. He made use of Greek, Hindu, and Islamic myths, as he had been exposed to all of these while growing up. Shahid's poems are highly allusive, and his allusions operate in a transcultural and transgeographic mode that weaves different locations, histories, and literary traditions into a richly complex artistic web. His readers come across frequent intertextual references to a host of canonical poets including W. B. Yeats, T. S. Eliot, G. M. Hopkins, W. H. Auden, Emily Dickinson, Faiz Ahmed Faiz, and Osip Mandelstam. But the greatest influence on Shahid's poetry came from the American poet James Merrill, who was in many ways Shahid's friend, philosopher, and guide. He once said to Christine Benvenuto: "I value [Merrill] immensely as a presence in my work, I would say he's in some ways the formal spirit guiding me through *The Country without a Post Office*."[8] Shahid dedicated this book of poems to Merrill. In his later poems, too, James Merrill, like Osip Mandelstam, makes significant appearances. However, Merrill's influence on Shahid's poetry was largely formalistic, while that of Mandelstam was political.

Exile, separation, loss (of home, history, and loved ones), evanescence, death and longing without limit reappear time and again as themes in Shahid's poetry, although from *Bone-Sculpture* to *Rooms Are Never Finished* the only subject that remains constant is Kashmir, his "imaginary homeland" whose geographical and cultural map he has drawn and redrawn like an expert cartographer. In reply to a question asked by Stacey Chase: "What do you regard as the major themes that you keep coming back to?," Shahid said, "It is a sensibility more than a theme. And the sensibility seems informed by a sense of loss. Things vanishing. Loss. And this can take place in an engagement with language, in an engagement with landscape, in an engagement with history, in an engagement with myth and legend. In all of them, there seems to be . . . this overriding sense of the evanescent, the vanishing. And I suppose that's what inspires me to write."[9] Throughout his poetic career Shahid followed the "route of evanescence" to draw a nostalgist's map of "separation's geography" and "desolation's desert." An acute awareness of transience and of ineluctable separation from, and loss of, persons and things one loves most is the central ontological condition of Shahid's poetry.

Agha Shahid Ali and His Work

Agha Shahid Ali's poetic career began with the publication of *Bone-Sculpture* in 1972. This volume (published in Calcutta by Writers Workshop) is the work of a budding poet who has not yet found his distinctive individual poetic voice. The influence of Euro-American modernists such as Eliot, Yeats, and Auden is too obvious to be overlooked. The opening poem "Bones," for example, is reminiscent of Eliot's "The Waste Land":

> The years are dead. I'm
> twenty, a mourner in the Mohorrum
> Procession, mixing blood with
> mud, memory with memory. I'm
> still alone. (11)

Loneliness, cultural dislocation, and separation from family and home coexist alongside the poet's personal obsessions with death, memory, history, ancestors, and a past he knows little about. "Bone" is a recurring image, and the volume features several poems about death and funeral pyres. A wry, cynical, almost Eliotian humor marks a poem named "Cremation" in which a person's bones refuse to burn when fire is set to his flesh. It evokes the speaker to remark caustically: "who would have guessed / you'd be stubborn in death?" There is no narrative link among these poems, and they "anticipate the surreal, somewhat grotesque lyricism" found in Shahid's later poetry.[10]

Shahid's focus in his second collection of poems, *In Memory of Begum Akhtar* (1979), is on Old Delhi and its Mughal history and culture. The title poem is an elegy for the renowned ghazal singer Begum Akhtar whom Shahid had idolized and who, like his own mother, had left a deeply abiding influence on his poetry. The news of the sad demise of Begum Akhtar, one of the finest ghazal singers in the subcontinent, who had "finally polished catastrophe, / the note [she] seasoned / with decades of Ghalib, / Mir, Faiz," made Shahid 'wish to talk of the end of the world.'" He also wrote poems on Thumri singer Rasoolan Bai, whose house in Ahmedabad was burnt during the riots in 1969; K. L. Saigal, who made Shahid nostalgic about his father's youth and his "wasted generation"; and Satyajit Ray's *Pather Panchali*. There are seven poems on the walled city, one each on Jama Masjid and The Jama Masjid Butcher. "Qawwali at Nizamuddin Aulia's Dargah" describes how the Mughal dynasty fell to the plunder of Persian Nadir Shah:

> That drunk debauched colourful king
> dances again with hoofs of sorrow
> as Nadir skins the air with swords,
> horses galloping
> to the rhythm
> of a dying
> dynasty. (29–35)

The partition of India, which also divided communities and cultures, features as prominently as Urdu and its most famous poet Ghalib, "who, at the crossroads of language, / refusing to move to / any side, masqueraded / as a beggar to see / our theatre of kindness." Two "Autobiographical" notes inform the poet's loss of faith in the family religion of Islam and its reason:

> Dreams of Islam crumbled for me
> when our servant, his shoes
> stolen at the mosque,
> turned deaf to the muezzin's call. (1–4)

After this incident his "tongue forgot the texture of prayer" and his "voice cracked on Ghalib." Once again, one finds the note of loss and nostalgia for pre-partition India with its rich Islamic culture and the poet's painful awareness of evanescence, of time passing. This second book also reveals Shahid's skill in weaving repetitive images and symbols as well as recurrent places, themes, and biographical details into the thematic structures of his poems.

Shahid became a recognizable poetic voice with the publication of two collections of poems in 1987: *The Half-Inch Himalayas* and *A Walk Through the Yellow Pages*. In fact, the years between 1987 and 1997 were the most productive in Shahid's poetic career. During this period, he published five anthologies—two in 1987—and translated Faiz Ahmed Faiz's Urdu poems into English (*The Rebel's Silhouette: Selected Poems by Faiz Ahmed Faiz*). Each anthology bears signs of the poet's gradually increasing maturity. By this time Shahid had settled permanently in the United States and, despite his annual visits to Srinagar, his relationship with Kashmir—and by extension India—had become tenuous. Kashmir was now, more or less, "an imaginary homeland" inhabited only in memory. But the poems written at this stage evince increased referential range, improved poetic technique, and confident use of American idiom. *The Half-Inch Himalayas* (1987) marks Shahid's transition from India to America. Of the thirty poems in this collection, twenty-three are set in India and the rest are located in his new home. The opening poem "Postcard from Kashmir" introduces the theme of the anthology: exile, loss of home, and the impossibility of reclaiming it except through memory, as the speaker in this poem laments that it is only the Kashmir printed on the postcard (which has now shrunk into his mailbox), a mere simulacrum of his native place, that is "the closest" he will "ever be to home." In a number of poems of this volume Shahid conjures up his past and family history. "A Lost Memory of Delhi," for example, describes the time immediately before the poet was conceived:

> I want to tell them I am their son
> older much older than they are
> I knock keep knocking
>
> but for them the night is quiet
> this the night of my being
> They don't they won't
>
> hear me they won't hear
>
> my knocking drowning out
>   the tongues of stars. (25–33)

In "A Dream of Glass Bangles" the poet imagines his mother wearing bangles, "like waves of frozen rivers," on her arms as a newly married bride. Both these poems are remarkable for their use of three-line stanza that Shahid now appeared to prefer. In some poems, he reminisces his ancestors ("Snowmen" and "Cracked Portraits") and family heirloom. An out-of-the-way reference to "Dacca gauzes" in Oscar Wilde's *The Picture of Dorian Gray* makes Shahid recall a family legend:

> Those transparent Dacca gauzes
> known as woven air, running
> water, evening dew:
>
> a dead art now, dead over
> a hundred years. "No one
> now knows," my grandmother
>   says. (1–6)

The grandmother "wore / it once, an heirloom sari from / her mother's dowry" and it "proved / genuine when it was pulled, all / six yards, through a ring." Years later, when this invaluable sari tore, the fragments were distributed as embroidered handkerchiefs among "the nieces and daughters-in-law." The familial loss is interwoven at the end with a cultural loss and a critique of colonialism as the lost heirloom becomes a metaphor of a greater tragedy underlying India's economy under British rule:

> In history we learned: the hands
> of weavers were amputated,
> the looms of Bengal silenced,
>
> and the cotton shipped raw
> by the British to England. (19–23)

Personal and familial history thus merges with the larger official history of the country. "After Seeing Kozintsev's *King Lear* in Delhi" begins with the heart-rending cry of the Shakespearean hero:

> Lear cries out "You are men of stones"
> as Cordelia hangs from a broken wall.

The poem then contrasts the former splendour of the capital of Mughal India with its present decadence and ends with a moving description of the tragic fate of the Emperor-poet Bahadur Shah Zafar:

> I think of Zafar, poet and Emperor,
> being led through this street
> by British soldiers, his feet in chains,
> to watch his sons hanged. (14–17)

The poet's imagined homeland is the multicultural and multiethnic prepartition India where his mother "played old records / of the Benaras thumri-singers, / Siddheshwari and Rasoolan, their / voices longing, when the clouds / gather, for that invisible / blue god." The poems set in America describe the poet's deracinated life that is always on the move, from one airport to another, from one apartment to another, constantly changing routes and locations, and completely devoid of memory. When he vacates an apartment, the cleaners "burn my posters / (India and Heaven in flames), / whitewash my voicestains, / make everything new, / clean as Death" ("Vacating an Apartment"). These poems reveal that by now Shahid has mastered an American poetic idiom and learned to connect poems metaphorically into loose narratives. But what is most remarkable about the poems in this volume is the poet's awareness that nothing has changed with the change of home and that "the moon did not become the sun" ("Stationary") despite his hectic, shifting journeys. His life remains as "stationary" as before, the exilic condition of a homeless foreigner haunting him as a constant reality.

A Walk Through the Yellow Pages (1987) is Shahid's all-American book, both thematically and stylistically. Published by a small Arizona press (Sun/Gemini Press, 1987), this chapbook is a collection of thirteen poems divided into six sections. The opening sequence "Bell Telephone Hours" breaks into five parts, each poem headed with a play on words taken from Bell Telephone advertisements: "Has anyone heard from you lately?"; "Call long distance: the next best thing to being there"; "It's getting late. Do your friends know where you are?" Failure of communication is a thematic trope of these poems, which often contain a grotesque humor. In the last poem of this section, a TV ad, "Today, talk is cheap. Call somebody," provokes the poet to dial the Information Desk in Heaven. But instead of the Angel of Love, it is the Angel of Death who receives his call:

> I said, "Tell me, Tell me,
> when is Doomsday?"
> He answered, "God is busy.
> He never answers the living.
> He has no answers for the dead.
> Don't ever call again collect." (15–18)

Two poems of this volume are based on language games, and one on graffiti ("Poets on Bathroom Walls"), while the last three poems are reinterpretations of Grimm's fairy tales about Hansel and Gretel and Red Riding Hood. The idiom and narrative style of these poems unveil the poet's fears and insecurities engendered by homelessness and cultural dislocation. The exilic condition prevails, and the anthology continues the surrealistic world of nightmare and fantasy that often appeared in his earlier poems.

A Nostalgist's Map of America (1991) is a collection of forty-two poems written in the years following Shahid's meeting with James Merrill, "the poet who was to alter the direction of his poetry."[11] Amitav Ghosh writes in his memoir of Agha Shahid Ali: "It was after this encounter that he began to experiment with strict metrical patterns and verse forms such as the canzone and the sestina. No one had a greater influence on Shahid's poetry than James Merrill."[12] For years Shahid would send his poems to Merrill, his American mentor. It is Merrill who wrote the blurb for *A Nostalgist's Map of America*:

> If I may speak for "America," it is a privilege to be held in so mercurial, many-faceted a gaze as this poet's, who goes to the heart of my troubles and turns them into bitter honey.

This book has a remarkable structure; it is divided into four sections with images and themes recurring in each. The epigraph to the anthology, "Eurydice," is a poem of forty-one lines that took Shahid an entire year to complete (Benvenuto). It is written from Eurydice's point of view and reworks the classical myth of Orpheus against the background of Nazi horror:

> I am a woman
> brought limping to Hell
>
> under the Night
> and Fog decree.
> But they've let him come
> here to Belsen, rare passenger
> in a river-green van. (1–7)

Belsen is a Nazi concentration camp that evokes the memory of mythical Hell. The first section of the collection is set in the American southwest, and the poems—five poems of unequal length—gradually move from personal history through myth to anthropology:

> When the desert refused my history,
> refused to acknowledge that I had lived
> there, with you, among a vanished tribe,
>
> two, three thousand years ago, you parted
> the dawn rain, its thickest monsoon curtains,
>
> and beckoned me to the northern canyons . . . ("Beyond the
>   Ash Rains," 1–6)

From recollection of "A Rehearsal of Loss," the poems trace the rituals of the Penitentes in New Mexico, "nomads of the Sangre de Cristos who / crucify, each Easter, one of their own," ("Crucifixion"), and the prehistoric culture of the Hohokam that centered along the hot Sonoran desert of Southern Arizona around 300 BC. Emily Dickinson's poem "A Route of Evanescence" serves as an epigraph for the title poem, which creates a city called "Evanescence" for the poet:

> I live in Evanescence
> (I had to build it, for America
> was without one). ("A Nostalgist's Map of America")

The poem employs Dickinson's language, images, and ideas to build a narrative of friendship that recalls a shared drive from Pennsylvania to Philadelphia. The second section, "In Search of Evanescence," consists of a sequence of eleven poems, all of which dwell on the poet's relationship with a friend named Phil who died of AIDS. He invents a hometown named Evanescence for this companion and puts it in his map of America:

>   But even
> when I pass—in Ohio—the one exit
> to Calcutta, I don't know I've begun
> mapping America, the city limits
> of Evanescence now everywhere. ("In Search of Evanescence,"
>   20–24)

The sequence follows a journey on a road through the deserts of southwestern United States and Georgia O'Keeffe crossing Howrah and Calcutta in Ohio to southern California. The sequence exemplifies Shahid's use of repetition and echo to intensify lyrical impact. The ninth poem in the sequence with its epigraph from Emily Dickinson imitates the slow motion of halting train wheels by using repeated dashes that are often found in her poems:

> The way she had—in her rushes—of resonance—
> I too—so want to eat—Evanescence—slowly—
> in the near—faraways—of the heart. Like O'Keeffe
> also—in her Faraway Nearby—that painting. (1–4)

The third section—"From Another Desert"—carries on the motifs of loss and desert, though now the locale is the Arabian desert, to re-create the legendary love story of Laila and Majnoon. In Shahid's retelling, Majnoon—literally the mad or the possessed one who sacrifices everything for love—is presented as a rebel and the loved one (Laila) as the revolutionary ideal that the rebel aspires to attain. The fourth section, containing eight poems, employs the earlier motifs of deserts, myths, sea, and water. Shahid imaginatively weaves past and present, myth and reality, American and Arabian deserts with their different histories and cultures, contemporary U.S. cities and extinct American Indian tribes and prehistoric oceans. As Bruce King rightly observes, "The poetry presents a world of mirrors in which each experience, object, person, place, time has reflections in the past and present, the here and there, the near and faraway."[13] Thus, when the poet looks at the sky, he sees the past because "Each ray of sunshine is seven minutes old" ("Snow on the Desert"). All existence becomes subjects of nostalgia just as former oceans turn into deserts and American towns in Ohio resemble the names of Indian cities. But the nostalgist, engaged in cultural cartography, does not ignore human suffering and loss. During his journey in search of Evanescence he sees "a woman climbed the steps to Acoma, / vanished into the sky. / In the ghost towns / of Arizona, there were charcoal tribes / with desert voices, among their faces / always the last speaker of a language" ("In Search of Evanescence"). "The Keeper of the Dead Hotel" describes in moving details the labor strike in the copper town of Brisbee in 1917 and the consequential human tragedy:

> The copper mountains echo with rifle shots:
> men on strike are being killed

in the mines, the survivors forced
into boxcars and left in the desert
without water. Their women are leaving
the city. (22–27)

The anthology ends with a poignant recollection of loss:

. . . a time
to recollect
every shadow, everything the earth was losing,
a time to think of everything the earth
and I had lost, of all
that I would lose,
of all that I was losing. ("Snow on the Desert," 74–80)

The ending of this book foreshadows the beginning of his next work, which deals with his devastated homeland, Kashmir, and his most overpowering personal loss.

The Beloved Witness: Selected Poems appeared in 1992, and was followed in 1997 by *The Country without a Post Office*, Agha Shahid Ali's "signature collection."[13] Written in response to the destruction, by fire, of one of Kashmir's most famous Muslim shrines, the mausoleum of Sheikh Nooruddin Wali, considered Kashmir's patron saint, along with an adjoining mosque, during the armed insurgency against the Indian state in May 1995, this volume uses letters as its key metaphor of communication—or rather a lack thereof—in politically troubled Kashmir, which is its central subject. There is a prologue, followed by five sections, each with a small group of poems followed by a few notes. The poems build up a loose narrative with seeming digressions that coalesce with the main theme through some recurring words, phrases, and images. Shahid here gives vent with a note of urgency and immediacy of impact to the feelings of loss, exile, and heartbreak that torment the people of Kashmir. Claire Chambers in her essay " 'It Is This': Agha Shahid Ali's Representation of Kashmir in The Country without a Post Office" has discussed the recurrent themes delineated by Shahid in this collection. What needs to be added is that the poet's intense emotional involvement with Kashmir's agony has led him to experiment with a variety of forms as attempts at depersonalizing his feelings, forms that include prose poems, letters, villanelle, sestina, pastoral, terza rima, ghazal, rhyming couplets and quatrains, sestets and octaves—some with regular rhyme schemes and some mixed—techniques that help him convey his convoluted emotions in a complex narrative structure. The prose poem "The Blessed Word: A Prologue" quotes the Russian poet Osip Mandelstam—"We shall meet again, in Petersburg"—to imagine a time when Kashmir, Shahid's homeland, will be free, although the "blessed word," presumably "azadi," is not mentioned anywhere in the poem. But the poet believes that "one day the Kashmiris will pronounce that word truly for the first time." In the Prologue, Shahid writes the name of Kashmir in all its variations of spelling, as a lover writes and rewrites his beloved's name. The history of Kashmir's subjugation by Mughal Emperor Akbar, which still lives in the songs of Habba Khatun that the rustic women sing together while gathering dry chinar leaves in autumn to use as fuels, commingles with descriptions of an army crackdown in search of "terrorists":

Srinagar was under curfew. The identity pass may or may not have helped in the crackdown.

> Son after son—never to return from the night of torture—was taken away. (Section III)

The poem is replete with gruesome pictures of Kashmir burning in the fire of freedom struggle:

> But the reports are true, and without song: mass rapes in the villages, towns left in cinders, neighbourhoods torched. (Section IV)

"Farewell," the opening poem of the first section, which is described by Shahid in the note as "a plaintive love letter from a Kashmiri Muslim to a Kashmiri Pandit," deals with the issue of mutual intercommunal suspicion and fear of animosity, which was not as real as it was imagined, that led to the near total exodus of the native minority Hindu population from the valley.[14] It ends with the poet's longing for a "return to harmony" and a faint hope of a possible rapprochement in future:

> If only somehow you could have been mine, what wouldn't have happened in this world? (38–39)

But, with the revocation of civil rights, enforcement of martial law, and mass-scale police killings, the legendary paradise on earth is turned into hell. In poem after poem, Agha Shahid Ali narrates the horrific, inhuman torture perpetrated on the Kashmiris by men in the Indian army, reducing them to objects robbed of all hopes of life:[15]

> Drippings from a suspended burning tire
> are falling on the back of a prisoner,
> the naked boy screaming, "I know nothing."
> ("I See Kashmir from New Delhi at Midnight")

> I beg for haven: Prisons, let open your gates—
> A refugee from Belief seeks a cell tonight. ("Ghazal")

> Hope extinguished, now nothing else remains—
> only nights of anguish, these ochre dawns.
> ("Ghazal," *adapted from Makhdoom Mohiuddin*)

The Country without a Post Office amply testifies to Shahid's reverence for Emily Dickinson, for whom "Cashmere" implied the nostalgia for the exotic, the strange, and the distant. In "Some Vision of the World Cashmere," he quotes Dickinson's lines as epigraph:

> If I could bribe them by a Rose
> I'd bring them every flower that grows
> From Amherst to Cashmere!

Shahid names another poem with a line from Dickinson: "Lo, A Tint Cashmere! / Lo, A Rose!" The poem describes Shahid's return to Kashmir from Amherst with his grandmother by way of "her dream within a dream within a dream." There is an autobiographical strain in many poems of the collection that include references to Amherst, to Begum Akhtar, and to his familial house in Srinagar, which had been forcibly converted into an army camp.

Events are presented in the poems of *The Country* from various perspectives in order to throw light on the grim situation in Kashmir. For instance, the cold-blooded murder of a Kashmiri youth named Rizwan by the Indian security forces is narrated from the point of view of friends, acquaintances, family members, and the narrator himself:

> You must have heard Rizwan was killed. Rizwan: Guardian of
> the Gates of Paradise. Only eighteen years old. ("Dear Shahid")

> From Zero Bridge
> a shadow chased by searchlights is running
> away to find its body. ("I See Kashmir from New Delhi at Midnight")

> I won't tell your father you have died, Rizwan,
> but where has your shadow fallen, like cloth
> on the tomb of which saint, or the body
> of which unburied boy in the mountains,
> bullet-torn, like you, his blood sheer rubies
> on Himalayan snow? ("I See Kashmir from New Delhi at Midnight")

Shahid repeatedly employs two synecdochal images for Kashmir as a paradise on earth: "saffron" and "paisley." These images appear in poems like "Farewell," "The Last Saffron," and "The Country without a Post Office." Again, there are recurrent evocations of a return to a devastated and lost paradise in the lines of many poems:

> "They make a desolation and call it peace.
> Who is the guardian tonight of the Gates of Paradise?" ("Farewell")

> "Kashmir is burning." ("I See Kashmir from New Delhi at Midnight")
> "See how your world has cracked.
> Why aren't you here? Where are you? Come back." ("A Pastoral")

Another important issue that Shahid takes up in this anthology is the poetic agenda of giving an international perspective to the struggle of the Kashmiris for *Azadi* (independence). He seeks to achieve this by comparing Kashmir to similar parts of the world such as Bosnia, Chechnya, Deir Yassein, Palestine, and Sarajevo. In "A Villanelle," for example, Shahid mourns the devastation of Chechnya ("Chechnya is gone") and Armenia ("Armenia . . . vanished"), linking their tragedy to that of Kashmir. Again, in "The City of Daughters," a four-part sequence of quatrains, his awareness harks back to centuries as he cries: "Say farewell, say farewell to the city / (O Sarajevo! O Srinagar!), / the Alexandria that is forever leaving." Although the places compared with Kashmir are predominantly Islamic countries,

Agha Shahid Ali's worldview is essentially humanist and internationalist, as is evident in the opening lines of the poem "First Day of Spring":

> "On this perfect day, perfect for forgetting God,
> why are they—Hindu or Muslim, Gentile or Jew—
> shouting again some godforsaken word of God?" (1–3)

Shahid's humanism is also expressed when he laments the gruesome murder of the twenty-seven-year-old Norwegian youth Hans Christian Ostro in Kashmir in August 1995 by Al-Faran militants with the same empathic intensity as he grieves the mass exodus of Hindu Pandits from the valley:

> By that dazzling light
> we see men removing statues from temples.
> We beg them, "Who will protect us if you leave?"
> They don't answer, they just disappear
> on the road to the plains, clutching the gods.
> ("I See Kashmir from New Delhi at Midnight," 41–45)

"The Correspondent" situates this cosmopolitan spirit amidst the disturbance in Sarajevo. The title character, a war correspondent, arrives in Srinagar to cover the conflict in Kashmir with video footage of Sarajevo:

> "I've just come—with videos—from Sarajevo."
> His footage is priceless with sympathy,
> close-ups in slow motion: from bombed sites
> to the dissolve of mosques in colonnades. (14–17)

The Sarajevo scene in "The Correspondent" presents not only the horror of war but also the problematic of war's representation by the media. The darkness of Kashmir throughout the poem, in contrast with the high-voltage coverage of the Sarajevo war, due to the Western powers' involvement in the politics of Bosnia, evinces Shahid's deep concern as a Kashmiri-American poet about the terror of war in the valley and its lack of proper representation in Western media. Delineating Kashmir's pain with a subtle, implicitly discriminatory contrast that reinforces its intensity, he seeks to draw the world's attention to the situations in other conflict-ravaged places in the East that are often overlooked. Kashmir, for most Western readers, is only an exotic, idyllic place, rarely represented in literary scenes. In "A Pastoral," Shahid gives vent to his grievance about this through a letter addressed to him by a friend in Kashmir:

> See how your world has cracked.
> Why aren't you here? Where are you? Come back.
> Is history deaf there, across the oceans? (41–43)

In his essay, "The Greatest Sorrow: Times of Joy Recalled in Wretchedness," Amitav Ghosh remarks: "If the twin terrors of insurgency and repression could be said to have engendered any single literary motif, it is surely the narrative of the loss of Paradise . . . The reason why there is no greater sorrow than the recalling of the times of joy, is . . . that this is grief beyond consolation."[16] Ghosh identifies Agha Shahid Ali as one of the writers who employ this trope of a lost paradise in their writings. The title poem of *The Country without a Post Office* is itself a disconsolate lament for the lost utopia. In section two of the poem, Shahid writes: "Everything is finished, nothing remains," which sounds like the wail of one who has returned to Kashmir in search of the keeper of an "entombed minaret." The line returns like a "mad refrain" in his narrative of the sad country:

> "Nothing will remain, everything's finished,"
> I see his voice again: "This is a shrine
>   of words. You'll find your letters to me. And mine
>   to you. Come soon and tear open these vanished
>   envelopes." And I reach the minaret:
>   I'm inside the fire. I have found the dark.
> This is your pain. You must feel it. Feel it. . . .
> This is an archive. I've found the remains
> of his voice, that map of longings with no limit. (Section 3)

Deeply buried within the "shrine of words" lies a "map of longing without limit." It is not the fall of the minaret but the loss of the map which, according to Shahid, is the real catastrophe, because with the map lost a future for "the country without a post office" has become inconceivable, and Kashmir is heading inexorably toward a new holocaust.

"The Country without a Post Office" employs letter as the central form that takes the volume to its emotional crescendo. The poem is the heart of the collection and it registers the poet's abysmal despair at the ruination of his paradisiacal homeland. "It's raining as I write this," he reminds the reader, and the rain pours throughout the poem as the objective correlative of the poet's own tears. Dedicated to James Merrill, his literary mentor and friend, the poem is divided into four sections, each part having three octaves with a rhyme scheme of ABCD DCBA. The speaker—a poet, probably Shahid himself—returns to Kashmir in a painful and futile search for the keeper of a destroyed minaret. He laments the dead muezzin, the crier who called the faithful for prayer five times a day, and the keeper of the minaret who appears as a disembodied voice desperately calling to the world outside Kashmir. The unconventional rhyme scheme echoes the movement of the speaker in and out of darkness and up and down the minaret. Each line in the poem has roughly ten syllables that impose a formal restriction on the poet. This self-imposed syntactical constraint generates a tight linguistic frame that parallels the asphyxiating emotional condition of the poet-speaker, who struggles hard to make sense of the war raging in his homeland for liberation along with its glory and the indefinable agony its consequences give rise to in his own heart:

> In this dark rain, be faithful, Phantom heart,
> this is your pain. Feel it. You must feel it.
> Nothing will remain, everything's finished. (Section 3)
> *or*
> I guide myself up the steps. Mad silhouette,
> I throw paisleys to clouds. The lost are like this:
> They bribe the air for dawn, this their dark purpose.
> But there's no sun here. There is no sun here. (Section 4)

Away from the world's attention, Kashmir in this poem is a ruined place where the communication system has completely collapsed. Each post office is boarded up, the letters rendered dead and left in piles, unable to reach their intended address, so that communication becomes impossible.

Again, no communication occurs between the Hindus and the Muslims, between the militants and the Indian state, between India and Pakistan—the two main parties in the whole controversy. Despite its focus on the local, the here and now, the poem achieves a universal dimension through reference to a poem by Gerard Manley Hopkins. Quoted from one of Hopkins's "terrible sonnets"—"I wake and feel the fell of dark, not day"—the lines are used as an epigraph and are also adapted in the final section of the poem: "And my lament / Is cries countless, cries like dead letters sent / To dearest him that lives alas! away." These lines depict an image of spiritual void as the speaker waits despondently for a reply from God. The unanswered prayers of a Jesuit priest are compared to the dead/undelivered letters that Shahid selects as the key metaphor in the poem. The poet's grief over the loss of the Muslim shrine—which is a deeply religious loss—and his longing for answers to his inconsolable lament find an echo in the profound anguish and despair which Hopkins's speaker feels for an ostensibly failed communication with God.

This overriding tone of loss and despair notwithstanding, the collection ends on a different note, if not explicitly of hope at least of a new possibility for a beleaguered homeland. In "The Prologue," Osip Mandelstam does not give any clue to the "blessed word":

> What is the blessed word? Mandelstam gives no clue.
> One day the Kashmiris will pronounce that word
> truly for the first time. (57–58)

In the concluding poem, "After the August Wedding in Lahore, Pakistan," which brings three strands—Islamic, Christian, and Jewish—of Shahid's cultural inheritance together through the reference to the loss of Eden, however, the poet utters the "blessed word"—*Azadi*—loudly and unequivocally:

> Freedom's terrible thirst, flooding Kashmir,
> is bringing love to its tormented glass.
> Stranger, who will inherit the last night
> of the past? Of what shall I not sing, and sing? (62–65)

Rooms Are Never Finished is Shahid's last book of poems published in his lifetime, a few months before his death in 2001. This book is divided into four parts. But, both thematically and structurally, central to this collection are two deeply moving elegies, each consisting of a sequence of poems. The first, "From Amherst to Kashmir," about the poet's mother, who died in an Amherst hospital after prolonged treatment for brain cancer and was buried in Srinagar, is structured around the tragic story of Karbala and moves in and out of time to knit past and present, personal and historical, into a unique narrative that transcends time. The second, "Eleven Stars over Andalusia," is an adaptation of Palestinian poet Mahmoud Darwish's original ode (*quasida*)—published in 1992—about the expulsion of the Moors from fifteenth-century Spain. The first poem of the collection, "Lenox

Hill," a canzone, serves as a prologue to the collection. This poignant elegy reveals Shahid at the height of his poetic strength. Dedicated to his dead mother, it is framed by her death in 1997 from brain cancer and the poet's own battle against the same fatal illness shortly afterward. Both merge into an exquisite meditation on life and death, on reclamation, exile, and memory.

From "Lenox Hill," the book moves to Part I, "From Amherst to Kashmir," a sequence that opens with an unparalleled prose poem, "Karbala: A History of the 'House of Sorrow.'" Using Karbala and Hussain's great sacrifice as a leitmotif to uphold Islam, Shahid takes the reader back to the historical moment (AH 61/AD 680). In elegant prose he reconstructs the story of Imam Hussain's self-immolation and the suffering of the survivors, particularly his sister Zainab, who was exiled in Damascus.

The next poem, "Zainab's Lament in Damuscus," is a translation of a Kashmiri elegy sung at Shahid's mother's funeral. This is followed by "Summers of Translation," which refers to Faiz Ahmed Faiz's poem "Memory," and recalls the poet's mother reading Faiz out to him and helping him to select poems for translation (which would later appear in *The Rebel's Silhouette*). He then goes on to provide a glimpse of Begum Akhtar, singing a meditative poem of Mirza Ghalib in Raga Jogia, and returns to Muharram and Kashmir's mourning again:

> I shelve "Memory" to hear Begum Akhtar enclose—
> in Raga *Jogia*—the wound-cry of the gazelle:
> "Not all, no, only a few return as the rose
> or the tulip." That ghazal held under her spell.
> But when you welcomed me in later summers to Kashmir,
> every headline read:
> PARADISE ON EARTH BECOMES HELL.
> ("Summers of Translation")

The revolving themes of death of the poet's mother, Muharram and Kashmir turning into Hell continue to be developed in subsequent poems, which are interspersed with glimpses of airports, old records, and black-and-white films. The poet's personal anguish becomes an expression of deeper, universal emotions and mysteries expressed in a wide range of style and forms. *Rooms Are Never Finished* is indeed remarkable for its exploration of a variety of poetic forms bound together with the prevailing motif of journey. In addition to Old English forms, the book includes poems written in canzone, sonnets,

Sapphics, ghazals, and terza rima, all of which were introduced to English from other literary traditions. Agha Shahid Ali's employment of various poetic forms from multiple literary sources corresponds to the transnational and transcultural itinerations that his poems map out.

Equally remarkable in *Rooms Are Never Finished* is Shahid's use of some elements of *marsiya* and *shikwa* in his lamentation for his mother. A *marsiya* is an Urdu elegy, long used as a medium of religious mourning. The *marsiya* tradition has Pre-Islamic Arabic roots as elegiac expression, which later became a predominant way to lament the death of Imam Hussain at Karbala. This lament for Hussain and the grief of his sister Zainab have for Shi'a Muslims a similar religious significance that the crucifixion of Jesus has for the Christians. With the twelve-part cycle of poems "From Amherst to Kashmir," Shahid layers his own and his family's grief for his mother's death and the cultural and religious tragedy they faced in early-1990s Kashmir with the tragic story of Hussain.

The poet's complaint in "Summers of Translation" that "God is a thief" brings his grief close to what in Urdu is called *shikwa* (grievance or grudge). It is a form of wailing protestation to Allah for having let the Muslims down through the ages. Again, in the three-part poem called "A Secular Comedy," Shahid lodges his grievance against God, calling Him "the final assassin." However, despite this unorthodox stance of the poet, the cycle "From Amherst to Kashmir" is characterized by a note of reverence for religious tradition. In the course of his journey, which is essentially a pilgrimage, Shahid moves back and forth in time, between the past and the present, alternating Muslim history and Christian allusions.

The second section consists of poems that observe the world from a distant plane in which the poet is but a passenger and "everything . . . fill[s] / [him] with longing, the longing to long, to be / flame, and moth, and ash" ("The Purse-Seiner *Atlantis*"). In the title poem, "Rooms Are Never Finished," which focuses on reality and illusion as well as incompleteness of life and life's work ("A house? A work in progress, / always."), a disembodied voice guides the poet somewhere in space and time.

Shahid was a playfully deceptive atheist, like Ghalib. He once asserted in a ghazal: "I . . . believe in prayer but could never in God." He countered Nietzsche, when he asked: "Now that God / is news, what's left but prayer . . . ?" Even a nonbeliever is tied up to a relationship of affection with this world, Shahid seems to believe. "This relation can make an ethical demand on him in the heart of a despairing, Kafkan moment—to pray in god's absence, to pray without hope, but pray nevertheless, as an unfathomable, mad duty towards the other. Shahid waits for us at the end of that prayer," remarks a discerning critic.[17]

Part III consists of "Eleven Stars over Andalusia," a hypnotic adaptation of an Arabic poem by Mahmoud Darwish. In an endnote Shahid explains that he was sent "a very literal version" and "asked to convert it into poetry." He finally found a way of tackling the task after reading Lorca:

> Some of my words of love will fall into
> Lorca's poems; he'll live in my bedroom
> and see what I have seen of the Bedouin moon. ("There is a
>   sky beyond the sky for me," 8–10)

The phrase "eleven stars" in the title comes from *The Quran* and alludes to Prophet Joseph's dream in which he saw eleven stars and the sun and the moon prostrate themselves before him. Like the Prophet, the poet has special insight into the meaning of Andalusia's fall for today's Palestinians. Al-Andalus has, as a literary and cultural topos, a long tradition in Europe and the Arab world, variably signifying loss and utopic longing. Shahid, however, turns Darwish's ode into a magical elegy mourning the loss of a once exalted culture and people now marginalized by history. "Eleven Stars" not only depicts the expulsion of the Moors from Islamic Spain after the Re-Conquest and their heart-rending farewell to the enchanting homeland but also cleverly draws an analogy between the homelands of the poet and of the translator—Palestine and Kashmir. The poem, with its brilliant interpretation of Darwish's lament over the Muslims' forced exodus, provides a significant tribute to Palestine's unofficially acclaimed national poet.

For all his sympathy for the deterritorialized and the dispossessed—both in Palestine and Kashmir—Shahid finally draws his consolation not from politics or religion but from art. This is hinted directly by the closing poem, "I Dream I Am at the Ghat of the Only World," which echoes James Merrill's "Changing Light at Sandover." It is a wonderfully meditative work dealing with memories of all that is dear to him, particularly people such as his mother, poet James Merrill, political thinker and activist Eqbal Ahmad, ghazal singer Begum Akhtar, all of whom have traveled to "the other shore." Shahid evokes their voices who urge him on in his journey toward his mother. The key figure that holds the poem together is Ghulam Mohommad, the waiting boatman who will ferry the poet across the water. "I always rowed you across / the Jhelum, of which this river's the ebony / ghost," the oarsman says. The poet moves in and out of conversation with the people whom he has loved and who have died. To his mother he cries: "Will I wait here, alone, by this ebony abyss, / abandoned by you, alone?" James Merrill appears posthumously to guide the poet beyond pain and despair. "WEEPING? YOU MUST NOT," he tells Shahid, who replies, "Which world will bring her / back, or will he who wears his heart on his sleeve eaves- / drop always, in his inmost depths, on a cruel harbinger?" As the poem closes, he receives a soul-soothing answer from the envoy: "SHAHID, HUSH. THIS IS ME, JAMES. THE LOVED ONE ALWAYS LEAVES." The article entitled "Epistemology of Mourning: A Reading of *Rooms Are Never Finished*" by Sisir Kumar Chatterjee and Sinchan Chatterjee discusses all the poems of this volume, offering a detailed, close and intensive reading of each individual lyric, in addition to indicating with illustrations the theoretical perspectives in which Shahid's poems in this collection can be placed.

Call Me Ishmael Tonight, a collection of Shahid's English ghazals, was published posthumously in 2003. Apart from these nine collections of poems, Shahid translated Faiz Ahmed Faiz's Urdu poems, *The Rebel's Silhouette: Selected Poems* and co-edited with Sara Suleri Goodyear *Ravishing DisUnities: Real Ghazals in English*. He was awarded Guggenheim and Ingram-Merrill fellowships and a Pushcart Prize, and his collection *Rooms Are Never Finished* became a finalist for the National Book Award in 2001.

Agha Shahid Ali's Contribution to English and American Poetry

Agha Shahid Ali's abiding contribution to American and English Poetry lies, perhaps, in bringing the ghazal to English, teaching Western readers its intricacies as well as its mysteries. He wrote his own ghazals and edited an anthology of ghazals in English with the objective of rescuing this Persian and Urdu lyrical form from the ill-use it had received from American poets. "The form has really been utterly misunderstood in America, with these free verse ghazals. I mean, that's just not the ghazal,"[18] Shahid said to Christine Benvenuto. He added: "The ghazal has a very strict formal unity, with a certain cultural location, and so James Harrison and Adrienne Rich, though I like things they have done with what they call ghazals, those aren't ghazals, they simply aren't." Shahid commended John Hollander as a poet who had produced a true ghazal. But he also said that once the form was understood, departures did not offend him: "People wrote sestinas of varying line lengths. Once you've seen a strict sestina such as Elizabeth Bishop's, then of course it's wonderful to keep experimenting. But at least we know what the real thing is."[19] It was with a view to giving American readers a taste of the "real thing" that he undertook, with Sara Suleri Goodyear, the "Ravishing DisUnities" project, published in 2000 as *Ravishing DisUnities: Real Ghazals in English*. This anthology includes traditional ghazals written by more than one hundred poets. In the introductory note, Shahid gives a brief overview of the ghazal, which "goes back to the seventh century Arabia, perhaps even earlier" (1). It is thus older than the European sonnet. Shahid believes that a ghazal cannot be written in free verse because of its clearly drawn rigorous rules. He explains the structure of a ghazal in this way:

> The ghazal is made up of couplets, each autonomous, thematically and emotionally complete in itself. One couplet may be comic, another tragic, another romantic, another religious, another political. There is underlying a ghazal, a profound and complex cultural unity, built on association and memory and expectation, as well as an implicit recognition of the human personality and its infinite variety. A couplet may be quoted by itself without in any way violating a context—there is no context, as such. One should at any time be able to pluck a couplet like a stone from a necklace, and it should continue to shine in that isolation, though it would have a different lustre among and with the other stones. (2–3)

What saves a ghazal from arbitrariness is its formal unity based on rhyme, refrain, and prosody. It is, however, its disunity—independent couplets held together in a shining fashion—that contributes to a ghazal its stunning beauty. Shahid worked assiduously to secure a place for the ghazal in American literature and *The Ravishing DisUnities* amply proves that his efforts have largely succeeded.

His own ghazals, collected in *Call Me Ishmael Tonight*, were edited by Agha Iqbal Ali (Shahid's brother) and Hena Zafar Ahmad. There are thirty-four poems in this collection that prove that writing successful ghazals in English, adhering to the traditional form, is not only possible but enjoyable and rewarding as well. The title is derived from the last line of the penultimate ghazal, "Tonight":

> I beg for haven: Prisons, let open your gates—
> A refugee from Belief seeks a cell tonight.
>
> . . .
>
> *Lord, cried out the idols, Don't let us be broken:*
> *Only we can convert the infidel tonight.*
>
> . . .
>
> In the heart's veined temple, all statues have been smashed.
> No priest in saffron's left to toll its knell tonight.
>
> . . .
>
> And I, Shahid, only am escaped to tell thee—
> God sobs in my arms. Call me Ishmael tonight.

The ghazal ends by invoking the famous opening lines of the classic American novel *Moby-Dick*, but it also alludes to a popular Islamic legend.

This cultural crisscrossing is undoubtedly a distinctive trait of Agha Shahid Ali's poetry, which often carves a passage across languages and civilizations. No language or civilization, Shahid believes, should be left alone with its inherent symbols, values, or assumptions. As he writes in a ghazal:

> No language is old—or young—beyond English.
> So what of a common tongue beyond English?
> I know some words for war, all of them sharp,
> but the sharpest one is *jung*—beyond English!
>
> . . .
>
> If someone asks where Shahid has disappeared,
> he's waging a war (no, *jung*) beyond English.
>
> ("Beyond English")

Significantly, these are not simply some time-worn clichés about the mutual coexistence of different languages and cultures. Urdu (from which *jung* comes) with its sound and rhythm is filtered into English so that readers are a bit confused about which language they are actually reading. In an age of global ascendancy, English writing (in prose and poetry) has, Shahid suggests, a moral responsibility to look beyond itself. The repetition of "beyond English" at the end of each couplet creates an insistence to open the door to other cultures, to look "beyond English."

Agha Shahid Ali's multicultural affiliations notwithstanding, his poetic sensibility is essentially that of someone steeped in Urdu poetry in the structure of his bones and flow of his blood. If one reads his poems carefully, one may detect the music of Urdu behind his English. Despite his lack of fidelity to any single aesthetic, use of American idiom, transnational journeys and allusions, and exploration of European poetic forms, Shahid's poems have a thorough Indianness about them. The poems in *The Half-Inch Himalayas*, *The Country without a Post Office*, and *Rooms Are Never Finished* bear ample testimony to this. Amitav Ghosh has rightly observed that

> Shahid thought of his work as being placed squarely within a modern Western tradition. Yet the mechanics of his imagination—dreams, visions, an overpowering sense of identity with those he loved—as well as his life, and perhaps even his death, were fashioned by a will that owed more perhaps to the Sufis and the Bhakti poets than to the modernists. In his determination to be not just a writer of poetry but an embodiment of his poetic vision, he was, I think, more the heir of Rumi and Kabir than Eliot and Merrill.[20]

Kashmir's political turmoil in the late 1980s and early 1990s made him grieve for his homeland, and this is especially evident in *The Country without a Post Office*, with its frequent references to army convoys, soldiers, curfews, police brutality, dead bodies with bullet holes floating in the rivers, boarded-up post offices, undelivered letters, unidentified graves, exodus of Hindus, killing of young and innocent foreign tourists by militants, deserted shrines, and a city in ruins. But, as already pointed out, sociopolitical concerns in Shahid's poetry are not limited to his homeland alone. Sarajevo, Bosnia, Palestine, Chile, Deir Yassein, Sabra-Shatila, and Chechnya feature prominently in his poetry. In *A Nostalgist's Map of America*, he writes of a strike of miners brutally put down in Brisbee, Arizona, in 1917, and of the native American cultures whose destruction is evoked by a drive through the desert. According to Shahid, an inclination to mourn historical loss was an inescapable part of his mental make-up. "I think of people who because of historical forces have lost so much," he said. "I mean, these things are in my way of looking at the world. I'm in one way or another obsessed with all that."[21]

In spite of his obsession with historical loss and the resultant nostalgia, overwhelming grief is not the most salient feature of Shahid's work. His poems wind through an intricate passage in which the initial response to loss gives in to a highly postmodern angst to retreat from that response. He is one of those poets "who of passion / never made a holocaust" ("Karbala: A History of the 'House of Sorrow'"). As he puts it:

When you're dealing with a painful subject matter . . . I would say definitely you need distancing devices. You can make that very choice to distance yourself from a subject matter, a thematic and aesthetic issue. But to actually serve that material you need a formal distancing device because otherwise you might end up sounding simply hysterical.[22]

Shahid justifies his point by citing the example of confessional poets such as Sylvia Plath: "Even someone like Sylvia Plath . . . is on the verge sometimes of something that may sound like hysteria . . . but everything is so finely tuned. Like it's on the edge, but there is also distance being maintained by that."[23]

Being on the edge was perhaps a geophilosophically immanent and psychologically inherent condition for a poet like Shahid, who always traveled between countries and explored the borders between geographical and cultural territories. But he remained unperturbed by the complications involved in such a condition. He always considered himself to be primarily a poet in English and gracefully accepted all other hyphenated identities (Kashmiri-American, Indian-American, Muslim-American, South Asian–American, and so on) so long as they did not attempt to pigeonhole him or his work. Being pigeonholed was a condition that this "beloved witness" detested most, as it was utterly alien to his poetic temperament. Perhaps it is this resistance to theoretical straitjacketing, resulting in the intellectual openness and aesthetic nonexclusivity of Agha Shahid Ali's poetry, that baffles the theory-obsessed critics of today.

Notes

1. Agha Shahid Ali's ancestors had migrated to Kashmir from Kashghar, now in Xinjiang, People's Republic of China, not from the Uzbek city of Samarkand that Shahid mentions in the poem "Snowmen":

> My ancestor, a man of Himalayan snow,
> came to Kashmir from Samarkand
> carrying a bag of whale bones:
> heirlooms from sea funerals. (16)

2. In his memoir "'The Ghat of the Only World': Agha Shahid Ali in Brooklyn," Amitav Ghosh narrates the story, which Shahid had told him, about the

origins of his family and that of his grandfather: "The story went that to sit for the examination, he had to travel all the way from Srinagar to Rawalpindi in a tonga. Later, he too became an official at the court of the Maharaja of Kashmir. He had special charge of education, and took the initiative to educate his daughter" (352).

3. "'The Ghat of the Only World': Agha Shahid Ali in Brooklyn," *The Imam and the Indian* (Delhi, Ravi Dayal Publisher, 2002), 353. Shahid also uses the line in his poem "I Dream I Am at the Ghat of the Only World" in *Rooms Are Never Finished*.

4. See Merchant's essay "Agha Shahid Ali's Gay Nation," *Forbidden Sex/Texts*, 2009.

5. Shahid said this in an interview with Stacey Chase (March 3–4, 1990), which was later published as "Agha Shahid Ali: The Lost Interview" in *The Cafe Review* (December 23, 2016).

6. "An Interview with Agha Shahid Ali." Interview by Christine Benvenuto, *Massachusetts Review*, 43.2: 261–268 (2002).

7. "The Ghat of the Only World," 354. During his terminal illness, when he was almost bed-ridden, Shahid said to Ghosh, "This dividing of the country, the divisions between people—Hindu, Muslim, Muslim, Hindu—you can't imagine, how much I hate it. It makes me sick. What I say is: why can't you be happy with the cuisines and the clothes and the music and all these wonderful things?" (346)

8. "Agha Shahid Ali: The Lost Interview," conducted by Stacey Chase, *The Cafe Review: A Maine-Based Quarterly Journal of Art, Poetry and Reviews* (Spring 2011); Shahid, December 23, 2016.

9. "An Interview with Agha Shahid Ali."

10. "Agha Shahid Ali: The Lost Interview."

11. Bruce King, *Modern Indian Poetry in English*. Revised Edition, 260.

12. "The Ghat of the Only World," 345.

13. Ibid.

14. It is important to note that Shahid lamented the forced departure of Hindu Pandits from the valley and mourned their loss. But he never suggested that Kashmiri Muslims were to blame for their indescribable misery, although this is the feeling that strongly prevails among exiled Pandits. Shahid does not counterpose the Indian army's brutality with the supposed brutality of the Kashmiri Muslims. On the contrary, he writes unequivocally: "In your absence you polished me into the Enemy" ("Farewell"). Although Shahid openly supported the Kashmiri cause of *Azadi* or self-determination, he never overlooked the horrors of terrorism. A glaring instance is his poem "Hans Christian Ostro."

15. The editors strongly felt the need to provide some serious historical overview of the sociopolitical scenario in Kashmir, as this context is integral to Agha Shahid Ali's poetry in general and *The Country without a Post Office* in particular. But the limitation of space restrained them. To read Shahid's poetic oeuvre more faithfully and in tune with his own stated political position, one should remember

that no simple separation can be made between his politics and aesthetics. There is no apolitical or neutral way to read Shahid's poetry. We therefore mention the following books as essential references to the Kashmiri struggle for self-determination and freedom, as well as the Indian army's attempt to suppress it:

> *Resisting Occupation in Kashmir*, ed. Haley Duschinski. Mona Bhan, Ather Zia, and Cynthia Mahmood (University of Pennsylvania Press, 2017).
> *Hindu Rulers, Muslim Subjects*, Mridu Rai (C. Hurst and Co., 2004).
> *Of Gardens and Graves: Kashmir, Poetry, Politics*, Suvir Kaul (Duke University Press, 2017).
> *Kashmir: The Case for Freedom*, ed. Hilal Bhatt, Arundhati Roy, Tariq Ali, Pankaj Mishra, and Angana P. Chatterjee (Verso Books, 2011).
> *Kashmir—The Untold Story*, Humra Quraishi (Penguin Global, 2005).
> *Curfewed Night*, Basharat Peer (Penguin Random House, 2008).
> *The Collaborator*, Mirza Waheed (Penguin Books, 2011).
> *The Ministry of Utmost Happiness*, Arundhati Roy (Hamish Hamilton, 2017).

16. "The Greatest Sorrow: Times of Joy Recalled in Wretchedness," *The Imam and the Indian*, 308–313.

17. Manash Bhattacharjee, "Looking for Shahid," *The Hindu*, December 3, 2011.

18. "An Interview with Agha Shahid Ali."

19. Ibid.

20. "The Ghat of the Only World," 360.

21. "An Interview with Agha Shahid Ali."

22. Ibid.

23. Ibid.

1

Ghazal for Open Hands

Martín Espada

In memory of Agha Shahid Ali
December 10, 2001
Northampton, Massachusetts

The imam stands above your grave to pray with open hands,
cupping your spirit like grain in the palms of these open hands.

Poet of Kashmir, the graveyard lathers my shoes with mud
as the imam calls to Islam's God and lifts his open hands.

Ghazal-maker, your pine box sinks into a cumulus of snow,
red earth thumping on the coffin, dropped from open hands.

There are some today who murmur of the cancer in your brain
but do not know the words for speaking to Allah with open hands.

We listen to Islamic prayers at the cemetery, as we pay for bombs
to blossom into graves in places where they pray with open hands.

Far from here, the bombs we bless are tumbling down in loaves
of steel to tear away the fingers from their hungry open hands.

Shahid, your grave multiplies wild as cancer cells across Afghani earth,
countless prayers reverberating in the well of the throat, in open hands.

I cannot scrape off the mud choking my shoes or blink away the vision
of reaching into the hole for you, my hands open to your open hands.

2

Shahid, Some Memories

PETER BALAKIAN

I had just returned from a semester in London back into the winter of central New York, back into snow and frozen roads, and I was just unpacking from months away when the phone rang. On the other end was a voice with an Indian brogue asking, "Are you Peter Balakian the poet?" I answered haltingly, not sure if this was some prank call, "Yes." The voice continued: "This is Agha Shahid Ali. Just call me Shahid. I'm calling because I'm the new poet at Hamilton College, and it is essential that we meet soon because we are neighbors and I like your poems." "Okay," I said. When the vibes were right, Shahid loved the community of poets. A week later we met at an Italian restaurant in New Hartford and talked for hours over wine and pasta.

Among other things, we discovered that we loved to cook, so a week later I invited Shahid to come to Colgate and cook with me at our new president's house on campus. In late January 1989 Shahid drove west down the road on a zero-degree night with snow banks high—to cook dinner with me for Colgate's new president Neil Grabois and his wife Miriam. They had arrived on campus in the fall when I was in London, so my first meeting with the new president turned out to be in his kitchen with my new friend Shahid. That evening we cooked up a wild combination of flavors and textures from Kashmiri and Armenian culinary zones. Shahid's chicken dopaise was hot, hot, and my imambylde was cool and sweet. Shahid's curried chickpeas were spicy and aromatic, and my lamb and cinamony green beans had melded to a sweet, savory stew. We drank wine 'til past midnight and talked poetry, and among other things we discovered that Shahid and I both had a love of textiles. The next time we met at my house in Hamilton a couple of weeks later, we read our textile poems to each other: Shahid's "The Dacca Gauzes" and my "The Oriental Rug." That winter of '89 we began our conversation about poetry and food, textiles and music and film, Armenia and Kashmir, genocide, exile, and diaspora, and we told our share of jokes to each other and laughed like hell.

Shahid's passion for cooking and for the gastronomic was large. He was one of the great makers and tasters of spices. He had no compunction about sending back a lamb vindaloo if it was not hot enough, as he did one night at a Pakistani restaurant near Union Square where we were having dinner with poets Elyse Paschen and Bill Wadsworth. I'll never forget the feast he cooked at his house in Northampton for me and Helen when we were visiting Shahid at his new home at the University of Massachusetts in Amherst. Shahid's brother and sisters, Jim Tate and Dara Wier, and various writers and friends were there, and we feasted on Shahid's chicken dopiase, lamb rogan josh, hot minced meatballs in a red sauce (which he always made with ground turkey), raita and great pilafs, and some sizzling okra. He was a great cook and a force for bringing people together, which is to say he was a great host. Shahid could entertain strangers as well as friends with just a pull of a phrase or an ironic quip, a parodic imitation, a deadpan foray. At a local restaurant in Hamilton he would say in his American nasal imitation, "Would you please bring the Moslem a dessert," or implore a waiter: "Whatever it is, just make it hot, hot." His fabled phone message greeting was part of his poetics: "Whoever you are, I need your message." Shahid's sense of the dramatic was brilliant. He loved an audience.

When Shahid came to our house, he loved to sit at the kitchen table with a scotch or a tea, depending on the time of day, and read a new poem. One day he came by having just returned from Delhi and Kashmir in late summer, full of energy and exclaiming: "From now on I will write only formal poems about love." And he started reading from a new poem, and then he stopped and said, "Listen to this," and he read the words: "It was a year of brilliant water." "Do you like it?" he asked me with his voice rising. "It's compelling," I said. It was a line from Thomas De Quincy, and it became a catalyst for a signature poem of his "In Search of Evanescence," a wildly associative, sequential poem, which I think opened up a new pathway for him. He kept reading his new poem:

It was a year of brilliant water
in Pennsylvania that final summer
seven years ago, the sun's quick reprints

in my attaché case: those students
of mist have drenched me with dew, I'm driving
away from that widow's house, my eyes open

to a dream of drowning. But even
when I pass—in Ohio—the one exit
to Calcutta, I don't know I've begun

mapping America, the city limits
of Evanescence now everywhere. It
was a year of brilliant water, Phil . . .

Another day, Shahid came over with a new poem about Kashmir. He was talking about Kashmir a lot in the early '90s as Kashmiri insurgents began to make their presence felt in the Jammu–Kashmir, India–Pakistan conflict. The poem was called "The Country without a Post Office," and when Shahid read it in the kitchen that day, I loved it on hearing it once, and I asked him if we could publish it in the poetry journal Bruce Smith and I then edited. He was delighted and handed me the manuscript. The poem appeared in *Graham House Review* 18 (Winter/Spring 1994–1995). Bruce and I were excited by the new range of Shahid's work, and the poem would turn out to be the title poem in his next book, *The Country without a Post Office*.

I think of Shahid's poetic voice as a prophetic one, opulent but controlled. He believed in poetry as annunciation and myth, chant and song—his poems have a high-voltage lyric voice—in a way that is against the grain of so much American poetry today with its more local, anecdotal, flat, conversational voice.

That was not Shahid. His sensibility was a unique fusion of American poetics and Persian, Urdu, and Arabic poetic modalities. He had made his own brew. He loved the realness of the world of objects, things, and artifacts, but he was also a fabulist. His visionary enumerations drew energy from his real and magical Kashmir. Out of that land and its historical predicament, he made a visionary language that was incandescent. He nourished a passion, as only a poet can, for loss and grief—hence, his love of Emily Dickinson and Begum Akhtar.

In his poem "The Blesséd Word," he captures that passion, and the title of the poem is a topos for Shahid's work; the poem has also an *ars poetica* embedded in it. Comparing himself with Mandelstam (oh, Shahid was never timid), he writes:

> He reinvents Petersburg (I, Srinagar), an imaginary homeland, filling it, closing it, shutting himself (myself) in it. For there is the blesséd word with no meaning. There are flowers that will never die, roses that will never fall, a night in which Mandelstam is not afraid and needs no pass. The blesséd women are still singing.

In Shahid's poems, desire, longing, and nostalgia can open into myth and history. His love of rhetorical tension and rhythmic compression led him to work in his favorite form: the ghazal. When he asked me to contribute a ghazal to his edited collection of ghazals in English, *Ravishing DisUnities: Real Ghazals in English*, I said I would. But circumstances in my life at the time made it impossible for me to get the poem to Shahid by his deadline. His anthology gave that classic Persian form a presence in the English language. I still owe him one.

On December 30 of 1999, Shahid dropped by our house on his way to New York City to celebrate the New Year, which that year was the fetishized moment of Y2K. Shahid was excited about his new appointment at NYU and moving to New York City, and Helen and I joined him in celebrating the moment with a very good bottle of scotch. We stayed up late catching up and celebrating the New Year early. A few days later, just after New Year, he called me to say that a strange thing had happened: he had passed out in his bathroom, and his father had found him on the floor. He was going to the hospital for tests the next day, but he was sure that he would be all right. "I'm going to lay off scotch for a while," he said. "Good idea," I said. "Insh Allah," he said as he hung up. The next day he was diagnosed with brain cancer, the same kind his mother had died of a few years earlier.

On May 1, 2000, Shahid joined me and several other writers, including Robert Pinksy, Rose Styron, Robert Jay Lifton, and Anthony Appiah, at the New York Public Library for an event I had organized. The event was a commemoration of the eighty-two Armenian writers killed in the Armenian genocide in 1915. We were reading from poems and prose by some of the Armenian writers killed by the Turkish government, and in doing so we were also commemorating a historical event that had proved ominous for writers and intellectual freedom in many histories of mass violence of the twentieth century. Shahid was noble to come out on that very hot early spring day. We were on a stage in the great Bartos Auditorium, which was crammed with about a thousand people on an oppressively hot day. Shahid was frail and undergoing chemotherapy, and his face showed it, but he read with deep feeling the poems of those Armenian writers. He remarked on the importance of his being a Muslim writer at this event, as in this case it was important for the voice of a Muslim poet to be heard since the perpetrators of the Armenian genocide were Muslim. After the reading we took some photographs together and spoke for a while as the noise of the crowd drummed over us. Shahid was running out of energy, so we embraced and said "see you soon." Although I spoke with him on the phone regularly over the following year, that day at the New York Public Library was the last time I saw him.

SILK ROAD

for Agha Shahid Ali
(1949–2002)

I drove in snow to Clinton.
My car slid into a field of buried stubble.
and cows disappeared in drifts

the color of your Dacca gauzes which were next
to nothing; for you they were all summer,
where the sun came like hammered gold on a broken dome.

You wrapped a shredded paisley—vermillion,
madder, cochineal—in a rag-worn prayer rug
I left in your car—for your trip to summer over there.

The white-out turned the bridge into a road
north to where Armenia was just a giant step
and bodies were ploughed crystal.

We drove from Bollywood to Deansboro
for scotch, and then the road turned
and you were driving through an undivided Punjab

where the wheat flared all summer
and you floored your Peugeot
outside of Armristar, that city of red silk

and gold from which the road north took you
to almost nothing—where silk worms disappeared
in rotting leaves and the voice of Begum Akhtar

was stinging air as you crossed the border
into your mother's monsoon which in Urdu
meant divergence and convergence of surface

heating air, and there and there and there
where the road sped up the way our extravagant passions
burn the esoteric leaves that fry our wires

till the car door opens and we're sucked out
into the unknown clouds over Calcutta
where the waterlogged slums are flooded

in the brain. That was your storm
of bangles, broken ghazal lines on prison walls,
vanishing elephants that were ploughed crystal.

3.

Shahid: *beloved* in Persian, *witness* in Arabic, you drove back
in the early upstate spring on the road to Hamilton
where the cows stared blankly at your car

the mud fields were plain and cold
pot-holes smashed the tires
the road was next to nothing,

and you asked me—staring through the window
at the trees and back roads: how can gray
drizzly light, just be gray drizzly light.

Reprinted from Peter Balakian's *Ozone Journal*, University of Chicago Press, 2015.

3

Somewhere without Me My Life Begins

DARA WIER

In the tiny spot I inhabit on Earth in North America in New England, in Massachusetts, in western Massachusetts, in Amherst, in North Amherst there's an ordinary autumn beginning to announce itself first with the tiniest hints of chills in the air, and crisper breezes, and new colors taking away greens to turn toward rust and red and yellow and bronze, pink and emerald, black and brown.

A young and handsome wild turkey woke me up this morning. He was trapped inside a terrace fence on the northwest side of our house. The crickets and frogs are louder in the evenings than any time they ever are, as if to announce the grievous time they are about to enter.

I think about Shahid in the fall most of all. And my first thought always is filled with the confusions impossibility presents to desire. I would like to speak with my friend, I believe I need him to understand—what? anything? everything? nothing? everything?

Though we first met in high summer, high up in the mountains of the American West, across the Great Divide in Aspen, Colorado, where we were both guests of a summer writing workshop run by the deceased and most generous poet and book lover Kurt Brown, it is in fall when Shahid's presence in his absence is most stark and melancholy.

I'd heard from Kurt that Shahid could, and would, cook. He'd told Shahid I could and would do the same. So in addition to what happens in books with our devotion to and love of poetry, what happens in the kitchen also brought us together. His greatest compliment to me was *Dara, you know what you are doing when you cook what you learned to cook as a south Louisiana girl.*

And likewise, the compliment I paid Shahid was that I was willing to be his sous chef anytime he would let me. And so it was I learned to cook many of his family's Kashmiri dishes. Both of our cooking styles shared love for delicious ingredients, and patience, and fearlessness with any pepper at the top of the Scoville scale. When we cooked, which it turned out was not often enough, we talked.

With Shahid, cooking qualified as dream cooking, a cook's dream—you knew what was coming would be delicious, you knew it wouldn't be timid or tamed down into innocuous generic anything, you knew it would be made lovingly and that it would take a long time, usually just enough time for us to share a bottle of wine once putting everything together ended and some slow simmering had begun. I loved the pace with which we cooked because it was never rushed; it was always as if Time itself was one of our chief ingredients.

And it would be during the simmering lulls when we talked and often laughed because Shahid's slightly wicked eye-gleaming moods could turn fantastically irreverent whenever necessary. We talked about poetry, family, friends, about what each of us was writing, reading, thinking, and hoping to find. Everything and everyone because of poetry, because of Shahid's belovedness, would be on intimate terms.

We worked together in other ways in other places. Our shared attention to our shared students, though equally ardent could not have been more different.

Our love of poems coincided often enough and differed often enough to surprise one another into second thoughts. After every one of our visits I would always find myself finding a book of poems he'd loved and wanted me to try again. Which I would. He wanted me to love James Merrill more, and so I did. He wanted me to know Faiz Ahmed Faiz, and so I do.

Poets who came to write at the university for which we taught were treated to what I believe was a rare and wonderful confusion of tastes, experiences, preferences, loves, dedications, loyalties, and styles; James Tate, Shahid, and me could never be mistaken for one another. Still, we shared some deep affections . . . for John Ashbery, for Elizabeth Bishop, for W. S. Merwin, for Marianne Moore, for James Merrill, for Yusef Komuunyaka, for C. D. Wright, to name a very few. We worked together easily, with pleasure and with love for poetry, and with simple responsibility to those poets who came to write in Amherst.

Once, on a quiet, slow day in the halls of the building in which our offices were housed, I heard the snap-snap-snap of popping bubble wrap, so with nothing in particular to do, I went looking for its source. Shahid's door was open. He was methodically popping one bubble after another, smiling at me, saying, *Oh, Dara, it can't be helped.*

Shahid always seemed to hold in reserve a quintessential melancholy mood and broadcast via a very particular tone of weary fatefulness. This is evident in the rhythms of his most grave poems, and it was evident in his eyes when he looked straight at you in order to tell you something words could not handle. This was rare, as in my all too brief time with him, he rarely wanted to bring doom or darkness into the proceedings.

He told me one night how he no longer felt *awe* over anything. That sent a chill through me I've never been able to shake. I knew he meant it. I knew it had to be true if he said it. To hear it was to understand he was choosing to begin a transitioning toward another plane of being. I believe it signaled a dark sadness he was unable to shake once he repeatedly couldn't help to encounter the unshakeable pain he suffered with the loss of his mother.

Though for all this relinquishing to the whims of fate, Shahid did not take to taking no for an answer. Once when he had embarked on a gathering of ghazals for his anthology of ghazals he came to be editing, he asked James Tate and me to provide him with ghazals of our own. At the time we were both deep into finishing books and didn't have the wherewithal to write something completely otherwise from what we were doing. So he wrote the poems himself—selecting lines and words from our poems, collaging these to suit a ghazal's form, and delivering to us for our approval ghazals we'd (not) written. He seemed pleased with the outcome, we seemed pleased with the outcome. He'd ghost-written for us because his kindness and love of poetry didn't want us to be left out. He wanted us and so brought us into the eternal world he was always making.

He lets go of the hundredth Name
which rises in calligraphy from his palm.

4

Beloved Witness, Beloved Friend

MAUREEN NOLAN

They met as junior members of Hamilton's faculty, living in college housing and settling into jobs in the English Department. Patricia O'Neill, who was hired to teach nineteenth-century British literature, had a year's head start. She came to campus in 1986. The next year, poet Agha Shahid Ali arrived bearing a manuscript of *The Half-Inch Himalayas*, a volume of his work soon to be published.

The Kashmiri-American Shahid was talented and sought after, with a growing reputation; it was O'Neill's first tenure-track job. They were friends from the first. Both loved Keats and Shelley; when each was trying to lose weight, they would run together; and O'Neill soon secured a spot at Shahid's table. A first-rate cook, he threw celebrated dinner parties with expansive guest lists. He'd invite everyone from kindred-spirit academics to the College administrator for finance, fearless in his desire to get to know everyone. By drawing in faculty from Hamilton, as well as Colgate and Syracuse universities, Shahid created the kind of lively intellectual scene that O'Neill had hoped for when she chose an academic's life.

Later on at Hamilton, Shahid would ask O'Neill to read drafts of his poems that would appear in *A Nostalgist's Map of America*, published in 1991. Not that she knew anything about writing poetry, she says, but Shahid wanted feedback from an intelligent reader. She enjoyed being in his sphere. "It was just fun—fun to be around a real artist and to think about it all."

Years later, Shahid dedicated "Farewell" to her, the first poem in *The Country without a Post Office*, published in 1997 and considered by many to be one of his best works. The dedication was a nod to his pilfering of a sentence O'Neill uttered in passing: "Your history gets in the way of my memory." "I said this in an argument with someone, and Shahid overheard it and used it in a completely different context," she says. It ended up in "Farewell."

Shahid was born in Delhi, and raised in Kashmir, a territory in chronic turmoil, claimed by both India and Pakistan. He came to the United States as a young man to live, study, write, and teach. Reviewers and readers speak of how Shahid inhabited multiple worlds, "shifting worlds," as Matthew Flamm wrote in the *New York Times* in 2001. What especially impresses O'Neill about Shahid the poet is how he found relationships among his Muslim, Hindu, and American cultural experiences, especially in his early works.

Shahid wrote in English, creating complex poetry about longing for home and family, strife and violence in Kashmir, loss and pain. He often chose to work in two extremely difficult forms, the canzone and, most notably, the ghazal, which dates to twelfth-century Arabia. O'Neill considers promoting the ghazal to be one of Shahid's biggest contributions to U.S. literature. She thinks Shahid's interest in poetic form offered a way to constrain the emotions he felt over the conflicts in Kashmir in the 1990s.

Lasting Influence

Hamilton students, it appears, loved Shahid as a teacher. "Shahid was brilliant and very, very funny. He treated poetry with total seriousness and most other things with great humor. It was an irresistible combination," says novelist Kamila Shamsie '94 (1994, the year Shamsie graduated from Hamilton College). She met him soon after she'd arrived on campus from a school in Pakistan. When he asked her to call him Shahid instead of Professor Ali, she explained she was still adjusting to American informality. And he said, "It's one of the things I love most about America," Shamsie recalls. "So he tried from the start to break down the teacher–student barriers."

Within the first few weeks of class, Shahid had shown students, as Shamsie puts it, "how to listen to the music of language." The lesson took hold. She still reads aloud much of her own writing. Shahid left Hamilton in 1993, her senior year, to teach at the University of Massachusetts, Amherst, and after Hamilton, Shamsie enrolled at UMass to pursue a master's of fine arts degree.

Anthony Lacavaro '94 (1994, the year he graduated from Hamilton College), who started writing poems in large measure because of Shahid, also followed him to Amherst to pursue an MFA. "He used poetry as a means to confront, make sense of and at times berate history, politics, instinct and memory; what 20-year-old isn't searching for that conduit?" asks Lacavaro, who still writes poetry and has published over the years. Fifteen or so of Shahid's graduate students went on to publish poems.

Shahid died of brain cancer in 2001 at the age of fifty-two, by then considered an important American poet of the late twentieth century. He lived long enough to learn that he was a finalist for the 2001 National Book Award for his collection *Rooms Are Never Finished*. In that book Shahid writes about Kashmir and his mother's death.

Safeguarding a Legacy

Professor O'Neill's friendship with Shahid continued after he left Hamilton, and when he got sick, she did what she could to support him. He dedicated his last poem, "The Veiled Suite," to her. "I think he did this because in his illness he was having trouble reading and writing. I was just typing his words and reading them back to him," O'Neill says.

During his illness she became close to Shahid's siblings, a relationship that grew into an enduring friendship. They were often around when she visited Shahid at his home in Brooklyn. In the final months of his life, he moved in with his brother, Iqbal, who lived in Amherst. "His brother was very generous, so when I would go to Amherst I would just stay at his house. I have to say, even up until the last month of Shahid's life, there was still a constant party going on; I mean his brother just sort of took over the cooking responsibilities," she says.

Even before Shahid grew ill, O'Neill had pondered how best to celebrate his time as Hamilton's poet. After he died, she landed on the possibility of creating a Hamilton archive of his papers, which were stored with his brother. In 2009, O'Neill approached Special Collections, but it was the College's Digital Humanities Initiative that became the first repository for a selection of the late poet's materials. Thus was born *The Beloved Witness*, an effort to explore the potential of digital scholarship in literature and to expand Shahid's audience. O'Neill and Shahid's sister Hena Ahmad co-direct the project.

"For the next two years I was able to get permission to digitize samples of the different formats in which Shahid's works and papers were held," O'Neill says. "The pilot project was really a proof of concept for the idea of digital archives and what they could do to make a writer's process available to an international community, something which seemed especially important in Shahid's case."

The digital archive includes select videos of Shahid introducing and reading his poems, drafts of his poems and other papers—and a "ghazal" that helps users write their own poems in the challenging form.

In 2011, O'Neill made another pitch to the College library about acquiring Shahid's collection, which his family had agreed to donate to Hamilton. By 2012, Shahid's siblings and the College signed a contract to create the Agha Shahid Ali Special Collections. O'Neill had worked for years toward that possibility; between 2009 and 2012, she made two or three trips annually to Iqbal Ali's attic to sort through the substantial collection.

"Mostly I remember being overwhelmed by the amount of material: hundreds of books, at least ten large plastic containers of papers, videos, audio tapes, at least three file cabinets full of papers, piles of telephone bills, mortgages, doctors' bills, student papers in boxes—and none of it organized at all," O'Neill says.

Shahid, apparently aware that he might someday be archived, saved a vast amount of materials. Among the stash were letters from prominent figures, including writer Salman Rushdie, poet James Merrill, and Edward Said, a Palestinian-American writer and scholar. The archive also includes correspondence and materials donated by Hamilton alumni, Shamsie and Lacavaro among them. (O'Neill is always looking for more.)

The final piece of the archive, Shahid's personal library, became part of the collection last summer. A number of scholars have traveled to Hamilton to work with the archive, including a Fulbright scholar from India. O'Neill is convinced the archive contains a trove of possibilities for Hamilton senior projects and for master's and doctoral work.

"It's fitting that Hamilton should host the archive," Lacavaro says. "It was a pivotal place for Shahid's development as a poet—his engagement with Kashmir, his engagement with form, which had all clearly been there in his early work, really exploded into what would become maybe his finest book, *Country without a Post Office*, which he began there."

Many Hands

Various students have worked on both sides of the archive—digital and paper—over the years. The first piece of *The Beloved Witness* was the senior project for English major Sarah Schultz '12—a digitized exploration of Shahid's poem "Snow on the Desert."

Will Newman '14 worked for about a year burrowing into boxes of Shahid's correspondences, trying to organize them without getting drawn into the letters, which was a challenge. He got involved after he took a course with O'Neill that focused on ways to work with literature beyond the printed book, for instance multimedia projects.

O'Neill retired from Hamilton in 2016, but she and Ahmad remain co-directors of *The Beloved Witness*. For a decade now, Shahid's poetry has informed O'Neill's academic work. These days she's revising a paper on using digital technology in literary interpretation of Shahid's ghazals.

The University of Michigan Press is collecting essays about Shahid's poetry for a volume, to which O'Neill contributed a short bibliography of his early publications. She's hoping the new book and the published work of scholars who have used the archive will spread the word about the collection.

"The Special Collections and the digital archives will, I hope, lead people back always to the poetry itself, which even now, after many readings, still moves me and reminds me that whatever concerns I have about the current political situation, Shahid knew how to hold on to the truth of our too-human condition," O'Neill says. "'Mad heart, be brave' is the final line of the poem 'The Country without a Post Office.' Good tagline for our days as well."

Ghazal

> *Feel the patient's heart*
> *Pounding—oh please, this once—*
> *—JAMES MERRILL*

I'll do what I must if I'm bold in real time.
A refugee, I'll be paroled in real time.
Cool evidence clawed off like shirts of hell-fire?
A former existence untold in real time . . .
The one you would choose: Were you led then by him?

What longing, O Yaar, is controlled in real time?
Each syllable sucked under waves of our earth—
The funeral love comes to hold in real time!
They left him alive so that he could be lonely—
The god of small things is not consoled in real time.
Please afterwards empty my pockets of keys—
It's hell in the city of gold in real time.
God's angels again are—for Satan!—forlorn.
Salvation was bought but sin sold in real time.
And who is the terrorist, who the victim?
We'll know if the country is polled in real time.
"Behind a door marked DANGER" are being unwound
the prayers my friend had enscrolled in real time.
The throat of the rearview and sliding down it
the Street of Farewell's now unrolled in real time.
I heard the incessant dissolving of silk—
I felt my heart growing so old in real time.
Her heart must be ash where her body lies burned.
What hope lets your hands rake the cold in real time?
Now Friend, the Belovèd has stolen your words—
Read slowly: The plot will unfold in real time.
(for Daniel Hall)

At the Museum

But in 2500 B.C. Harappa,
who cast in bronze a servant girl?
No one keeps records
of soldiers and slaves.
The sculptor knew this,
polishing the ache
Off her fingers stiff
from washing the walls
and scrubbing the floors,
from stirring the meat
and the crushed asafoetida
in the bitter gourd.
But I'm grateful she smiled
at the sculptor,

as she smiles at me
in bronze,
a child who had to play woman
to her lord
when the warm June rains
came to Harappa.

Notes

This article first appeared in the *Hamilton Alumni Review* magazine, Spring–Summer 2017. Here it is reprinted with permission of the author.

Poems reprinted with permission. Originally published in *The Veiled Suite: The Collected Poems* (New York: W. W. Norton & Co., 2009).

5

Agha Shahid Ali

Notes and Anecdotes on the Growth of the Poet

FATIMA NOORI

The ancestors of the Agha family migrated to Kashmir from Kashghar, Central Asia (poetry reading 0011) (currently in Xinjiang, PRC) as opposed to the ancient Uzbek city of Samarkand that Shahid refers to in his poem "Snowmen" (HIH, 34).[1] The Agha family was one of the most educated ones around, Shahid's great-grandfather being the first Kashmiri Muslim to matriculate. His grandmother was the first educated woman of the Valley and later became an inspector of women's schools and recited poetry in four languages. Shahid's father was the first man from the Valley to earn a PhD abroad. To this educated, culturally rich, Shia-Muslim family was born the poet Agha Shahid Ali on February 4, 1949. When Shahid was very young, perhaps three or four, the family traveled to London. An amusing story that Shahid's brother, Agha Iqbal Ali, likes to recount (hinting at a career of attention-grabbing antics the poet frequently indulged in) is about a train journey when Shahid was hardly three years old. Baby Shahid was trying to talk to a Londoner who preferred to be engrossed in his newspaper. Young Shahid did not like this and slapped the man in the face, to the embarrassment of his parents and the puzzlement of the poor man! (private conversation, Agha Iqbal Ali, 2015). Shahid would always find a way to make himself heard and noticed. Along with his parents, he lived in Muncie, Indiana, for about three years while his father was earning his PhD there. The family returned to Kashmir, where Shahid completed high school at a Roman Catholic school in Srinagar, the CMS Tyndale Biscoe Memorial School. Later, in 1968, he graduated from the University of Kashmir, studying history, philosophy, and general English. He earned a Master's in English from the Hindu College in 1970. In the same year, the college employed Shahid as a Lecturer, and he continued teaching there until 1975. This period and place spurred Shahid's creativity. In the year 1972, the Writers Workshop in Calcutta published his first collection of poems, *Bone-Sculpture*, while Shahid was still in Delhi. Amitav Ghosh reports that Shahid was a sort of "campus celebrity" there. He had made many friends and would frequently host dinners and also attend them elsewhere, often including poetry-reading sessions. This period, however, was also "deeply conflicted" for Shahid as he had to face certain "rebuffs and disappointments," "betrayals and unhappiness." He was thus happy to move to the United States. Meanwhile, another volume *In Memory of Begum Akhtar and Other Poems* came out in 1979, again published by the Writers Workshop in Calcutta. These early poems earned Shahid credit as a poet and fetched some reviews that lauded his distinct voice but were critical of his craft. Shahid was self-confessedly under the influence of Shelley and T. S. Eliot.

In 1981, Shahid earned a second Masters in English from Pennsylvania State University, and also completed his PhD there in 1984. His dissertation *T. S. Eliot as Editor* was published in 1986 by UMI Research Press. Shahid spent the year 1984–1985 at the University of Arizona earning a Master's degree in Fine Arts in Creative Writing. His revised thesis was published by Wesleyan University Press in 1987 as *The Half-Inch Himalayas*. The excitement of being published by such a reputed publisher after a long wait and several rejections is seen in a letter dated February 14, 1986, in which Shahid writes to his parents: the Wesleyan Press is like "the Rolls Royce of University Presses." The publication of *The Half-Inch Himalayas* immediately shot him to fame. The book earned positive reviews from many American poets, such as James Merrill, Hayden Carruth, Mark Strand, W. S. Merwin, and Forrest Gander, and was included in the *Oxford Anthology of Twelve Modern Indian Poets* edited by A. K. Mehrotra in 2011. Needham Lawrence, an ardent reader and critic of Shahid's poetry, found *The Half-Inch Himalayas* to have "historical and political awareness" (*Satanic Verses*, 12).

Shahid was gradually acknowledged as a major poetic voice in India, as could be deciphered from Eugene Dutta's letter dated August 4, 1997, in which he asks Shahid to send him copies of his poems so that Shahid could be included in the autumn collection of an anthology of poetry and fiction. Dutta sounds upset about Salman Rushdie naming only three notable poets in India: Arun Kolatkar, Jayanta Mahapatra, and A. K. Ramanujan. "While I share Rushdie's despair, I definitely do not agree with his list of notables because I have read your poetry, among others'. Also, I am surprised Nissim Ezekiel's name escapes him. Or that of Dom Moraes, for that matter, whose early poems are quite accomplished."

In March 1985, Shahid married a fifty-two-year-old woman, "Jamie" Stanley Taylor, in Arizona, and she became his close friend and housemate. The marriage was important because it allowed Shahid to remain in the United States as a legal migrant. (His student visa had expired.) The marriage was much more a legal formality than an emotional bond. A letter written by Jamie in January 1986 reveals much about the real nature of the relationship. Jamie was supposed to be a close friend to Shahid but not a real "wife." In many of her letters, Jamie shared her personal problems and discussed her English readings with him. It seemed that the bond between them was a cherished one, as Shahid's 1991 volume *A Nostalgist's Map of America* was dedicated to "Jamie Stanley, 'who brings polish to her every insight.'"

Letters from around the same period (1984–1985) reveal Shahid to be in a love relationship with a certain "Lawrence" (or "Larry") that ended rather painfully. Yet, other letters from late 1992 appear to suggest a rebound. However, partly because Larry's handwriting was often illegible, not much is known about the reasons that ended the relationship. One letter (typed) from September 1992 mentions Larry's fear of contracting HIV. This may or may not be the reason behind Shahid's break-up with Phil, an episode that caused an emotional disaster for the poet. (This story is related in the poem "In Search of Evanescence" in *A Nostalgist's Map of America*.) In his poetry readings, too, Shahid refers to a heartbreak that made him cry all the way during a drive to upstate New York.

> Arizona appealed to my melodramatic nature; the landscape had the same scale and drama as Kashmir . . . I have been to Utah three times before. I came here in 1986 to the Writers at Work Conference as a fellow and then I came back in 1987 and that was when I was about to leave. I was in Arizona at that time. I was about to leave for upstate New York, and when I was here in 1987, I was going through a terrible crisis because just before—I was about to leave for upstate New York and

this love relationship I was in fell apart so I was cutting an exquisite tragic figure in Utah at that time, I came here though I didn't smoke regularly, I suddenly brought a packet of those wonderful luxurious Dunhill cigarettes and I was smoking all the time. You could smoke indoors those days and people said whenever there was a cloud of smoke, they knew I was behind it." (recording 007)

As described, in 1987 Shahid moved from Arizona to Hamilton College in Clinton, New York, to join the teaching faculty. The journey from Arizona to upstate New York forms the skeletal framework of *A Nostalgist's Map of America*. This volume's structure is much like a road trip, the poet experiencing several interesting and fascinating tales during the drive, and the poetry emerging out of it. Thematically based on the northwest American desert, the poems include a few pieces of revisionist reading of popular mythic figures. Many of the stories and circumstances of poems described in the readings were crowd pleasers and were the reason why Shahid became "beloved" to American poetry readers. The story behind the poems "Crucifixion" and "The Keeper of the Dead Hotel" derives from a particular occasion that Shahid describes in this way:

. . . because we had to go through New Mexico and through the Sangra, the Crest of Mountains through New Mexico, I discovered that there is a tribe described as Nomadic Hispanic Catholic [who] came there in the 16th century and they are very secretive and they re-enact the crucifixion every Easter. I saw a photograph of one of the crucifixions done in 1890 something—you see, the Penitents—a group of them in [the] Philippines—they still do it too. Anyway, they are very very secretive and they invariably choose a bachelor to be the Christ figure—the parents never know their son has been chosen but if the child—the boy—the man dies—they leave his sandals outside the door and in the morning the parents know their son has died. And his grave remains secret for one entire year. And as I said they always chose a bachelor, so my epigraph says, "Among the Penitentes, in New Mexico—just before Easter—there is a flurry of marriages."

Bisbee, Arizona . . . a ghost town . . . was a very thriving place at the turn of the century as it was a copper mining town and was a fashionable stop for trains from New Orleans to San

Francisco. There was a strike there in 1917 which was put down really brutally and people in Bisbee really don't like to talk about it now. What they did was—it first was put down and then all the surviving members of the family were put into box cars and sent away to New Mexico deserts, a hundred miles away and so their families had to leave Bisbee to look for their men and their pictures of it—it really looks like it's of Nazi Germany and it's called the Bisbee deportation of July 1917 . . . there's a marvelous hotel in Bisbee called the Copper Queen Hotel—so there is a mixture of facts and fantasy in the poem. (recording 002)

The occasion of poems always made an interesting discussion. Many poems came to Shahid in inspired moments, while others took several months to reach their final form. Reworking the Medusa poem took Shahid some two years and forty-eight drafts. Introducing the poem in a reading, Shahid says that the theme of loneliness in the story of the mythical character appealed to him. He thought about those villains who no one generally identifies with. Eurydice again is one such character that Shahid worked on. "A woman's one chance of getting out of Hell but she could not because of one foolish act by the man who was not trustworthy enough." "The character is placed," Shahid explains, "in the modern equivalent of Hell which would be a concentration camp" (recording 002).

The poetry-reading sessions exhibit much about the art and craft of the poet. The poems frequently discussed included "Snowmen," "Prayer Rug," "Stationery," "Dacca Gauzes," "A Butcher," "Resume," "Medusa," "Hansel and Gretel," "Wolf's Postscript," "Eurydice," "The Country without a Post Office," and the ghazal "Tonight." The early poems from *The Half-Inch Himalayas* volume were revealed to be loosely based on his family history and characters. Shahid sometimes fused figures into one: grandmother from father and mother's side, grand fathers and great-grandfathers, and sometimes imaginary lands were created by fusing two places or events were situated in different contexts. "A Butcher" is one such poem. Shahid explains that while waiting on the steps of Jama Masjid in Old Delhi "a man who did not look so literate asked 'O respected brother, what are you thinking?' Shahid begins to quote a line from the poet Ghalib—*daer nahi, haram nahi, dar nahi, aastan nahi*—and the man immediately completes the line—"*baithen hain reh-guzar pe, koi hame uthae kyun?*" (It is not a temple, nor is it the mosque / Neither it is a door nor the threshold / It is the passage that I sit on, / Why then, am I asked to go away?) (recording 004, Ball State

University). This, Shahid claims, was a very exciting moment. Later they went to a butcher who was "very eloquent with the Urdu language," and he fused the two episodes and figures into one moment that evokes a lost era of poetic grandeur. The poem "Story of a Silence," Shahid explains, is an "attempt to recover the lost women. We were always told about the ancestor men—not women. This is one of my pre-feminist poems" (recording 002).

In a casual talk, Daniel Hall, poet and academician at University of Massachusetts, Amherst, who wrote the introduction to *The Veiled Suite: The Collected Poems* (2009), claims that *A Nostalgist's Map of America* is the book he likes least. *Nostalgist's Map* earned Shahid much fame as a cosmopolitan poet, as a new American voice, and as a chronicler of loss, but as a poet, Shahid felt he needed more restraint in his craft. Daniel Hall knew Shahid's dilemma: "He himself said he was bored with the free verse. It was getting too easy for him, too easy to write a line, too easy to break a line, he needed some constrictions, for his poetry to come alive. He felt he was coming to the end of a phase. There is this long series in *Nostalgist's Map* where lines are just chopped into couplets or tercets not meaning much. It actually is like a long country drive: a lot of it is boring but then something comes up and you say this is interesting but then you are back on the drive again" (Hall, 2015).

Hall was one of Shahid's poetry-confidants; he along with James Merrill and a few others had the privilege of discussing Shahid's poems in their making. These few opinions did matter to Shahid and certainly helped him in chiseling his poems into better works. There is a famous incident in which Shahid sends a poem to James Merrill, who returns it with the comment: "And while you can't really do much about Bosnia, can you improve this poem?" (October 30, 1992). In the same letter, Merrill promises to gift Shahid a rhyming dictionary to help him improve his craft. Shahid met Merrill at a poetry reading and later cooked for him to grab his attention (Ghosh, 5). His friendship with Merrill was important for him as a poet, as Merrill both influenced his craft as well as the content of his poetry. After Begum Akhtar and Faiz Ahmed Faiz, Merrill is the third poetic figure that features in Shahid's poetry. The volume *The Country without a Post Office* was dedicated to Merrill. The poem "I Dream I am at the Ghat of the Only World" is an elegy to Kashmir, its people, the poet's mother, Eqbal Ahmed, the academician, as well as Merrill. According to Amitav Ghosh, Merrill was "the poet who was to radically alter the direction of his poetry: it was after this encounter that he began to experiment with strict metrical patterns and verse forms such as the canzone and the sestina. No one had a greater influence on Shahid's poetry than James Merrill. . . ." Their relation was not unidirectional: Merrill was equally interested in Shahid's work. Ghosh notes that Merrill, who was the best-known living poet in America at that time, was present at Shahid's first poetry reading at the Academy of American Poets. "My stock in New York went up a thousand-fold that evening," Shahid told Ghosh (5).

The year 1991 saw Shahid's translations of Faiz Ahmed Faiz's Urdu poems published by the University of Massachusetts Press as *The Rebel's Silhouette*. This volume has a long introduction that clarifies Shahid's position and his intention as an Indian-American poet. He wanted to bring to the Western world the knowledge of one of the finest poets of the subcontinent, and while doing so make his two worlds meet: to "repay the loan" of the two cultures. This was also the period of severe hostility in Kashmir. The inland trouble in Kashmir, the political uprising of the common people to claim independence, the brutal suppression of the uprising by the Indian army, and the travails of the Pandits who had to leave their home in the Valley to become refugees in Jammu and Delhi deeply affected Shahid, providing a political flavor to his poetics. At a reading in Salt Lake City, Utah, in 1996, Shahid endorsed the idea of an independent Kashmir:

> Usually in India, marriages are held in winter because it is cooler in winter but not in Kashmir and therefore I say, Kashmir should be independent. (reading 007)

> Bill Clinton used to support Kashmir because it was allies with Pakistan but now that the cold war is over, India has become a market for all its goods—but he know[s] how to smile—that was my political comment. I hope I have offended somebody. (reading 0013)

This political pungency is different from his earlier stance where Shahid accepted Kashmir as a state of India. The two passages quoted below are from a talk where Shahid describes his sense of belonging and the privilege that comes with it. Noteworthy is that Shahid acknowledges his affinity with the Indian poetic fraternity and realizes the responsibility that he owes to the Indian poetry.

> When I am writing in English I am very much aware of contributing to Indian literature that is being written in English,

considering English as an Indian language and my idiom is not particularly American, though it has influenced me of late. When I write, I am very much aware now that I am in a position that I can do it or not or people like me are in a position to enrich the English language to contribute to it and do things with it in terms of image, in terms of metaphor, in terms of phrasing that has just not been attempted by . . . let's say, American English, or British English or Irish English etc., etc. I am very much aware that I am writing and because there is an absence of a tradition in English, I am very much aware that I am being given historically a unique position to do something very fresh. Whether I do it or not is my personal failing but I am in a position to do it now and in that sense I come back to the point of being—my having inherited three major world civilizations through certain permutations in India and I am very much aware that I am contributing to Indian English and therefore also to World English in one way or the other.

My sense of self is very much defined by the fact that I belong to a group in India that speaks English and is by and large an affluent group of India. And that creates a certain kind of tension, because as a poet I am actually aware that I belong to a privileged group and that privilege is defined by fact that I speak English and speak it in a particular manner and I cannot really reach the masses of India as poets in India do as there are poets who have millions of people as audience and can be quoted by them. And also, my sense of self is very much defined from the fact that *I am a Muslim from India* and it could be a negative situation because I have to appeal. I mean my audience is largely the audience that has drawing rooms and has English Literature background etc., etc. but I think on the international level, this could be used positively because by writing in English I could reach out to a large audience in the world. I am very much aware that I have inherited three major world civilizations; the Islamic, the Hindu, the Western. Much as I don't like any of these terms, I have used them for fresh purposes in the English language and I am very much aware as I write that I have to one way or the other, either reconcile them or make a virtue of the contradictions and write about them. That's my sense of self I suppose. I am also aware that I am a kind of a multiple exile. I am an exile in India because I am in a sense on loan to English language and I am for whatever reasons—I am also an exile in the sense that I tend to get very attached to places, I can be in a place—I was in New Orleans just for a day and I thought I could live there forever. So I left Cashmere, I went to Delhi, I became an exile from Cashmere—exile is not the right word exactly because exile really means you are forced into a situation. I am more an expatriate, I have chosen to be here and then from Delhi I went to Pennsylvania, from Penn I went to Arizona and now I am in upstate New York and each place I have left behind I feel exiled from one place to the other to the other. So I suppose, that's as vague as I can be. (reading 005)

From acknowledging his roots as "Indian" to getting specifically "Kashmiri-American," somewhere during the 1990s turmoil Shahid's fidelities changed and his allegiance to his homeland and its cause for independence concretized. The political trouble in Kashmir changed much in all who were associated with the land. Shahid could not remain unaffected despite being thousands of miles away. Poems like "I See Kashmir from New Delhi at Midnight," "Dear Shahid," "Return to Harmony," "Muharram in Srinagar," "A Villanelle," and "Hans Christian Ostro" are heavily borrowed from real-life events. The surrealistic episodes and the people who populate the poems are very much real. The land that Shahid constructed in *The Country without a Post Office* oscillates between a utopian paradise and a demolished palace. The word "country" in the volume reveals Shahid's politics at the time, favoring an independent rule. However, unlike "nation" or "state," "country" is a rather mellowed and apolitical term, signifying natural affinity and not the militant pride or control that the other terms denote.

> I come from Kashmir, which is a very troubled place these days. There's a big freedom struggle going on there and much to my incredible disappointment because I have been very fond of India, India has cracked down in very, very ugly ways in Kashmir. (reading, 007)

The Kashmir episode brought in a sense of real exile in Shahid, as it blocked the way of the "return." For migrants with a no-return option, the homeland is frozen in time and memory at the point when he sees it the last time or had their happiest, saddest, most interesting memory. In

Shahid's case, these memories were reinforced by his annual trips to Kashmir. The home was therefore not actually lost; the memories were updated, fluid, in formation. The idea of separation from home hits him only when the political situation becomes so intense that the passage to the Valley is shut off to the rest of the world. There was a period when even post offices were shut down, leading to the genesis of *The Country without a Post Office*, published in 1997.

> My new book is called *Country without a Post Office*—the entire book is a response to these events in Cashmere. The reason for the title is . . . there has been no mail delivered for six months from the local post office across the river so he went there and he looks down and there were bags and bags of mails lying down there and there was a letter addressed to my father, so he picked it up and kept it till he could give it to my father." (recording 002)

The sense of "exile" therefore sets in late in Shahid's work. The bloodshed and killing were brutally suppressed by the deployment of the army, and the bitterness of the aftermath changed the cultural composition of the land. Shahid was in constant reception of the several newsletters and reports that were brought out by the native Kashmiri freedom fighters—an entire pile of such documents and reports lay at the Hamilton College archive.

Interestingly, Shahid met and interviewed Palestinian-American academician Edward Said.[2] The unpublished interview, *The Art of Criticism*, conducted in 1993 in three rounds, is a lengthy discussion between two minds that knew their preferences and positions but were struggling to define their identities according to the demands of their international situation. Shahid appears to stand aligned with Said on the issues of exile and identity, as Said confesses that "exile need not mean deprivation; it could, in fact, mean a multiplication of awareness." However, the 1967 war in Palestine is what triggered Said's identity and changed his personal politics:

> I felt a shattering disorientation as a result of the war [1967, Palestine]. I was given a sense of being claimed by the Arab world. Don't forget I had lived away from it for almost seventeen years in this country. I mean I would still go back but my work and my career had been entirely Western and American. And all of a sudden these events which affected my whole family over there

had radically affected me. And one of the things that affected me was the sense that my rather precariously formed identity as an American and as an academic had suddenly given way to this extraordinary intervention in my life formed by the '67 war. . . . (Said, 41)

A similar pattern is evident in Shahid's case; it was after the Kashmir turmoil (1989–1992) that his poetry gained an unprecedented intensity. When the situation in Kashmir subsided, Shahid's mother, Sufia Ashraf, developed a brain tumor and, after undergoing treatment in the United States for nearly a year, passed away in April 1997. The volume *Rooms Are Never Finished* (2000) is dedicated to her memory and relates to the event of her passing away and the rituals afterward. According to Shahid, he could not write for an entire year. The elegy that he composes after that spell of mourning comes in the form of a *marsiya*, a Persian or Urdu elegiac form. Shahid pays tribute to not only his mother but to his roots as well by including that form into the frame of his work. This poetic form, along with its traditional narrative of the death of Imam Hussain, a legendary figure of sacrifice in Islamic history, at the battle of Karbala, and the tropes of lament and mourning that it offers were well suited to Shahid's poetic theory at that point. The principal poem of the volume, "Lenox Hill," is a canzone—an elaborate and intricate Italian form attempted by only six poets before Shahid: Auden, Merrill, Anthony Hecht, Marilyn Hacker, and John Hollander. Shahid himself wrote three canzones: "After August Wedding," "Lenox Hill," and "The Veiled Suite." The latter was written in his last days, when he had almost lost his vision and needed a scribe to pen his poem. Patricia O'Neill, to whom the poem is dedicated, accomplished the task. These stringent forms were a harness to Shahid's raw emotions, but it was ultimately the ghazal that fulfilled his needs as a poet and craftsman. As an Urdu-speaking Indian, Shahid felt he could not let go of certain emotions, ideas, images, and traditions; he felt compelled to introduce the ghazal form to his English-speaking audience. This project of "repaying the loan" of one culture and language to another began with the translation of Faiz's Urdu poems in *The Rebel's Silhouette* (1991). The next important step was bringing the ghazal to the American scene. The contributors to *Ravishing DisUnities* (2000) were poets and students of Shahid from the various American universities and colleges where he had taught. Shahid took great efforts to teach the peculiarities and requirements of the form to them. However, most of the ghazals in this volume lack an Indian, Persian, or

Urdu subject matter, metaphor, or mood. The metaphorical East does meet the West, but the exchange remains strained, as the emotional ground of the ghazal is completely bypassed by the American poets. The "loan of the two languages and cultures" that Shahid referred to in his introduction to *The Rebel's Silhouette* is ultimately and fully paid off only in the last volume, *Call Me Ishmael Tonight*, where the English language is molded and suffused with the syntax and idiom of the Urdu to produce the ghazal in English.

Some of Shahid's personal relations appear to dictate his poetics, if not the poetry. Begum Akhtar and Faiz Ahmed Faiz are mentioned profusely, showing Shahid's involvement with them at several levels. Faiz taught him that the central theme of his poetry could be multifocal—the beloved can be a woman, God, home, or revolution, and in Shahid's case, home and homeland. From Begum Akhtar he learned to harness his pain. Just as Akhtar's ghazals were sung in classical Indian ragas, Shahid's poetry happened in the compulsions of strict metrical forms. She features in his poems repeatedly as a figure that haunts him as well as grounds him. She symbolizes loss, beloved, and art in his poems, as well as the perfection of art. The diamond on her nose, her blue sari, and her voice singing classical tunes are motifs that signify both indulgence and control. Merrill is the other important figure whose presence is felt in Shahid's work. He was a father figure who played a major role in giving the right direction to Shahid's poetry. From lending Shahid a rhyming dictionary to fine-tuning his words and ideas to chiseling the entire volume, Merrill was perhaps the greatest influence on Shahid—after, of course, his mother. From Merrill, Shahid learned the craft of writing poems that were "deeply personal but not confessional," as well as infusing his poems with what T. S. Eliot called the "objective correlative"—the emotions conveyed through images, events, tonality, and even form. The "I" in Shahid's poetry is different from the "I" of Sylvia Plath, Robert Lowell, or Adrienne Rich, or even Nissim Ezekiel or Kamala Das. Shahid's "I" is much more in the tradition of Whitman and Frost, Ghalib and Faiz. Shahid is deeply aware of his political position as an Indian-Muslim-Kashmiri-Shia having an English-medium education and living in the United States. (Shahid became an American citizen only after his death on April 4, 2001.)

Harold Bloom, who included Shahid's *The Veiled Suite* in his collection of last poems *Till I End My Song: A Gathering of Last Poems* (2010), commented that the mother was the person Shahid was closest to in life. None of Shahid's readers would miss that point. She was a contributor to Shahid's poems both as inspiration and driving force. She was even more significant if one keeps in view Shahid's homosexuality and the absence of a long-term partner. (He was close to two or three men, deciphering from the letters, but none of the relationships appears to have worked out well.) Hoshang Merchant has written an excellent essay, *Agha Shahid Ali's Gay Nation* (2009), delineating Shahid's sexual "subtext" and overt "mother fixation."

When trying to capture the complexity of Shahid the man, one thing that deserves special mention is his impish humor and ingenious wit. As a person, Shahid was not just friendly and good natured, but he tended to be the center of attraction at all parties. Daniel Hall grudgingly admits how bad he felt when he went to a party with Shahid and everybody in the room seemed to know him and wanted to talk to him while Hall just tailed behind holding Shahid's jacket! Some of his poems, too, emerge from his comfort with the ludicrous. "Poets on Bathroom Walls" (95) is a perfect example. In the ghazals, as well, the ludicrous is taken much seriously and provides a necessary angle to the poet's personality. "White men across the U.S. love their wives' curries— / I say *O No!* to the turmeric of it all" ("Of It All," 329). "I, from the upper birth, slip 'down into her dream.' / Choo-choo 'Goes the train towards' some déjà-vu things" ("Things," 333). His poetry readings gathered huge audiences mainly because of his open demeanor, vividness, and brilliance. Some of his witty comments need to be reproduced verbatim:

> I don't want to be a demanding Third Worlder but I'd like some water somehow—the things you can get away [with] if you are a foreigner. I have always told people it's an advantage to be a foreigner. You can act as eccentric as you can and everyone will think it's a cultural thing. (reading 004)

While reading out his poems to a packed hall, Shahid pauses to notice two more men entering the hall. They were probably standing at the back of the hall (not visible in the video), but Shahid is concerned for them: "Oh, come and sit in the front. There is an empty chair here. And if one of you wants to sit here (pointing to the space before the front row), I don't mind a white man at my feet" (reading 007). At the same session (007), before reading "The Last Saffron," Shahid takes delight in claiming that the best saffron is produced in Iran and Kashmir and that Spanish saffron "if I may hurt people" is not good enough. Later he pauses and says, "Oh! I was hoping I would come to Utah and be the darkest thing here, but it isn't possible anymore." Shahid draws a roguish pleasure in speaking the unspeakable: "Are you all nervous, now? You see, I can say things that are politically incorrect. You can't—being so white. What a pity! I offer you my sympathies." These details of Shahid's wit and informal humor, sometimes direct and thus inappropriate, reveal an aspect of his personality, what Ghosh called "transmuting the mundane into magical" (3). Shahid was fond of cooking and hosting, songs and singing, dancing, and getting in front of the camera; he never missed an opportunity to show off and would frequently get himself "clicked" to send pictures to his family. The occasion for the title poem of the volume *Rooms Are Never Finished* is a relished story and throws light on Shahid's wit, ingenuity, and process:

> This longish introduction is to introduce my next poem, which is the title of my new book, which is not out; it will be out in a few months. It so happened that I got a telephone call from a guy and he said "I'm the literary editor of a new magazine of interiors, called *Nest* and we would like you to write a poem to go with this feature we are doing on some billionaire's house." And I was sort of hesitating and humming and he said "Well, you know, we'll pay you fifteen-hundred dollars, and I said "well I'm not on sale, but I am for sale." But I did tell him "please send me material, send me stuff, send me interviews with the designer" so he sent me two interviews with the designers, two different designers and sent me cuttings, fabrics, pictures, all kinds of things. And as I was writing this, I was looking at it and one of the designers said "well you know rooms are never finished." And I said: "Oh, Rooms are never finished! that could be the title of this poem." So I wrote down "rooms are never finished" and then, the other designer said: "many of my favorite things are broken." And I said, "Aha, that could be the epigraph of my poem." So now I have the title, I have my epigraph, "many of my favorite things are broken" and now to write the damn poem. Then I was at the same time, working on a ghazal, in which my rhyme scheme was the 'I' sound, like I, sigh, die, and the refrain was the word 'in,' cry in, die in. So I said, "well why don't I discard the ghazal and create my own form, remembering the word "stanza" in Italian means rooms. So—*Rooms Are Never Finished*, I create my own poem in which no stanza really ends; it always leads to the next room with the

word in. I'm telling you all this to show you how ingenious I am. (reading 012)

Two major Indian traditions found in Shahid's poetry contribute to his persona of a post-independence and postcolonial product—the Urdu Ghazal and the Bollywood cinema. "There were certain things—images, ideas, or people that Shahid felt he just could not miss," says Shahid's brother, Agha Iqbal Ali.[3] Images of bangles, diamonds glittering, watching movies, mirror-studded quilts, performance on stage, postcards—that create an echo of Hindi cinema. On several occasions, phrases hint subtly to a common Bollywood image: "And my memory will be a little / out of focus, in it / a giant negative, black / and white, still undeveloped" ("Postcard," 29). "Mughul ceilings, let your mirrored convexities / multiply me at once under your spell tonight" ("Tonight," 374). This image is a direct reproduction of a scene from a song sequence from the popular Bollywood movie *Mughal-e-Azam* (1960).

Most Bollywood devouts would sniff the heavy loan in Shahid's poetic imagery as well as his poetic temperament. Sheila Dhar, the Indian classical singer and a friend to the Agha family, once sent a ghazal to Shahid (Letter June, 1980) by Asghar Gondvi "*Husn ban kar khud ko aalam ashkara kijiye / phir mujhe parda bana kar mujhse parda kijiye.*" This finds resonance in his last poem "The Veiled Suite"—"Make me now your veil, then see if you can veil / yourself from me." (23) The lines from the ghazal "From the Start," "I am mere dust. The desert hides itself in me. / Against me the ocean has reclined from the start" (339) are a transcreation of a Ghalib *sher*: "*Hota hai nihaan gard mein sehra mere hotel ghista hai jabeen khaak pe dariyan mere aagey.*" "Something like smoke rises from the snuffed-out distance" ("For You," 328) is from a Mir couplet: "*Basti basti khaak udi hai, jungle jungle aag / Ye dhuan balkhata uthey jaise kaaley naag.*" Similarly, "Ghazal . . . wears her grief, a moon-soaked white . . ." ("In Memory of Begum Akhtar," 53). "In the lake the arms of temples and mosques are locked / in each other's reflection" ("Farewell," 176) and "If clouds were boats, / one would row them // with rods of lightning / across the world ("Flight from Houston in January," 69) are re-creations of very popular images from Bollywood. These are but a few examples, and readers will find such hidden and layered images at many places. Many are translated and used in italics or within double-quote marks.

Shahid died just as he lived: full of wit and humor, living instantaneously and yet living largely. Almost two hundred people attended his funeral, "all claiming to be Shahid's close friends," recounts Daniel Hall. Agha Iqbal Ali and Patricia O'Neill repeat the story almost verbatim. He was on his way to class when he had his first blackout. "I'm dying," was his realization at the moment, but he tells himself, "No. First I'll teach my class, then I'll die" (Katyal, 2011). "The University at Utah [where Shahid held his last academic position as a professor] was very good to Shahid in retaining the position, the health insurance. Shahid's brother was a godsend!" claims Daniel Hall (letter, October 19, 1998).

Shahid's brother, Agha Iqbal Ali, himself a professor at University of Massachusetts, Amherst, is the chief source of all the small stories that are so important to understanding Shahid and his poetry. Iqbal, like Shahid, is popular for his digressive narration. The setting up of a temple and then a chapel in his room, the mother dressing Shahid as Krishna, the occasion of poems, the fusion of imageries from different sources, the influences of people and poets on Shahid's work are all such stories. The brother himself was quite a support to Shahid. Apart from being a companion and a nurse to his brother in his last days, Iqbal also managed the organization of *Call Me Ishmael Tonight*, published posthumously. While trying to explain how Shahid came to use Islamic references in his later poetry, Iqbal recounts:

> The whole thing about Ishmael also comes in from my mother because she knew the Quran completely. She had her scotch but she also prayed. So, she was a cosmopolitan and a devout in a true sense. She had grown up in a very devout family so she knew tradition inside out, she had her own practices and there is a sense of spirituality in the house. There was a sense of spirituality in the sense of *praja* (subjects). There were simple things. So basically, when we'd arrive Mummy used to *utharo the aarti* (a Hindu ritual of welcoming the members/winners). She said touch the rice, touch the money and then give it away to the servants and tell them to find a fakir. . . . We were not raised to be practicing Muslims in everyday life. We were exposed to some episodes. Invited to Ashura. Hearing the Marsiya. We started offering *namaz-e-janaza* with the political trouble in Kashmir before my mother's death. I don't think as a child *Bhaiyya* ever went to *Namaz-e-Janaza*. He had no sense of that. At that time, he was more into Jesus and Krishna. The awareness of Islam comes in much later and it is the sense of history that kicks in. What is the history of Islam? He goes through a

lot of books and there is a poetic aspect of it all and it comes from my mother. When she was ill, she made this remark: "O, Allah has promised *Houris* to men but what about me? What do I get?" It is then Shahid makes that comment, "Wide-eyed *houris* and immortal youths" ["In Arabic," 372]. Bhaiyya brings in the men! That comment did not come in from Bhaiyya; it's an awareness that comes on from my mother.

There is a marked absence of discussion of the personal and love relationships in letters exchanged with his parents. It was only on one occasion that his mother casually mentions at the end of a letter (June 2, 1979): "When do you contemplate marriage—if at all! You know I am not either impatient or anxious on that score but if one has to—then certainly it should be before you are 33—I have read somewhere that each couple produces its most brilliant 'product' when the father is 33 or 34!!!" Apart from this, there are no references to Shahid's relationships in his letters. The content of most letters revolved around Shahid's visit to India, or asking them to come and visit him, his publications, fellowships, awards, jobs, and a frequent inquiry into the well-being of other family members and friends in Kashmir and Delhi. His poems too never take up his love relationships directly. Unlike most contemporary postmodern poets, who express anxiety about marriage and love relations, show affection or fear of childbearing or children, or even make efforts to come to terms with their sexuality—excesses, lacks, diversions, or just expressions, Shahid never really enters that arena. He instead carefully and meticulously builds up a form of poetic idiom reworking the Urdu-Persian model that suits his suggestive temperament. The ghazal with its exigency of emotional indulgence, the forbidden love relations, the ever-evasive beloved, the ever-pained lover, and most importantly, its either male-to-male or nongendered address, allows Shahid the scope to remain ambiguous. It was not that he was ashamed or uncomfortable about his homosexuality; most friends attest Shahid to be very overtly gay, especially in his later days. Shahid, however, had a clear agenda from the beginning: he was aware of the privileges of the colonial heritage he was a legacy of, as well as his unique in-between "witness" position as a diasporic, multicultural Indian, and also due to his learning in more than one language. Shahid's aim was to bring this aspect to the forefront. This was where Shahid becomes political even while evading the gender politics.

The poet Hoshang Merchant wrote several letters to Shahid from 1991 to 1997 asking him to allow him to include his work in an anthology of gay writings from Indian writers he was putting together. The poem "The Country without a Post Office" was included in *Yarana: Gay Writing from India*, published in 2011. However, reading the letters (only Hoshang's) reveal that Shahid did not acquiesce easily. Shahid also rejected the proposal to include his name in an anthology of gay men and their religions—*Wrestling with the Angel*—compiled by Brian Bouldrey in 1993 (letter, October 30, 1993).

Agha Shahid Ali's sexuality and its consciousness in his poetry remains an unexplored area by critics other than Hoshang Merchant. Shahid's vision about the necessity of his poetry seems to be working at a level different from that of militant literary politics where the "personal" is put up to feed the "political." Shahid's poetry was trying to rekindle that *lihaz*—culture-induced reverence of Urdu poetry cultivated by master poets Ghalib and Mir—sexuality remains an undiscussed topic even when love is the thriving emotion.[4] Here are a few sample lines from *Call Me Ishmael Tonight* that hint slantingly to the sexual orientation of the poet:

> Elusively gay but not quite presently straight,
> one is stone in his own forest stream about me.
> ("About Me," 353)

> Ah, bisexual Heaven: wide-eyed *houris* and immortal youths!
> To your each desire they say *Yes! O Yes!* in Arabic.
> ("In Arabic," 372)

> If you wish to know of a king who loved his slave,
> you must learn legends, often-sung, beyond English.
> ("Beyond English," 361)

Notes

1. Poetry Reading Sessions 001 to 015 are videotapes of Shahid's poetry readings at several locations across the United States.

Please note that I am attempting in this chapter to compile a biographical essay of Agha Shahid Ali primarily from the bits of information I collected during the tenure of my Fulbright Fellowship in the United States. This chapter thus may not entirely conform to the expectations of academic writing. The information recollected here is from disparate sources including videotapes of Shahid's poetry readings, interviews, class notes, letters, and official documents. Also included here are bits from discussions with Shahid's brother Agha Iqbal Ali (professor, MIT, Amherst);

poet Daniel Hall, who teaches/taught at Amherst College; Patricia O'Neill, a friend to Shahid and my supervisor at Hamilton College in Clinton, New York. The Burke Library at Hamilton College holds the digital archive of Shahid's manuscripts and letters. These anecdotes, I believe, help to capture a sense of Shahid's personality.

2. The Edward Said interview, *The Art of Criticism*, was recorded on August 24, 1993; September 27, 1994; and December 16, 1993.

3. Conversations with Daniel Hall and Agha Iqbal Ali took place on November 11, 2015, during my Fulbright Fellowship tenure in the United States. As mentioned earlier, O'Neill was my supervisor at Hamilton College.

4. Translations of Urdu are mine.

Works Cited

Ali, Agha Iqbal, Casual Talk. Amherst, Massachusetts. November 11, 2015.
Ali, Agha Shahid. Introduction to *Ravishing DisUnities: Real Ghazals in English*. Wesleyan University Press, 2000.
———. *The Veiled Suite*. New York: W. W. Norton, 2009.
———. trans. Introduction to *The Rebel's Silhouette: Selected Poems by Faiz Ahmed Faiz*.
———. Recording 002, New Worlds of New Literature, New York.
———. Reading 004, Ball State University, Munice, Indiana.
———. Reading 005, unnamed, undated.
———. Recording 007, *Anne Newton Sultan Poetry Series*, Westminster College, March 6, 1997.
———. Reading 012, Baruch College, New York City. Undated
Bloom, Harold (Ed.). *Till I End My Song: A Gathering of Last Poems*. Harper Perennial. 2011.
Hall, Daniel. Casual Talk. Amherst, Massachusetts. November 11, 2015.
Katyal, Akhil. "'i swear . . . i have my hopes': Agha Shahid Ali's Delhi Years." *Kafila*. Blog, January 30, 2011. https://kafila.online/2011/01/30/'i-swear-i-have-my-hopes'-agha-shahid-ali's-delhi-years
King, Bruce. Agha Shahid Ali's Tricultural Nostalgia. 2001. http://www.jstor.org/stable/25797511
Mehrotra, Arvind Krishna, ed. "Agha Shahid Ali." *The Oxford India Anthology of Twelve Modern Indian Poets*. Delhi: Oxford University Press, 1992.
Merchant, Hoshang. "Agha Shahid Ali's gay nation." *Forbidden Sex/Forbidden Texts: New India's Gay Poets*. Routledge, 2009.
Ghosh, Amitav. "'The Ghat of the Only World': Agha Shahid Ali in Brooklyn." *The Annual of Urdu Studies* 17 (2002): 1–19.
Said, Edward, "The Art of Criticism." Interview by Agha Shahid Ali, New York, 1993.

6

"Separation's Geography"
Agha Shahid Ali's Scholarship of Evanescence

Amy Newman

> It seems proper that those who create art in a civilization of quasi-barbarism, which has made so many homeless, should themselves be poets unhoused and wanderers across language.
>
> —George Steiner

It is tempting to read Agha Shahid Ali as an Indian poet writing in English, poised under the mantle of postcolonial literature, or as a Kashmiri-American poet, the title he finally settled on himself.[1] Equally tempting is to read Shahid as an exile in the conventional sense of the term, since his homeland was not North America, though he spent most of his adult life there. Although his poetry is dense with the landscapes of pre- and post-partition India and of his travels through and transitions to America, his nostalgia is extraterritorial. It is not limited to the borders and water bodies between countries but extends to the boundaries of human longing, dissolving postcolonial categorizations and etching poetry of a geophilosophical rather than a geographic exile. In an article in *Middle East Report*, Michael Fischer suggests that Shahid "reminds us of the ways in which so many different identities suffer in a family of resemblance that makes all of us family, however woundedly antagonistic."² Shahid's championing of the ghazal form is especially significant, as the ghazal and its history mirror the physiological state of the human in eternal exile, in a nostalgic search for a lost paradise. The poet's career is a narrative of the intricacies of loss, the evocation of estrangement as the true state of the human condition, and the drive to reassemble the world as a response to such dispossessions. As his oeuvre matured, his reliance on traditional forms increased. In Shahid's three books, *A Nostalgist's Map of America* (1991), *The Country without a Post Office* (1997), and *Rooms Are Never Finished* (2001), the poet houses his increasing awareness of dislocation and death in a number of poetic forms, offering temporary shelter for a voice that sings of the transience of existence.

In *Reflections on Exile* Edward Said defines exile as "the unhealable rift forced between a human being and a native place, between the self and its true home: its essential sadness can never be surmounted. . . . Like death but without death's ultimate mercy, it has torn millions of people from the nourishment of tradition, family, and geography."[3] By conventional definition, an exile is one separated from his country; the term houses both those who have chosen to live elsewhere and those banished by decree. Yet we limit its possibilities when we endeavor to understand exile only in its conventional usage.

The Bible begins as a story of exile, and exile may gloss the burden of the unknown, the nongeographic wandering and wondering that humans experience. Though established categories are useful for critical approaches, when studying the poetic voice, one must consider the condition of the human in spiritual as well as in secular terms. The doctrine of salvation underlying the world's major religions postulates that in our earthly forms, we are in a spiritual condition of pre-fulfillment and that the human condition is saturated with this sense of the limits of knowing. The garden, the mother's womb, the childhood home, and the countries one leaves may each be read as a stage in a journey away from or toward perfection, as though when we were driven *from* paradise, we were exiled *into* the human condition. Poetry, concerned with the human voice, is a record of that journey.

Shahid created a renaissance of sorts for the ghazal, a form of poetry that he dates back to seventh-century Arabia.[4] While the United States had its dabblers in the form, for Shahid, those dabblings were hardly writing ghazals at all. There was first the matter of the rules of the form, as Shahid notes:

> The opening couplet (called matla) sets up a scheme (of rhyme—
> called qafia; and refrain—called radif) by having it occur in both

lines—the rhyme IMMEDIATELY preceding the refrain—and then this scheme occurs only in the second line of each succeeding couplet. That is, once a poet establishes the scheme—with total freedom, I might add—she or he becomes its slave.[5]

There are additional conditions (the poet names himself in the last couplet, for instance), yet as with contemporary sestinas that are simply six-line stanzas, or sonnets whose sole adherence to the form is to be found in the poem's having fourteen lines, some ghazals are considered ghazals simply because they are so called. But to discard the formal requirements is to miss the point of the form, which is to contribute to the poem's series of competing forces. To avoid the *matla*, *qafia*, or *radif* is to ask the ghazal to lose its blood, its underlying resemblance to life itself. In a 2002 interview with Christine Benvenuto, Shahid takes issue with poets such as Adrienne Rich and James Harrison for this very reason: "Though I like things they have done with what they call ghazals, those are not ghazals, they simply aren't."[6]

At the same time that the poem is expressing an underlying fidelity within its ranks based on this interwoven pattern of rhyme and repetition, each couplet within must express a notion of sovereignty, of independence. This internal complication generates an accumulating sense of simultaneous disunities and unities. A true ghazal insists on both the rule of rhyme and repetition and the autonomy of each couplet in the form. Laced together, the couplets merge into a fully realized ghazal, resonant of both independence and a near simultaneous resolution of repeated sound. A ghazal's *radif* and *qafia* give it, as Shahid writes in *The Rebel's Silhouette: Selected Poems by Faiz Ahmed Faiz*, a "peculiar fragrance . . . its constant sense of longing."[7] The self-reliant couplet sings its sovereignty, yet the *radif* and *qafia* confirm repeatedly that the couplet is in fact enslaved. Roam in autonomy as the couplet may, it will always be reminded of return. A form that simultaneously embraces independence *and* linkage would be attractive to a poet who is so deeply interested in the condition of the exile and its attendant heartbreak, as Shahid writes in *Ravishing DisUnities: Real Ghazals in English*: "Remember one definition of the word ghazal. It is the cry of the gazelle when it is cornered in a hunt and knows it will die. Thus, to quote Ahmed Ali: 'the atmosphere of sadness and grief that pervades the ghazal . . . reflects its origin in this' and in the form's 'dedication to love and the beloved.'"[8]

It is no coincidence that Shahid should have found in this form his strength as a writer. In the first ghazal he wrote,[9] the final couplet is a telling discovery for both the poet and his readers. "They ask me to tell them what Shahid means— / Listen: It means 'The Beloved' in Persian, 'witness' in Arabic."[10] That Shahid should be a witness, and also stand for love, underlines Ahmed Ali's reminder that the ghazal is both "melancholic and amorous."[11] One may imagine that the cry of a gazelle when it is cornered and foresees its death would contain something akin to witnessing: fear, knowledge, regret, and grief, and then, certainly, love for the vanishing world.

The arc of Shahid's poetic career may be read as the personal evolution of this condition. The poet was an exile in the conventional sense of the term, having spent most of his adult life in a country that was not his own. His poetry reflects back on the changing landscapes of India, initially focusing on his childhood in New Delhi but shifting in later works to the Kashmir he loved, which since 1947 had suffered brutally in the dispute between India and Pakistan. He consciously plays with the term of exile: in some places he refers to himself as a "multiple-exile"[12] and yet with Benvenuto insists that the condition didn't apply to him or his work. "I say please don't be so fussy about it. The airplanes work. I mean, if you have a certain kind of income, whether you live in Bombay and fly to Kashmir, or you live in New York and fly to Kashmir, for a certain group it really makes no difference."[13] Readers familiar with Shahid's work can identify his roots—his family, friends, and his beloved Kashmir. Yet the creation of and insistence on the existence of roots is a part of the "emotional resonance" of the exile;[14] if he is to endure life, an exile must attempt to deny his essentially rootless, wandering state.

One who is both rooted and emotionally exiled therefore roosts in contradiction, a landscape of tension between continuity and dislocation. Similarly, since form offers the comfort of a historical and social body, Shahid's later appropriation of, in addition to the ghazal, complex traditional forms such as canzones, pantoums, sestinas, terza rimas, and villanelles suggests that the poet sought traditional structures of solidity within which the present could exist, however temporarily, a home within which the individual's voice wanders, grieves, and ultimately sings.

Initially Shahid uses the word *exile* as belonging to the poetic vocabulary. Bruce King finds in Shahid's early work *Bone-Sculpture* (1972) "clichés of exile and biculturalism" but also the "stronger images" of "a now dead world that will not reply to his interest."[15] Early in his career his poetry locates the past in India, in his mother's and father's homelands; later his experience places the transparencies of his past over his present in a shifting of alternative landscapes. The differing topographies share amassing histories of loss. In his penultimate collection, *The Country without a Post Office*,

Kashmir stands for all landscapes of suffering and for the lost paradise. In his final book, *Rooms Are Never Finished*, the poet returns with his mother's body to their devastated homeland for her burial, this journey a bereavement of his two essential roots. The nostalgias the poet practices begin as memory for lost cultures and peoples, and become over time the nostalgia of the heart, a cry like that of a gazelle for its accumulated losses.

One may study the titles for a short narrative of compounding ruptures: *A Walk Through the Yellow Pages* (1987) will share with Shahid's future book titles a desire to grasp distance through contrivance (here the telephone, and in later work the postcard, the post office, the map) and the hollow substitutes for traversing, recording, and overcoming distance that these resources may provide. As does a true postcard. The postcard trope of *The Half-Inch Himalayas* (1987) evokes distance and homesickness, suggesting we are severed from home's true dimensions. The title is from the fourth line of "Postcard from Kashmir":

> Kashmir shrinks into my mailbox,
> my home a neat four by six inches.
> I always loved neatness. Now I hold
> the half-inch Himalayas in my hand.
> This is home. And this the closest
> I'll ever be to home.[16]

Here the poet finds his origins neatly arranged for him in a limited space. It is a considerable act of physics to shrink the Himalayan mountain range down to two dimensions. Whatever is real, textural, tactile, and memorable about the vast range of mountains is lost in this tiny reproduction, shrunk from the true subject; implicit in the act of reduction is the accompanying lifelike dissolution of a landscape of home. True color or not, a picture can only contain an image, after all. All else associated with the Himalayas must relocate to memory and imagination and, therefore, find a home now only in desire. The poet thus implies connection and distance simultaneously. As witness and storyteller of family and continental history, and as one who through this retelling continues to embrace the dissolving past, Shahid conjures himself as representative for those who experience a persistent loss.

The shift from *The Half-Inch Himalayas* to *A Nostalgist's Map of America*, a shift in the connotations of home, records the poet's transition from geographic exile to spiritual exile as he becomes aware that, eventually, *everything* will vanish.

While he is more at home in America now, as the collection proceeds he reveals that home is not immune to loss and that the world offers only the mirage of stability. We may read Shahid's gesture away from the unrhymed stanzas and syllabics of his first books to the more increasingly complex traditional constructions in *A Nostalgist's Map of America*, *The Country without a Post Office*, and *Rooms Are Never Finished* as a distinct maturation of voice, as well as the poet's greater acknowledgment of the themes of disruption, violence, and death. The tightly weaving forms that Shahid increasingly employs are patterns of turn and return, of echo and of interlocking: the ghazal's doubling voices of *qafia* and *radif*; the villanelle and terza rima's rhyme and repetition; the pantoum's reprised, alternating lines; the canzone's five end words in a spectacular arabesque. In such poetry, the intricacies of form interweave to construct an embodiment in mid-air, creating a temporary region of braided stabilities.

Shahid would eventually employ poetic form as harbor, as house, holding evocations of the past in its patterns. The ghazal is a shaped terrain through which such masters as Begum Akhtar and Faiz Ahmed Faiz have traveled. A form recalls legacies: the canzones of "After the August Wedding in Lahore, Pakistan" and "Lenox Hill" revive the tradition of the exiled Dante Alighieri's use of the same form in "Amor, Tu Vedi Ben Che Questa Donna," to say nothing of Dante's invention of terza rima, a form that Shahid revives in, among other poems, "A Fate's Brief Memoir," "I Dream I Am the Only Passenger on Flight 423 to Srinagar," and "I Dream I Am at the Ghat of the Only World."

As a unifying dynamic in poetry, form merges disparate parts into an historical, objective whole. One task of the poet is to achieve a flexible residence therein, maintaining the richness of individual voice without compromising the structural requirements of the form. Mutually captivated, constantly aware of the geography they traverse, theme partners form as though the two were one anatomy, voice singing within body, establishing and fixing design for the duration of the poem. A tense, vivid, exquisite, and fleeting equilibrium is thus achieved.

Such equilibrium would prove increasingly necessary in Shahid's oeuvre. At the point at which he writes *A Nostalgist's Map of America*, the poet understands that the bonds of love may remove the sting of geographic exile but will prove increasingly helpless in the path of human loss. The title poem and "In Search of Evanescence" are testimonies of the grief of human experience in language at times bejeweled with love. Shahid's epigraph to the section is Emily Dickinson's "A Route of Evanescence," a flashy poem that stars a hummingbird whose speed is so incredible that it might have brought the mail from as far away as Tunis this morning. That the bird metaphorically carries a paper representation of another continent proves compelling for the writer who has titled his first full-length book after a postcard of his missing home and his second after an imaginary map of his current one. Described in vibrant terms of "emerald" and "cochineal,"[17] the hummingbird's most marked quality is its transience: the colors we admire we must admire quickly, for they disappear as the tiny bird speeds off, and this is the scholarship of evanescence. For Shahid, the hummingbird is both beauty and loss. Shahid and Dickinson's appreciation of transience is bittersweet—such a bird may stand for the temporary nature of experience itself, illustrating that part of what is lovely about the world is that it vanishes, leaving nostalgia and homesickness, the longing after what is gone.

Apprehension of such transience occurs in "A Nostalgist's Map of America," wherein Shahid recalls driving with his friend Phil across America. The vehicle of memory is useful for the poem; it evokes evanescence since it conjures existence and diminishment simultaneously. Shahid creates a city named Evanescence as they drive through Pennsylvania: "Let's pretend your city / is Evanescence—there has to be one—."[18] At once, this seemingly solid moment is revealed as vaporous memory: the present day intrudes through the means of a telephone conversation "six, perhaps seven years since then," when the companion reveals he is dying.[19] In response to this confrontation with mortality, Shahid offers the reader three endings to the poem, each false, thereby echoing the beguiling nature not only of the imaginary city but also of the solidity of poetic invention. While his first two endings do revise the city of Evanescence—"I had to build it, for America / was without one," and "which I found—though / not in Pennsylvania"[20]—the ending he settles upon is an apology to Phil:

> . . . Please forgive me, Phil, but I thought
> of your pain as a formal feeling, one
> useful for the letting go, your transfusions
> mere wings to me, the push of numerous
> hummingbirds, souvenirs of Evanescence
> seen disappearing down a route of veins
> in an electric rush of cochineal.[21]

Shahid attempts to inoculate his grief by employing evanescence to decorate the truth of illness into something beautiful, diverting: if Phil's affliction can be revised as the vibrant colors of the hummingbird, it might also adopt the bird's capacity to suddenly disappear in a blur of wings. As he wished to transform the landscape of Pennsylvania so that it might contain an imaginary city, Shahid wishes to transform his friend's illness and discomfort. Shahid confronts the nature of transience: both the imaginary city and Shahid's beautiful words exist in time, and as time passes, both will fail. Shahid asks forgiveness not for his actions but for their inefficacies.

"In Search of Evanescence" conjoins the drive across America with the attempt to memorialize Phil. Within this poem, landscape resolves and dissolves in a series of mirages, underlining beauty and then its disappearance, as Shahid makes nascent moves toward a larger appreciation of the depths of personal loss. Shahid revisits the highways of America; this time he's on Route 80: "I don't know I've begun / mapping America, the city limits / of Evanescence now everywhere."[22] This evanescing landscape strikes within him an awareness of dematerializing, "such a cadence of dead seas at each turn."[23] "The mythic terrain of the book is not the actual historian's terrain," Shahid explains in *Himalmag*:

> The superstitious mountains of Arizona are not the Karakoram Range or the Hindu Kush mountains but there are so many similarities in mythic structures across the world. . . . This cry to be remembered and the language to be remembered, seen in terms of my friend's death, acquired other dimensions.[24]

Such inclusive gestures acknowledge that, in spite of the seeming solidity of territory, geography, or family, the capacity to pass out of existence is shared by all tribes. Shahid's poetry acquires dimensions of longing and regret; he grasps a world of perceptible erosions and recognizes that losses are tragic and bittersweet, standing for the absences of things loved, and further, for absences embedded in history and consciousness.

Within "In Search of Evanescence" Shahid's rhetoric takes its first steps toward the post-Edenic. Moving between joyous memories and the coming losses, Shahid will face the rupture of Phil's illness in terms of the loss of Eden: "there's everything in this world but hope."[25] While in future work this fissure will compel Shahid toward the stabilities of form, for now it evokes fracture and the attempt to heal such fracture in response. In section nine of the poem, the two take a train tour through an imaginary landscape of famous paintings, works of art that will, as the journey proceeds, gradually disappear. Through his reinvention of Emily Dickinson's lines as well as of her anacoluthon, Shahid establishes fissures: "After great pain—a formal feeling does come—I— / the society—of that sheer soul. The soul selects."[26] Shahid conjures Georgia O'Keeffe's paintings as a figurative landscape, a place of temporary spiritual beauty through which he and Phil travel (on her "Train—in the Desert— / at Night").[27] O'Keeffe's paintings of animal skulls and mute deserts are apt in their evocation of "ghost towns," those icons of interruption and interregnum. As the poem nears its end, all the beauty the two have traveled through is revealed as fugitive: "I give our tickets to Fog. / When he leaves, we see Light Coming on the Plains, / the last painting we own. As it too vanishes."[28] The increasingly vaporous piece is grounded in the final stages by couplets, yet as the paintings through which they have been riding vanish entirely, the final couplet holds only Phil's pain, against what is left: the disappearance of beauty.

The final poem of the collection, "Snow on the Desert," merges two significant moments: a drive through fog to Tucson International Airport and a memory of Begum Akhtar singing "during the Bangladesh War."[29] The fog of desert and its perceived history mingle in his mind with the moment of Akhtar's voice, "like this turning dark / of fog, a moment when only a lost sea / can be heard, a time / to recollect / every shadow, everything the earth was losing."[30] Personal loss enlarges to touch a universal, earthly loss. As the poem ends, the poet merges the dispossessions of the earth with his own: "everything the earth / and I had lost."[31] In these poems America's topography has dissolved to include Delhi, Calcutta, Kashmir, Santiago, Chile, and elsewhere, so one continent's evanescence may stand for all others, and we behold the antecedent promise of the ideal with the nostalgia of the human for its losses. *A Nostalgist's Map of America* plots a homesickness of a global kind; anyone may navigate with it toward a history of irretrievables.

In *The Country without a Post Office* Shahid returns to Kashmir in a series of dream states, finding war-torn desperation: dismembered bodies float down the Jhelum; fires encompass houses; the population diminishes before his eyes. The ostensible subject of the collection, the devastation of Kashmir, becomes a metaphor for the world at large, unmoored from its paradise, where the fates are parentless and the gods asleep. The poet's use of voices from other troubled landscapes (such as Yeats, Zbigniew Herbert, and Chechnyan Elena Bonner) further enlarges the collection's terrain. His homeland becomes a metaphor for the first lost landscape, his sadness the nostalgia of the expulsion and its subsequent miseries. In a conversation with Eric Gamalinda in *Poets and Writers*, Shahid exhibits this imaginative linkage between Kashmir and the troubles elsewhere: "I'm always talking about the troubles of Kashmir. I remember when I was eight or nine my parents talked to me about the execution of the Rosenbergs. That's left quite an impact on me."[32] The Rosenbergs' link to Kashmir is not direct but exists in terms of the universality of inhumanity. Thus *Kashmir* in his poetry may stand for all places where devastation evokes the felt sense of the flawed human, where paradise exists as possibility, ever present in mind, though the landscape reflects only its absence. The letter writer in "Dear Shahid" writes, "I am writing to you from your far-off country. Far even from us who live here."[33] In "After the August Wedding in Lahore, Pakistan," Shahid clarifies the link between pre-devastation Kashmir and paradise and their shared sense of impasse, a final time: "banished from Eden (on Earth: Kashmir)."[34]

In the face of disorder, a poet may turn to order. As Shahid's apprehension of disorder increases in scope, postcards and maps prove useless, and the poet inevitably seeks other methods of order, grafting subcontinental tragedy onto a number of traditional verse forms; as witness to the devastation of Kashmir, Shahid now sings in a variety of tribal structures. More so than in previous collections, *The Country without a Post Office* is sustained by its abundance of forms. Ghazals, quatrains, pantoums, villanelles, sestinas, and terza rimas accumulate and lend the book the grounding required to hold its fluttering, shimmering quality, such as exists in a candle's dying and recuperating light. Kashmir and paradise pass into and out of existence, offering beauty and then its disappearance, like Shahid's totemic hummingbird.

In a 2003 interview with Anton Shammas for the *New York Times Sunday Magazine*, Theodor Adorno noted the tradition of homesteading implicit in the relationship between the writer and his work: "In his text, the writer sets up house.... For a man who no longer has a homeland, writing becomes a place to live."[35] The duration of the text is the duration of the haven; the voice will eventually stop singing. Cued to the comfort of the fabricated structure, the reader experiences a syntactic transience: building and building, the poem ends.

Form's contribution to the duration of the poem's theme is as important as its role as temporary haven. In "The Country without a Post Office," "nothing remains"[36] but letters, the written words of now-lost inhabitants; such messages, Shahid contends, in echo of his previous book, are "maps of longings with no limit."[37] The borders of longing may be limitless, but the physical borders created by the collapse of the postal system effectively cut off communication. Yet the locus of the nomad is a reckoning of hopelessness underlined with hope: "These words *may* never reach you" (my emphasis).[38] Thus Shahid embodies pattern to ward off utter hopelessness in his apprehension of ruin, rendering absolute grief over such exile into a fine and tragic beauty.

The poem's eight-line stanzas establish a reflecting rhyme scheme of *abcddcba* that mirrors itself in an interior conversation held forever within its pages, similar to the soliloquy of an undelivered letter that may never reach its "doomed / addresses."[39] The poem's mirror form establishes a call and a response, the call of "lamps" satisfied by its rhyming mate "stamps."[40] Though Shahid employs rhyme to ground the desperation in a sense of harmony, he is equally careful to include oblique rhyme so that the poem does not become misleadingly harmonious. "[P]lains" is mated with "flames,"[41] "wrote" will find "smoke,"[42] and most remarkably, "mirror" will be fulfilled by "letter,"[43] commenting on the poet's own mastery of form.

Such interrelatedness of form and theme inhabits the book. The sestina of "The Floating Post Office" masterfully intensifies the poem's glimpses of hope appearing in the midst of disorder. In this poem, the landscape is fertilized with unanswered questions: "Has he been kept from us?"[44] "Who has died? / Who'll live?"[45] The postman emerges silently, ghostlike; he will disappear again into the "fog of death."[46] Yet in this landscape of uncertainty, "rumors,"[47] and "ambushed letters,"[48] the postman asserts a hope in the weave of the unknown: "he gives his word: / Our letters will be rowed through olive / canals, tense waters no one can close."[49] A sestina's six end words coalesce in a pattern of sound and meaning, enlarging the theme of the poem by their repetitions, in this case: *live* (which Shahid conjugates with *alive* and *olive*), *close* (*disclose*), *road* (*rowed, erode*), *word* (*password*), *portents* (*sentence, penitent's, tense, pretense*), and finally, *letters*.[50] Significantly, one particular end word is never changed: "letters" remains "letters" throughout the poem. Amid the poem's whirlwind, "letters" appears, occasionally but continually. Here, form evokes content: the sestina's braided pattern of words creates a litany of obsession and relief, as the end words offer occasional glimpses of letters, in John Hollander's terms, a "light" at "stanza's edge"[51] of the dense forest the form creates, emphasizing the significance of the post office for the exile: letters offer potential evidence of survivors, community, and the possibility of sending out the barest hope to others. Such hope is fleeting, however, and as Shahid confronts increasingly dispirited landscapes, his use of poetic forms intensifies. The "Ghazal" that ends section four opens with dispossession: "The only language of loss left in the world is Arabic— / These words were said to me in a language not Arabic."[52]

In *Rooms Are Never Finished*, Shahid returns to a devastated Kashmir, traveling with his mother's body to bury her in her homeland, as she wished. Foregrounded now is the post-paradise wreck of time; his return home leaves him twice rootless, and grieving. In 2001, Shahid would learn that he had less than a year to live (he was suffering from the same type of brain cancer that took his mother's life).[53] In a 2001 article in *Postcolonial Studies*, Amitav Ghosh describes how Shahid acknowledged that the poems he was writing would be his last.[54]

In the canzone "Lenox Hill," a record of his mother's last days, the poet reveals his private grief: "I swear, here and now, not to forgive the universe / that would let me get used to a universe / without you."[55] In a striking echo of parallel descent, both Kashmir and Lenox Hill become linked landscapes of affliction, as the sirens outside her hospital window remind his mother of the wails of the elephants of Mihiragula as they are driven off the cliffs. Kashmir has become a fading promise, and paradise and the universe are both to be "considered a tomb."[56] But for Shahid the mother is the true home, and in her suffering and her vanishing, all is lost. "For compared to my grief for you, what are those of Kashmir, / and what (I close the ledger) are the griefs of the universe / when I remember you—beyond all accounting—O my mother?"[57] Nowhere is the poet's desire for home and form more needed; nowhere is the poet more aware of the absolute rupture of experience. The canzone form Shahid employs for the poem achieves, as Amitav Ghosh writes, "a soaring superstructure, an immense domed enclosure, like that of the great mosque of Isfahan . . . and the meter is the mosaic that holds the whole in place."[58]

The conceit of "From Amherst to Kashmir" is to examine mourning, which may be the catalyst for both faith and the loss of faith. Against the backdrop of the poem—the lament of the sacrifice of Hussain, his family, and his followers—Shahid positions the devastating loss of his mother. The history of the Passion magnifies the existence of faith, though Shahid will relinquish this at the close of the poem as he relinquishes his mother; it is not possible to judge which sacrifice is greater. Shahid records how the death of one's mother severs stabilizing roots such as faith and home. At the close of this poem he admits he is entirely exiled from the world.

The cry of the gazelle, an animal noted for its tenderness and beauty, echoes throughout: the animals weep to foretell Hussain's massacre;[59] Begum Akhtar's raga evokes "the wound-cry of the gazelle";[60] Zainab's cry is that of a gazelle, recollected in the cries the *majlis*;[61] the "wounded gazelle" wail is evoked at the mourning of his mother.[62] The poem is awash in the creature's tragic sound, which stands for the simultaneity of love and loss in the ghazal. Both "amorous" and "melancholic,"[63] the gazelle's cry is in the contradiction of the two, and it is the sting that lies beneath grief. Yet here, and in "I

Dream I Am at the Ghat of the Only World," Shahid exiles the gazelle from its ghazal. The animal tries to temporarily shelter here, where Shahid employs the Sapphic stanza in several sections to great effect. Coming as it does after three lines of eleven syllables each, the Sapphic stanza's short final line of five syllables implies a cessation, and a succession of Sapphics presents a series of diminishments. John Hollander finds in the form's first three lines "heartbeats," which the fourth line "tenderly end[s]."[64]

Having taken the titular journey back home and experienced only true loss in the final section of "From Amherst to Kashmir," the poet confronts the question of compound exile: "So what is separation's geography?"[65] Beginning at the waters of Kashmir, he ponders the river and its history, from its headwaters to its mouth. That all things flow into one another, implies cohesion and a design which is to him contradictory. Similarly, though the reflected moon colors the river "steel" and "silver," he finds only "Black Water" and "black waves," which he glosses in his endnotes as *kalapani*: "*Kalapani*, or black water, referred to the stretch of ocean between mainland India and colonial Britain's most notorious prison on the Andaman islands. To cross *kalapani* meant being condemned to permanent exile."[66] Located securely in his homeland (the landscape of his dreams in his previous books), he concludes the poem not with a cry of homecoming but with a wound-cry of the boundless exile, crushed, annihilated:

> that *How dare the moon*—I want to cry out,
> Mother—*shine so hauntingly out*
> *here when I've sentenced it to black waves*
> *inside me? Why has it not perished?*
> *How dare it shine on an earth*
> *from which you have vanished?*[67]

Edward Said writes, "The exile knows that in a secular and contingent world, homes are always provisional";[68] the constant is that one's deeply felt desire for home will forever be frustrated. A structure that is both ruptured and ongoing would therefore constitute the true estate of the exile, though it seems an impossible feat to manufacture dislocation within infinity. Yet in "Rooms Are Never Finished," a tribute to writing as an evocation of the irremediable desire for home, Shahid creates a form both broken and continuous, a flirtation with the infinite. Within this title poem of the volume, the stanzas (Italian for "rooms") begin broken and do not end. The last line of each stanza enjambs across white space to the first line of the stanza that follows, which then opens with a prepositional phrase beginning with "in," creating a constant entrance to the room of continual rupture.

The poem's epigraph invokes interior designer Mario Buatta: "Many of my favorite things are broken."[69] The speaker has welcomed a visitor to his house, and together they admire the rooms while the speaker comments on his interior decorating. "You were / led through all the spare rooms I was to die / in. But look how each room's been refurbished[.]"[70] Indeed, as the two walk from room to room, the reader and Shahid move from stanza to stanza, admiring the ornamentation as well as the odd navigable quality of the walls: "in (How one passes through such thick walls!)."[71]

Shahid is long familiar with a stanza's ability to enclose. But in creating stanzas that have both entrance ("in") and absence of ending (each stanza's enjambed final line) he has mastered the limitations of the form, creating a Möbius strip of home; a "house," he writes here, is "a work in progress, / always."[72] Further, because the poem's last line—"in. But for small hands. Invisible. Quick . . ."[73]—ends with an ellipsis, indicating omission and therefore implying continuity; the poem doesn't actually end at all. Said notes, "Borders and barriers, which enclose us within the safety of familiar territory, can also become prisons, and are often defended beyond reason or necessity. Exiles cross borders, break barriers of thought and experience."[74] We may consider Shahid's form in this poem an exile's tour de force, an eradication of the border that ends a poem and hence ends the stabilizing experience.

The book closes with "I Dream I Am at the Ghat of the Only World," wherein Shahid, on a journey, rows toward his mother, and toward his own end. On the way the poet invokes Eqbal Ahmad, Begum Akhtar, James Merrill, all beloved figures who have passed on and whose absences he feels most keenly. If heaven exists, Shahid's excursion would be toward a homecoming that would put an end to wandering, but since the poet tells us this is the "Only World," we may understand his death as the final banishment. As he rows toward Kashmir; he finds "desecration, God's tapestry / ripped"[75] and "only the wind . . . in one awed / fright of boots, of soldiers."[76] Denied his paradise, he perceives his journey as that of perpetual exile: "I always move in my heart between sad countries."[77] Shahid had fixed his love to Kashmir, extended his love to the world; now he encounters an ultimate loss. He is joined in this banishment by a familiar creature: there is "the cry of the gazelle— /it breaks the heart into the final episode."[78] Even the wound-cry of Shahid's gazelle, exiled now to the terza rima of this poem, remains here a wanderer in an alien poetic form.

The invention of terza rima is credited to Dante for his *Divina Commedia*, another epic journey.[79] Yet while Dante eventually reaches his paradise, as "I Dream I Am at the Ghat of the Only World" ends, Shahid has not yet done so. In this final poem he declares, "*To be rowed forever is the last afterlife*" (emphasis in original).[80] Said writes, "The pathos of exile is the loss of contact with the solidity and the satisfaction of earth. Homecoming is out of the question."[81] Shahid allows the poet James Merrill to speak the last line in Merrill's signature majuscules: "SHAHID, HUSH. THIS IS ME, JAMES. THE LOVED ONE ALWAYS LEAVES."[82] We understand the "LOVED ONE" is Shahid, as he exiles himself out of the poem, leaving readers to experience only the poet's vanishing.

Notes

1. An early version of this article was published in *The Hollins Critic*, Hollins University, Virginia, Vol. XLIII, no. 2, April, 2006. Here it is reprinted with the permission of the contributor.

2. Michael M. J. Fischer, "Orientalizing America: Beginning and Middle Passages," *Middle East Report* 178 (1992): 32.

3. Edward Said, *Reflections on Exile* (Cambridge, MA: Harvard University Press, 2000), 173–174.

4. Agha Shahid Ali, *Ravishing DisUnities: Real Ghazals in English* (Hanover, NH: Wesleyan University Press, 2000), 1.

5. Ibid., 3.

6. Christine Benvenuto, "Conversations with Agha Shahid Ali," *Massachusetts Review* 21 (2002): 261–268.

7. Agha Shahid Ali, introduction to *The Rebel's Silhouette: Selected Poems by Faiz Ahmed Faiz*, trans. Agha Shahid Ali (Amherst: University of Massachusetts Press, 1995), x.

8. Agha Shahid Ali, *Ravishing DisUnities*, 3.

9. Ibid., 8.

10. Ibid., 9.

11. Qtd. in ibid.,4.

12. Agha Shahid Ali, *The Country without a Post Office* (New York: W. W. Norton, 1998), 96.

13. Benvenuto, "Conversations with Agha Shahid Ali," 261.

14. Eric Gamalinda, "Poems Are Never Finished," *Poets and Writers* (March/April 2002): 44–51.

15. Bruce King, *Modern Indian Poetry in English* (New Delhi: Oxford University Press, 2001), 260.

16. Agha Shahid Ali, *The Veiled Suite: The Collected Poems* (New York: W. W. Norton, 2009), 29.
17. Qtd. in Ibid., 118.
18. Ibid.
19. Ibid., 119.
20. Ibid., 120.
21. Ibid.
22. Ibid., 122.
23. Ibid.
24. Qtd. in Rehan Ansari and Rajinder S. Paul, "Ahga Shahid Ali: Calligraphy of Coils," *Himalmag* (March 1998): 2.
25. Agha Shahid Ali, *The Veiled Suite*, 135.
26. Ibid., 131.
27. Ibid.
28. Ibid., 132–133.
29. Agha Shahid Ali, introduction to *The Rebel's Silhouette*, xxiv.
30. Agha Shahid Ali, *The Veiled Suite*, 167.
31. Ibid., 168.
32. Gamalinda, "Poems Are Never Finished," 49.
33. Agha Shahid Ali, *The Veiled Suite*, 194.
34. Ibid., 240.
35. Anton Shammas, "The Lives They Lived: Looking for Someplace to Call Home," *New York Times Sunday Magazine*, December 28, 2003, 25.
36. Agha Shahid Ali, *The Veiled Suite*, 204.
37. Ibid., 205.
38. Ibid., 206.
39. Ibid., 202.
40. Ibid.
41. Ibid.
42. Ibid., 203.
43. Ibid., 204.
44. Ibid., 207.
45. Ibid.
46. Ibid.
47. Ibid.
48. Ibid.
49. Ibid., 208.
50. Ibid., 207–208.
51. John Hollander, *Rhyme's Reason* (New Haven, CT: Yale University Press, 1981), 41.
52. Agha Shahid Ali, *The Veiled Suite*, 225.

53. Amitav Ghosh, "The Ghat of the Only World," *Postcolonial Studies* 5 (2002): 319.
54. Ibid.
55. Agha Shahid Ali, *The Veiled Suite*, 247.
56. Ibid., 248.
57. Ibid., 249.
58. Ghosh, "The Ghat of the Only World," 320.
59. Agha Shahid Ali, *The Veiled Suite*, 250.
60. Ibid., 257.
61. Ibid., 258.
62. Ibid., 275.
63. Agha Shahid Ali, *Ravishing DisUnities*, 4.
64. Hollander, *Rhyme's Reason*, 18.
65. Agha Shahid Ali, *The Veiled Suite*, 276.
66. Ibid., 379.
67. Ibid., 278.
68. Said, *Reflections on Exile*, 185.
69. Agha Shahid Ali, *The Veiled Suite*, 279.
70. Ibid.
71. Ibid.
72. Ibid., 281.
73. Ibid.
74. Said, *Reflections on Exile*, 185.
75. Agha Shahid Ali, *The Veiled Suite*, 319.
76. Ibid.
77. Ibid., 318.
78. Ibid., 319.
79. Alex Preminger et al., eds., *Encyclopedia of Poetry and Poetics* (Princeton, NJ: Princeton University Press, 1965), 848.
80. Agha Shahid Ali, *The Veiled Suite*, 321.
81. Said, *Reflections on Exile*, 179.
82. Agha Shahid Ali, *The Veiled Suite*, 321.

7

Agha Shahid Ali
and the Ghazals in English

SAGAREE SENGUPTA

Agha Shahid Ali taught us to write ghazals in English. By "us," I mean poets and students of poetry in America. It is true that there are odd examples of people trying ghazals in English before Shahid, notably in translations from Persian and Urdu that tried to look like the original verses.[1] But it is ghazal-composing in English by the few simple rules that Agha Shahid Ali distilled (from the forest of possibilities in Urdu and Persian) that gives one the sensation of a living new form. Shahid, a poet in English but attached to a deep South Asian literary heritage, eschewed the complex way Urdu counts ghazal meter and gave us a simpler formula. He trusted the English language to do its own patterning if the lines were kept (more or less) the same length. In addition, many American poets, not just the ones featured in Shahid's edited book *Ravishing DisUnities: Real Ghazals in English* (2000), have tried the form. In fact, after I began writing this, a friend posted an English ghazal on her social media page: the poem "Sorrow" by Shara McCallum, from the poet's 2017 book *Mad Woman*. McCallum's poem had been the day's feature on the popular National Public Radio program *The Writer's Almanac*. Interestingly, the specific poetic form—ghazal—was neither mentioned nor expounded upon in the broadcast.[2] Several ghazals in English, by Agha Shahid Ali, Kazim Ali, and Patricia Smith are also featured in this year's America-wide school poetry recitation contest known as *Poetry Out Loud*.

I feel that the reason Agha Shahid Ali's ghazal "lesson" succeeded in English is his creation of soft rules based on what he saw the ghazal doing in Urdu and in other Indian languages. He saw potential in the elasticity of the form and in its not-quite-accidental layers of meaning; these meanings emerge with subtle variation when separate stanzas of a particular poem are recited or evoked in free combination. Shahid's lesson on writing ghazal in English, "Ghazal: The Charms of a Considered Disunity," appeared in Robin Behn and Chase Twichell's poetry lesson book *The Practice of Poetry: Writing Exercises from Poets Who Teach*.[3] Using syllable count over any definite metrical pattern, the lesson was instrumental in my trying English ghazal composition with my own students. Shahid solely uses *form* as the basis of transferring ghazal to English rather than promoting the set scenario of the ghazal *world*, populated by figures such as the bereft lover, the unprincipled rival, and the cruel beloved. The practicality and transferability of Shahid's lesson—that I and many of my college and high school students have followed—come from this emphasis on form and his preemptive promotion of "disunity." The latter notion keeps the student from trying to "add up" the couplets at the end to force a conventional narrative pattern out of them.

I always start by asking my students to pick a "beloved or terrifying" object, beast, or person. Interstate highways, alcohol, and pet cats have all been chosen by college-level writers. Even when a pedestrian topic—love or a dreaded exam—is chosen, the compulsion of the form (syllable count, end rhyme) tends to fruitfully distort any ready clichés. I tell my students to write a few lines, and then select and polish one attractive one. They count this line's syllables and use it as the pattern for the rest of the ghazal. I also explain qafiya-radif, the penultimate few syllables and repetitious end rhyme of ghazal, simply or elaborately depending on the age and grade I am teaching. In a hurried middle school class, a simple rhyming word (e.g. fair, lair) would be enough to propel the exercise forward. In a longer session, or in a college class where Urdu language is the matrix in which we are experimenting with English ghazals, basketfuls of qafiya-radif matches ("charm university," "farm in adversity") are worked out prior to the actual composition. Interestingly, the poetry does not sound as forced as one might suspect because, once begun, the process of rhyme generation continues naturally for those gifted with sonic sensibility. This new way of producing rhymes of several syllables is bound to result in novelties. It is with glee that I listen to the inventions of more sophisticated students in this part of the exercise, because they cause all of us to hear *English* differently.

In his lesson for English ghazal, Shahid emphasizes the semantic disunity of the verses, apparently so strange to the English poetic universe. My personal conjecture is that "disunity" is an overstatement that Shahid uses to get past the resistance of readers to a form in which stanzas hang together so subtly that an assiduous pursuit of definite meaning-making is futile. The title of his lesson on ghazal writing, and the name of the anthology *Ravishing DisUnities: Real Ghazals in English,* both contain the term "disunity," and both celebrate the ravishing charm of (in theory) fracture and disarray. But rather than fracture and disarray, what I have felt while writing and teaching a simplified ghazal form is simultaneity or drifting from one aspect of an invisible theme to another. Shahid claims, "[a] couplet may be quoted by itself (anytime, anywhere) without in any way violating a context—there is no context, as such"[4] But when we think about how a ghazal singer, Begum Akhtar in particular, seems to pluck a couplet from a cloud of floating thought, the idea of simultaneity becomes useful for the writing process as well. The leaping of couplets from one focal point to another is parallel to the way the mind muses on a problem: the meter and rhyme unify, and connection invisibly shifts into place. Love, desertion, or renewal can be viewed from many philosophical angles, at different stages of development, or through the lenses of different emotional states. The speaker in the poem can meander through hope and hopelessness and back again. In my view, the phrase "pearls on a string" to stand for the separate couplets of a ghazal is an old cliché. True, the words are strung on the string of meter and rhyme. But as far as meaning is concerned, each couplet is more like a single ray shooting out of one moment of experience. Yes, the verses are strung on the string of time—it takes so many minutes to go through five verses, especially if the audience is a traditional one, vocally appreciating and repeating some of the words after the poet has spoken—but it is not necessary to claim bead-like discreteness.

As an example of "plucking thoughts" in English, one *Ravishing DisUnities* poet, William Matthews,[5] takes the very word *ghazal* and uses irreverent rhymes of it as titles of his seven free-spinning but grounded-by-form contributions, "Dazzle," "Frazzle," "Guzzle," "Muzzle," "Puzzle," "Drizzle," and "Nozzle." In "Frazzle," he appropriates well-known sayings to illuminate a familiar-sounding resignation:

All for one and one for all was our motto after all
Our tribulations. And then we'd each go home, after all.

By the people. For the people. Of the people. Grammar—
But politics is an incomplete sentence, after all.[6]

For Matthews, statements of solidarity and democracy do not add up to much. They are merely wishful thinking that is never realized. The bonds of social unity fray and frazzle.

Matthews ends the ghazal "Frazzle" with the following two couplets:

The love of repetition is the root of all form?
Well, liturgy and nonsense are cousins, after all.

"I cannot tell a lie," he said, which was a lie,
but not the kind for which the bill comes after all.[7]

The string of worn-out old phrases—"*All for one and one for all*," "I cannot tell a lie"—leads to a comic resignation to the falsity of their heroic claims. Any repetitious set of words can be magical or meaningless, be they a religious incantation or a rhyme-repeating ghazal. Then in "Guzzle" (the title is a dipsomaniacal pun on the name of the poetic form), Matthews seems to rewrite each couplet in the subsequent one; each couplet brings to light the various struggles of an indigent drunkard—or poet, with Rilke for context—

I need a loan. I need a drink. I need
not to be perceived to be in need.

You must change your life, scolds Rilke.
Just how big a diaper will I need?

There's skill and merit and, of course, good looks,
and charm, and nepotism. Also, need.

Ant to grasshopper: How about some bread?
Grasshopper to ant: Whatever you knead.[8]

The slightly outrageous narrator above is not that remote from the hapless beggar/mystic/lover of traditional Urdu and Persian ghazals. In "Muzzle,"

Matthews explores the motif of silence, enthroning the word in the end rhyme. In English, the final rhyme of the ghazal frequently seems to become the theme word as well—not at all a given in Urdu or Persian, where the final word is often a simple verb. In spite of being "muzzled," the poet keeps talking about silence!

> Some people like the idea of silence.
> Let them try the drab thin itself: silence.
>
> A cat stalking a roach, ears up, bell
> Dusting the floor—a statue of silence.

Matthews continues through several more couplets and ends the poem with the following two:

> OK, Mr. Know-It-All, let's compromise.
> Tell all but translate it into silence.
>
> A tree falls where no human hears it crash;
> Do its siblings mourn for it in silence?

The conundrums in both verses could be any rebellious poet's own paradoxes—most of us suffer the challenges of surviving as a whole human being, telling the truth in our art but without pretense, and finding an audience. Do we speak up or swallow our thoughts? Are the falling trees of our poems heard by anyone?

The English ghazals that result from Shahid's instructions *do* have some of the ineffable coherence that we all know Indian and Persian ghazals to have. Even without a trace of the "profound and complex cultural unity"[9] that the South Asian prototypes inhabit, many of the new English poems still resonate with a regretful ethos. Other English ghazals seem to fall into wry reflections as in the apparently self-deprecating ghazals of Ghalib and Mir—I may be influenced by my prior reading and cultural baggage, but so is every reader. Yet defensible intercultural and interlinguistic satisfaction (or discovery, for those new to the form) can result from tracing "typical" South Asian ghazal emotion in a new English ghazal. Ghazals in South Asian languages can be imbued with irony and rueful feelings of all kinds; involving English in this weighty tradition is a coup—take for example the final two couplets from Paul Jenkins's ghazal in Shahid's collection:

> The poet's taped voice from beyond death itself
> Fills the chapel with his whole being as the final words come back
>
> And back to haunt me because what are we but voice
> Amazed final bodies that are never coming back[10]

The motif of "coming back"—of seasons, or migratory birds, of athletic prowess—that Jenkins has accessed through his rhyming word "back," weaves through the poem. So, even without a unified subject, we are left with the final experience of a poet's taped voice outlasting his life, and Jenkins's application in the last verse of that experience to all poets, and perhaps to all people who have spoken, conversed, and died. The floor of familiar reality falling away underfoot, and only a voice remaining, is very like the unbearable and transcendent truth Persian and Urdu ghazal poets and mystics have been facing for centuries.[11]

Speaking of endings, *Ravishing DisUnities* includes John Hollander's performance on paper, which cleverly evokes the anticipation for the end of the line that characterizes engaged ghazal audiences. An acculturated audience expects the ghazal poet or singer to introduce twistings and turnings of the initial verse. Anticipation is built into an oral performance, notwithstanding how self-deprecating (ironically, since the poet is the center of attention at that moment) the poet's tone may be.

> "Ghazal on Ghazals"
> For couplets the ghazal is prime; at the end
> Of each one's a refrain like a chime: "*at the end.*"
> But in subsequent couplets throughout the whole poem,
> It's this second line only will rhyme at the end.[12]

Hollander, an expert in meter and form[13], extends his classical English virtuosity by describing the format of the ghazal *in* a ghazal. His emphasis on *the end* of each line entwines written form with an evocation of live performance.

In the absence of sung ghazal, the ghazal on the page, or the ghazal read by a poet at a microphone, still has a foot in the world of modern English lyric. Auditors supply the narrative that connects, like a trembling spider web, the little shiny moments of desolation or desire that the couplets hint at. Agha Shahid Ali's own English ghazals provide a concrete formal link to South Asia, balancing the tragic laments of much of his other poetry, poetry that often uses bits and pieces of the ghazal's scenario (hapless lover, tragic ends, vanished beloveds) to evoke the real losses of an immigrant from Kashmir. "A Pastoral"[14], for example, looks back to Shahid's family home in strife-torn Kashmir, emptied of family and occupied by fighting forces. In this poem, Shahid adapts traditional Urdu poetic metaphors for emotional desolation, which are forced to revert back to the literal here: "Again we'll enter / our last world, the first that vanished / in our absence from the broken city." Let us, however, look at a few stanzas of Shahid's well-known English ghazal, "Tonight."[15] The poem is a rich entwinement of Laurence Hope's (actually Adela Florence Cory's[16]) popular turn-of-the-century poem "Kashmiri Song" (which became a very popular song in English-speaking countries in the early decades of the twentieth century), cited in the epigraph, with the rest of Shahid's world:

> Where are you now? Who lies beneath your spell tonight?
> Whom else from rapture's road will you expel tonight?

Compare the mock-Kashmiri quatrain by Cory/ Laurence Hope that Shahid's head couplet derives from:

> Pale hands I loved beside the Shalimar,
> Where are you now? Who lies beneath your spell?
> Whom do you lead on Rapture's roadway, far,
> Before you agonise them in farewell?[17]

There are echoes of Ghalib and Mir. Praising the beloved by enumerating the many lovers she has been able to make miserable is a centuries-old pattern in the court ghazal. The heartbreaks caused raise the (cruel) beloved's status. But after this elegant rewriting of what was already a strange intercultural product, Shahid switches to his own mixed world in later stanzas:

> I beg for haven: Prisons, let open your gates—
> A refugee from Belief seeks a cell tonight.

Belief is what has torn Kashmir apart, he seems to say. Prison would be better than the contention outside. The nonbelieving narrator would rather be jailed than declare himself the member of a faith. In a further verse, idols themselves pray to a God:

> Lord, cried out the idols, Don't let us be broken;
> Only we can convert the infidel tonight.

"Idol" in the traditional ghazal can refer to Hindu or Buddhist sacred images, or to "beloveds," or those who live by their beauty. The breaking of idols only continues the war—the poet begs for them to remain if anyone is to come to belief. Or, love is the only common religion, in the poet's eyes. The loss of a homeland, of union, and of peace haunts this gripping couplet.

As some American poets borrow bits and pieces of the ghazal world's traditional scenario, adding to the basic structure laid out by Shahid, the new poems can begin to resonate aesthetically with a South Asian ghazal follower. The repetition in the form connects easily to prayer and lamentation genres—many Urdu ghazals have "hai hai" (alas, alas) as part of the end rhyme. Whatever the repeating word a ghazal poet uses, its repetition often seems to suggest regret. The poet's persona is still that of an outsider to society in the world of English-language poetry, and meshing that state with the true lover-mystic of the ghazal world is not difficult. David Raphael Israel's contribution to *Ravishing DisUnities* points us toward the merger:

> Once I get walking, I could walk for miles, this mild night.
> What keeps me caught in the net of tears & smiles, this mild night?
>
> . . .
>
> Again the moon is waxing. Immaculate lunacies loom.
> Spool out the oldest yarn: it still beguiles, this mild night.[18]

Above, the narrator is a fool who is beguiled by the false charms of a beautiful night, charms that promise some kind of romance, only to disappoint . . . a reader familiar with the South Asian ghazal can fill in the scene. And in another ghazal (II) Israel makes a poet conscious of the hapless lover in the lane of the beloved, just as in the Urdu poems of Ghalib and Mir:

> It's a dangerous business, wandering into the lane of poetry.
> First there's a dazzlement; then: surprise! The pain of poetry.
> I kept on passing this vacant alley, thinking I'd find some enterprise!
> Each time, I lost something else. My loss was the gain of poetry.[19]

The beloved in the ghazal above, of course, is poetry itself. Just as the cruel beloved of the traditional South Asian ghazal "wins" every time the hapless lover is humiliated, poetry "wins" when Israel's narrator loses. Meanwhile, Eleanor Wilner valorizes the "losing" position of both lover and poet, and thus completes the circle:

> Risk it? What, after all, have you got to lose?
> With a time-honored form, you ought to lose.[20]

In traditional gambles such as love, or trying out the ghazal form, losing is a given. The poet is ennobled, or has her identity affirmed, by such defeats. Along with Wilner, any poet writing English now has compelling exemplars of a new form. Diane Ackerman, Molly Bendall, John Canaday, G. S. Sharat Chandra, Katharine Coles, Keki Daruwalla, Annie Finch, Marilyn Hacker, Paul Muldoon, Elise Paschen, John Edgar Wideman, and dozens of other poets contributed fine ghazals to *Ravishing DisUnities*. Since that volume was published, younger poets continue to float successful ghazals into the English-reading world. Older poets reach for the form too, for welcome variety. Writing in English, we learn from each other, and from the South Asian tradition. Thanks largely to the liberal structure demonstrated and taught by Agha Shahid Ali, the ghazal is now enmeshed with poetry in English.

Notes

1. Peter Avery et al. *Hafiz of Shiraz: Thirty Poems* (London: John Murray, 1952) is an example of translation from the Persian in which English couplets appear. Many other translations were actually prose explanations. With regard to Urdu, Aijaz Ahmad's edited volume of translations *Ghazals of Ghalib* (New York: Columbia University Press, 1971) featured a number of well-known American poets interpreting the ghazal form.

2. It may be possible to hear Shara McCallum's poem online at https://writersalmanac.org/episodes/20171010

3. New York: Harper Collins, 1992

4. Behn and Twichell, eds., *The Practice of Poetry*, 205.

5. Agha Shahid Ali, *Ravishing DisUnities*, 104–110.

6. Ibid., 105.

7. Ibid., 105.

8. Ibid., 106.

9. Behn and Twichell, eds., *The Practice of Poetry*, 205.

10. Agha Shahid Ali, *Ravishing DisUnities*, 85.

11. In a famous passage from the *Gulistan*, Sa'adi Shirazi has a dervish saying "My state is that of leaping lightning. / One moment it appears and at another vanishes. / I am sometimes sitting in high heaven. / Sometimes I cannot see the back of my foot. / Were a dervish always to remain in that state / He would not care for the two worlds" (chapter 2, story 10. Translator unknown).

12. Agha Shahid Ali, *Ravishing DisUnities*, 76.
13. See, for instance, John Hollander, *Rhyme's Reason: A Guide to English Verse*. 4th edition. (New Haven, CT: Yale University Press, 2014)
14. Agha Shahid Ali, *The Veiled Suite: The Collected Poems* (New York: Norton, 2009), 196–197.
15. Ibid., 374–375.
16. "Laurence Hope." *Poetry Foundation*. 2017. https://www.poetryfoundation.org/poets/laurence hope
17. Laurence Hope, "Kashmiri Song," *Poetry Foundation*. 2017. https://www.poetryfoundation.org/poems/53821/kashmiri-song
18. Agha Shahid Ali, *Ravishing DisUnities*, 79.
19. Ibid.
20. Ibid., 172.

Works Cited

Ahmad, Aijaz. *Ghazals of Ghalib*. New York: Columbia University Press, 1971.

Ali, Agha Shahid. "Ghazal: The Charms of a Considered Disunity." In Robin Behn and Chase Twichell, eds., *The Practice of Poetry: Writing Exercises from Poets Who Teach*, 205–209. New York: Harper Collins, 1992.

Ali, Agha Shahid (Ed). *Ravishing DisUnities: Real Ghazals in English*. Hanover, NH: Wesleyan University Press, 2000.

Ali, Agha Shahid. *The Veiled Suite: The Collected Poems*. New York: W. W. Norton, 2009.

Avery, Peter and John Heath-Stubbs. *Hafiz of Shiraz: Thirty Poems*. London: John Murray, 1952.

Behn, Robin, and Chase Twichell, eds. *The Practice of Poetry: Writing Exercises from Poets Who Teach*. New York: Harper Collins, 1992.

Hollander, John. *Rhyme's Reason: A Guide to English Verse*. 4th edition. New Haven, CT: Yale University Press, 2014.

McCallum, Shara. "Sorrow." *The Writer's Almanac*. October 10, 2017. https://writersalmanac.org/episodes/20171010

Sa'adi (Muslihuddin Sa'adi Shirazi), (Translator unknown) *Gulistan*. (Persian/English) http://classics.mit.edu/Sadi/gulistan.3.ii.html

8

"I will open the waves"

Examining the Hybrid Forms in Agha Shahid Ali's Poetry

ABIN CHAKRABORTY

In the opening poem of his third collection, *The Half-Inch Himalayas*, Agha Shahid Ali writes:

> Kashmir shrinks into my mailbox,
> my home a neat four by six inches.
>
> I always loved neatness. Now I hold
> the half-inch Himalayas in my hand. (29)

This self-confessed love of neatness subsequently develops into a fascination with intricate verse patterns through which Shahid weaves for his readers, patterns as lovely as the paisley designs for which Kashmiri fabrics were famous. Beginning with free verse, Shahid then goes on to foreground in his later anthologies a series of other verse forms such as the sestina, the canzone, the villanelle, and most importantly the ghazal. In typically postcolonial fashion his "biriyanized" English (Mehrotra, 4) molds itself into a wide variety of formal combinations that crisscross between subcontinental and Euro-American traditions with as much felicity as his own sweeping imagination, which can claim that "By the Hudson lies Kashmir, brought from Palestine" (VS 297). What thus emerges is a sense of hybridity intrinsic to both the diasporic and the postcolonial imaginary, which not only finds poetic manifestation through his thematic explorations and the affective cartography that his lines sketch, but also through the formal structures he so carefully cultivates. As this chapter will demonstrate, such formal experiments and innovations testify to the poet's unique preference for enriching artistic fusions as well as the defiant confidence of a postcolonial poet who manages to mold the English language into difficult forms while retaining his own cultural specificity.

These formal experiments are part of an exciting personal artistic trajectory for Shahid who began his career by exploring the nuances of free verse as exemplified by the already quoted lines from *The Half-Inch Himalayas*, with its rich notes of nostalgia. Even in his subsequent anthologies, such as *A Nostalgist's Map of America* or the subtly humorous *A Walk Through the Yellow Pages*, Shahid continues to play with various affects and moods carried by free verse. By consistently varying line lengths and syntax he manages to extract from the lines an array of diverse emotions and tenors. From telling one-liners like "I innovate on a noteless raga" (VS 54) or "You cannot cross-examine the dead" (54) to halting, pause-laden, three-line stanzas made up of just one sentence—Shahid uses all possible varieties:

> Somewhere
> without me
> my life begins. (79)

Here too, however, alongside the hesitant groping for origins, characteristic of diasporic sensibilities, one also needs to notice the slowly ascending number of words in each line, which recurs in other stanzas as well, signifying the increasing accumulation of building blocks with which identity is shaped. On the other hand, in a poem like "Advertisement (Found Poem)," the same free verse is used to replicate the language of *menus* and *fliers* with remarkable comic effects:

> DIM SUMS are different to instant noodles
> or instant soups
> Our DIM SUMS are freshly frozen food
> AND need only 15 minutes of steaming to eat (90)

On other occasions, with similar dexterity he uses enjambment in such a way that the line breaks off immediately after a resonant verb or noun, thus generating multiple connotations, which the reader is urged to ponder. For example, a poem called "A Call" begins with the following lines:

> I close my eyes. It doesn't leave me,
> the cold moon of Kashmir which breaks
> into my house (76)

The verb "breaks" in the second line here not only refers to the creeping moonlight that enters the house but also suggests the torn relationship between migrant and homeland as well as the inner loss that the speaker himself experiences, away from homeland and parents—a loss intensified by the image of the moon as seen from Kashmir.

However, poets do not always remain shackled to the same form for their entire career, no matter how much successful their handling of such forms might be. Whether it is T. S. Eliot or W. B. Yeats, Ted Hughes or Seamus Heaney—most major twentieth-century poets have repeatedly experimented with several different forms, and for many the search for new forms has coincided with new directions in their poetic careers. Beginning with *The Country without a Post Office*, Shahid's poetry also moves in a different formal and thematic direction altogether as the subjective voice merges with a larger rubric of collective suffering initiated by the violence and injustice faced by the people of Shahid's homeland, Kashmir, in the wake of insurgency and counter-insurgency military operations that began since the end of the 1980s and escalated in the 1990s, virtually turning the fabled "paradise on earth" into an infernal war-zone. Shahid's attempt to poetically express the horror and the suffering of the people of Kashmir led him away from the province of free verse to continued experiments with prose poems, sestina, terza rima, canzone, ghazals, and many other forms, all the while retaining the lyrical melody of his verse and the specificity of the cultural context from which it had sprung. It almost seemed as if the unprecedented violence and horror being experienced by the people of Kashmir demanded the rigors of strict verse forms for the successful transmutation of that personal anguish that Shahid himself experienced. It must be noted, too, that such an artistic choice was also influenced by Shahid's friendship with the multiple award–winning American poet James Merrill, who was also Shahid's mentor in many ways. The kind of formal dexterity that one witnesses in Merrill's poems, especially his earlier works, is something that the maturing Shahid replicates in his later collections. Particularly significant in this context is one piece of advice that Merrill sent to Shahid after receiving from him a poem on Bosnia that he disliked for its weak rhymes. Merrill wrote: "There's not much you can do for Bosnia, but you can make this a better poem" (Hall, 18). Throughout the rest of his career Shahid would pay heed to such advice by pouring his deeply personal and sensitive poetic voice into a series of finely chiseled poetic forms.

Significantly, the opening sections of *The Country without a Post Office* capture this voice not through verse forms but rather through a number of prose poems of varying intensity that spell out the speaker's longing for the inflamed, suffering valley of Kashmir, a space that appears in Shahid's text with almost as many names as a god:

> Let me cry out in that void, say it as I can. I write on that void: Kashmir, Kaschmir, Cashmere, Qashmir, Cashmr, Cashmire, Kashmere, Cachemire, Cushmeer, Cachmiere, Casmir. Or Cauchemar in a sea of stories? Or: Kacmir, Kaschemir, Kasmere, Kachmire, Kasmir. Kerseymere? (VS 171)

This anguished invocation also attests to the heteroglossic cultural matrix that constituted Kashmir and contributed to its unique cultural identity. Furthermore, this voice, while registering the agony of a migrant who painfully witnesses from a distance the metaphoric disappearance of the homeland he knew, at times modulates into a hallucinatory voice as well, almost collapsing under the weight of emotions, as evident in the following lines of "The Last Saffron" where the speaker prophesies his own death, even as he laments the burnt saffron fields of Pampore:

> He'll sever some land—two yards—from the shore, I his last passenger. Suddenly he'll age, his voice will break, his gaze green water, washing me: "It won't grow again, this gold from the burned fields of Pampore." And he will row the freed earth past the Security zones, so my blood is news in the *Saffron Sun* setting on the waves. (182)

This consciousness of conflict also reappears through other kinds of formal variations. Particularly significant is the poem "Farewell," written in single-line stanzas or monostich where the poet plays with repetitions of "memory" and "history" in order to create a recognition of antagonistic histories and conflicting communal or ethnic memories:

> Your history gets in the way of my memory.
> I am everything you lost. You can't forgive me.
> I am everything you lost. Your perfect enemy.
> Your memory gets in the way of my memory. (176)

The competing constructs of "self" and "other" thus find their way into the carefully paired repetitions and antitheses that resemble the image of the lake where "the arms of temples and mosques are locked in each other's reflections" (176). The self-conscious artistry of the poet thus merges with a playful self-reflexivity that also points toward his fascination with syncretic fusions of one kind or another. This is evident in a poem like "The Last Saffron" where the prose section in the middle is flanked by two verse sections of different rhyme schemes. While the opening section works on the basis of alternately rhyming quatrains, the concluding section changes into two-line stanzas where every second line rhymes with the concluding line of the next stanza:

> On everyone's lips was news
> of my death but only that beloved couplet,
> broken, on his:
> "If there is a paradise on earth,
> It is this, it is this, it is this." (183)

A similar rhyme scheme is witnessed in "I Dream I Am the Only Passenger on Flight 423 to Srinagar," where again it fuses with occasional tercets or consistently alternately rhyming lines:

> Could she have then foreseen
> the tongue survive its borrowed alphabets?
> She blessed her true heir: Sheikh Noor-ud-Din (186)

It is also important to note how effortlessly Shahid seems to weave into his lines names like Noor-ud-Din or Begum Akhtar, while preserving the original patterns of pronunciation, or place-names like Chrar-e-Sharif or Zabar wan. These proper nouns are also indicative of a particular kind of geocultural specificity that ties the lines to their local origins even while opening the channels of "glocal" interactions that the English language almost inevitably secures.

These "glocal" intersections also become visible in a poem like "First Day of Spring," carrying lines from *King Lear* as epigraph, where the terza rima is used to enfold within itself the speaker's rejection of any kind of militant religious rhetoric that only inflicts godless violence upon others:

> On this perfect day, perfect for forgetting God,
> why are they—Hindu or Muslim, Gentile or Jew—
> shouting again some godforsaken word of God? (227)

It is perhaps deliberately ironic that the terza rima, as a form, gained prominence through Dante's divinely inspired masterpiece *The Divine Comedy*, which functions on the basis of unperturbed foundations of faith. In contrast, Shahid's poetry repeatedly plays with the sheer irrelevance of terms like "paradise" and "inferno" in today's chaotic world, prompted by the recognition of infernal violence in Kashmir, often in the name of God:

> You spent these years on every street in Hell? How odd,
> then, that I never saw you there, I who've loved you
> against (*Hold me!*) against every word of God. (227)

Such lines further testify to Shahid's nuanced deployment of enjambment in his stanzas, which contributes to a wonderful colloquiality within formal strictures. This is evident also from other poems in terza rima such as "A Fate's Brief Memoir" or poems like "The Floating Post Office," written in an equally demanding form, the sestina, where words that end each line of the first stanza are used as line endings (made bold for clarity) in each of the following five stanzas, rotated in a set pattern:

> Has he been kept from us? **Portents**
> of rain, rumors, ambushed **letters** . . .
> Curtained palanquin fetch our **word**,
> bring us word: Who has died? Who'll **live**?
> Has the order gone out to **close**
> the waterways . . . the one open **road**?
>
> And then we saw the boat being **rowed**
> through the fog of death, the **sentence**

passed on our city. It came **close**
to reveal smudged black-ink **letters**
which the postman—he was **alive**—
gave us, like signs, without a **word** (207)

Queries regarding the post boat that would call at each houseboat to deliver and collect letters offer the poet yet another opportunity to lament the predominance of death and uncertainty in the valley of Kashmir and, much like the fog that rolls over Dal Lake, the rhyming words of each stanza continue to roll into the succeeding ones, signifying also the mechanical regularity with which nightmare stalked the valley of Kashmir. Significantly, the repetitive rhymes demanded by these forms are also commensurate with the *radif* that constitutes an important part of that heritage of Urdu poetry that Shahid's poetry so consistently embraces. The term "radif" refers to the repeating of common words in the ghazal, a typical Arabic and Persian form that Shahid himself uses with exquisite success. These strict verse forms with intricate rhyming patterns, which Shahid so frequently uses, thus operate as cross-pollinations between European verse traditions and those of Persia and the Indian subcontinent. This is precisely what Jahan Ramazani was hinting at when he discussed how Shahid participates in a "dialectics of indigenization" where each tradition becomes enriched and influenced by the other, a "transformative twinning of the Euro-modernist with the postcolonial" (Ramazani, 107). Thematically and formally, Shahid thus contributes to a typically postcolonial transnational poetics where one is moved by intimately felt notes of cultural multiplicity.

Such interlacing of heterogeneous traditions is also significantly witnessed in the three major canzones written by Shahid, which also operate as poetic milestones in his artistic trajectory. As Caleb Agnew notes: "The canzone is a sixty-five line form in six stanzas with five refrain words, essentially a much more difficult version of a sestina. Every line must end with one of the five end words, so five twelve-line stanzas and a five-line envoi shuffle these end words in a motivic progression" ("The Refrains of Kashmir"). One of these three canzones is "Lennox Hill," the opening poem of the collection *Rooms are Never Finished*, where the separation from the motherland fuses with the speaker's autobiographical agony of losing his mother to create cosmic resonances of loss. Almost inevitably, "Kashmir" features as one of those five end words that are arranged and rearranged throughout the poem, emphasizing the yearning of the exile as well as the multiple significations that Kashmir possesses in the psyche of the speaker:

> For no verse
> sufficed except the promise, fading, of Kashmir
> and the cries that reached you from the cliffs of Kashmir
> (across fifteen centuries) in the hospital. Kashmir,
> *she's dying*! How her breathing drowns out the universe
> as she sleeps in Amherst. Windows open on Kashmir:
> *There*, the fragile wood-shrines—so far away—of Kashmir! (248)

Kashmir here alternates between the promised final destination of the exile, a source of historical memory transmitted through anecdotes, an apostrophized beloved to whom a complaint may be voiced and a space that seems to swirl into infinite regression ("so far away"). It is the choice of the rhyme scheme that allows these multiple connotations to percolate and proliferate and the form thus plays a vital role in the unfolding of that elegiac aesthetic which Shahid mastered so carefully. The same pattern also reappears in another canzone, "After the August Wedding in Lahore, Pakistan," where the invocation of Kashmir is complemented by the images of glass in which are reflected the binaries of self and other as well as the mirroring of past and present that poetry might offer:

> With a rending encore, she closed the night.
> There was, like this, long ago in Kashmir,
> a moment—after a concert—outside Kashmir
> Book Shop that left me stranded, by midnight,
> in a hotel mirror. Would someone glass
> me in—from what? Filled, I emptied my glass,
> lured by a stranger's eyes into their glass. (240)

Kashmir becomes the portal through which the past ("long ago") and the present ("like this") are fused in the consciousness of the speaker who finds himself stranded, "by midnight / in a hotel mirror." But what does the mirror hold? Does it reflect the anguish of the speaker who remains aware of his own exilic location, especially in the eyes of the native? Or does it resemble something akin to the "looking glass border" (Ghosh, 233) invoked by Shahid's dear friend Amitav Ghosh, signifying those illusory images of self and other that continue to fuel hatred and violence across the subcontinent? Is that the fear that Shahid registers when the speaker wonders about being glassed in? But as always, Shahid's lines, like opened waves, find an escape from restrictive strictures and merge with the image in a stranger's glass which perhaps transports one to a place where there is "no border between oneself and one's image in the mirror" (Ghosh, 29). Therefore, by the time Shahid pronounces the final lines,

> Freedom's terrible thirst, flooding Kashmir,
> > is bringing love to its tormented glass.
> Stranger, who will inherit the last night
> of the past? Of what shall I not sing, and sing? (VS 241)

The answer is already evident: the exilic poet will reflect through the formal symmetries of his verse images of both beauty and terror, of the past that is lost and the horror that is present, so that, like Yeats, he too may raise a toast (a glass also refers to a glass of wine, an oft-repeated image in traditional Persian poetry) to a terrible beauty being born.

This is of course true of Shahid's wonderful ghazals, which not only dazzle readers with hybridized eloquence born from a diction streaked with Arabic and Urdu terms, but also repeatedly foreground the traumatic ruptures of dehumanizing, sectarian violence and its corrosive consequences. This is evident from the ghazal opening with "Where are you now? Who lies beneath your spell tonight?," which conveys his lamentation regarding competing religious and nationalist absolutisms and the havoc they unleash:

> Has God's vintage loneliness turned to vinegar?
> He's poured rust into the Sacred Well tonight.
>
> In the heart's veined temple all statues have been smashed.
> No priest in saffron's left to toll its knell tonight.
>
> He's freed some fire from ice, in pity for Heaven;
> he's left open—for God—the doors of Hell tonight.
>
> And I, Shahid, only am escaped to tell thee—
> God sobs in my arms. Call me Ishmael tonight. (VS 193)

As Shahid himself explained, the ghazal is composed of a series of autonomous or semi-autonomous couplets in a strict rhyme scheme that the opening couplet inaugurates by having it in both lines while the succeeding couplets repeat it in every second line. This is precisely why the word "tonight" is repeated in the aforementioned stanzas, which are also remarkable for what Jahan Ramazani identifies as their "ghazalified, modernist syncretism" (Ramazani, 105). What is equally remarkable, however, is how Shahid manages to combine within these lines echoes of Job, *Moby Dick*, and of course his own Islamic tradition, especially through the adoption of the name Ishmael, which, as Ramazani mentions, functions as "an intercultural node in which Judaism, Christianity, and Islam intersect, as they have in the poem's formal junctures and syncretic layerings" (105). These intercultural fusions are seen in many of his ghazals where he also includes a series of Arabic and Urdu terms, as examples of postcolonial code switching, to hybridize or "biriyanize" the English language. This is particularly true of the ghazal dedicated to Arabic that continues to remain relevant in this post-9/11 era of trumped-up (pun intended) jingoism and rampant Islamophobia:

> When Lorca died, they left the balconies open and saw:
> his *qasidas* braided, on the horizon, into knots of Arabic.
>
> Memory is no longer confused, it has a homeland—
> Says Shammas: Territorialize each confusion in a graceful Arabic.
> Where there were homes in Deir Yassein, you'll see dense forests—
> That village was razed. There's no sign of Arabic.
>
> I too, O Amichai, saw the dresses of beautiful women.
> And everything else, just like you, in Death, Hebrew and Arabic.
>
> They ask me to tell them what *Shahid* means—
> Listen: It means "The Beloved" in Persian, "witness" in Arabic.
>   (VS 225–226)

This trend is extended in other poems as well, where he uses terms like "al-Mustalim" or "ar-Rahim," proper nouns like "Hallaj" or "Jamshed" to create an English diction that successfully transmits his cultural heritage, in defiance of the imperialist baggage associated with the English language. This is most explicitly achieved in the ghazal entitled "Beyond English":

> No language is old—or young—beyond English.
> So what of a common tongue beyond English?
>
> I know some words for war, all of them sharp,
> but the sharpest one is *jung*—beyond English! . . .

Go all the way through *jungle* from *aleph* to *zenith*
to see English, like monkeys, swung beyond English . . .

If you want your drugs legal you must leave the States,
not just for hashish but one—*bhung*—beyond English . . .

If someone asks where *Shahid* has disappeared,
he's waging a war (no *jung*) beyond English. (361–362)

All these examples illustrate that not only was Shahid able to successfully transplant the Arabic-Persian form of the ghazal into English, but consequently modified the English language as well by infusing into it the flavors of Arabic and Persian languages. In this way, too, his poetry continues that trend of polysemic plurality that stands out as a feature of much of the diasporic, postcolonial poetry being written in English. Never one to be fenced by limiting definitions, Shahid's poetry functioned as an eclectic confluence where one could meet the waves from different cultural streams that together composed his heritage. Agha Shahid Ali thus emerges not just as a "laureate of loss" (Patke, 232), as he has sometimes been called, but also as a virtuoso and daring craftsman whose poetry champions hybridity through both themes and forms. Paraphrasing one of the most iconic couplets on Kashmir, a couplet that Shahid himself has used as well, a reader might well claim that if one is searching for poetry that amalgamates cultures and continents at ease, in both structure and sensibility, it is this, it is this, it is this.

Works Cited

Agnew, Caleb. "The Refrains of Kashmir: Agha Shahid Ali's Canzones and the Forms of Exile." *Arcade: A Digital Salon*. April 16, 2016.
Ali, Agha Shahid. *The Veiled Suite: The Collected Poems*. New Delhi: Penguin, 2010.
Ghosh, Amitav. *The Shadow Lines*. New Delhi: Oxford University Press, 2006.
Hall, Daniel. Foreword. *The Veiled Suite: The Collected Poems*. New Delhi: Penguin, 2010.
Patke, Rajib S. *Postcolonial Poetry in English*. Oxford: Oxford University Press, 2006.
Ramazani, Jahan. *A Transnational Poetics*. Chicago: University of Chicago Press, 2009.

9

Out of Focus

Agha Shahid Ali's Queer Optics

GAYATRI GOPINATH

This essay draws from my book *Unruly Visions: The Aesthetic Practices of Queer Diaspora*, in which I consider the ways in which queer visual practices negotiate diasporic movement in multiple geographic locations.[1] This book suggests other possibilities of being in and moving through these spaces that deviate from the straight lines of hetero- and homonormative scripts that typically determine one's life trajectory.[2] These practices disrupt the normative ways of seeing (and hence knowing) that are the legacy of colonial modernity, and that have been so central to the production, containment, and disciplining of sexual, racial, and gendered bodies. Crucially, they do so through a deployment of queer desire and identification that renders apparent the intimacies of our conjoined pasts and potential futures.

One of my central arguments in *Unruly Visions* is that the aesthetic practices of queer diaspora enact a complex interplay between the concepts of archive, affect, and region. When I speak of "region" in this context, I refer to both subnational and supranational spaces that exceed the boundaries of the nation. I argue that the aesthetic practices of queer diaspora mobilize new ways of seeing both regions and archives, and put into play an intimate relation between the two through an affective register. Such practices engender a queer optic that brings into focus nonconforming bodies, desires, practices, and affiliations that emerge in the space of the region and are concealed within dominant nationalist narratives. This queer optic thereby conjures forth *a queer regional imaginary*, one that suggests the possibility of tracing lines of connection and commonality, a kind of south–south relationality, between seemingly discrete regional spaces that in fact bypass the nation. This mode of seeing the queer aesthetic is necessarily disorienting in that it surfaces the connections between seemingly disparate geographic locations, temporalities, and sites of power. While the aesthetic practices of queer diaspora reorient us away from the straight and the narrow, they do not instead offer recourse in the fictions of stable identity or the security of homecoming. Rather they demand that we dwell, perhaps uncomfortably, in the space of disorientation that they open up. As such, this project is very much in conversation with other authorities of queer scholarship that treat queerness itself as a form of disorientation, of getting and staying lost, that diverges from the straight and narrow paths prescribed by heteronormativity.[3] I use "queerness" here to name not just non-heteronormative sexualities and genders, but rather to a way of seeing that I am calling a "queer optic." It also names a state of being out of place, of being disoriented in the landscape of heteronormativity. Thus we might explore what emerges when we see queerness as a process of both dwelling in those off-center spaces and of staying lost, and thereby perhaps even stumbling into new worlds of possibility.

I turn to the work of Agha Shahid Ali to investigate the productively disorienting effects of a queer regional imaginary, as it emerges in queer visual aesthetic practices. While Shahid, of course, was a poet and not a visual artist, I situate his work as paradigmatic of such practices precisely because of the way in which it allows us to see differently, through a queer optic. In fact, Shahid's poetry suggests a complex theorization of the interface between queerness and region, and the queerness *of* region, in the context of diasporic dwelling and displacement. His work allows us to explore a queer diasporic relation to a region from which one is forcibly removed, and how this displacement occasions a disorientation of a metronormative vision that we can identify as a queer optic.[4] Shahid was compelled to leave Kashmir first for New Delhi, and then for the United States, where his peripatetic existence took him to Pennsylvania, Utah, Arizona, and New York, before he died of brain cancer at the age of fifty-two in Northampton, Massachusetts, in October 2001. The point of departure in much of Shahid's poetry is his forced exile from Kashmir, a region that was and continues to be a casualty of both successive waves of colonialism and the dueling postcolonial nationalisms of Pakistan and India. Significantly, it is the region of Kashmir—not the nation-states of India or Pakistan—that provides the anchor for Shahid's diasporic vision and sensibility.[5] Similarly, his sense of "Americanness" is exquisitely attuned to the contours of region: much of his poetry evokes the landscapes and layered histories of the U.S. Southwest or Midwest alongside those of Kashmir.

When I was beginning to contemplate writing on Shahid's work, I was struck by the ways in which questions of sexuality and queer desire both appeared and disappeared in the critical scholarship about his work. A few critics have commented in passing on the homoerotic undertones in his work, as well as on his close, decades-long friendship with his mentor, the gay poet James Merrill. But for the most part, Shahid's homosexuality is seen as tangential or irrelevant to the themes of exile, loss, nostalgia, and trauma that echo so powerfully throughout his work.[6] In a departure from this non-engagement with the question of sexuality in relation to Shahid's work, I want to take queerness seriously as a mode of reading Shahid's poetry. As I suggested earlier, I understand his poetry as exemplary of the aesthetic practices of queer diaspora not simply because of the orientation of his own desire, but also because of the way in which his work demands a disorientation of normative ways of seeing, and of seeing the "region" in particular. His 1987 collection of poetry, entitled *The Half-Inch Himalayas*, for example, opens with the poem "Postcard from Kashmir":

> Kashmir shrinks into my mailbox,
> my home a neat four by six inches.
> I always loved neatness. Now I hold
> the half-inch Himalayas in my hand.
> This is home. And this the closest
> I'll ever be to home. When I return,
> the colors won't be so brilliant,
> the Jhelum's waters so clean,
> so ultramarine. My love
> so overexposed.
> And my memory will be a little
> out of focus, in it
> a giant negative, black
> and white, still undeveloped.

For the speaker, "Kashmir" as home is multiply mediated, relayed through various technologies of representation. Thus even actual return will not return home to him; the landscape will never be as perfect as it is in his memory. Indeed the postcard, this mundane representation of Kashmir as a picturesque landscape, is for the speaker the closest he will ever get to home; actual return only accentuates the disjuncture between the "giant negative" of home installed in his memory and the lived, messy reality of the place itself. The poem is a recognition of the impossibility of return even if and when geographic, physical return happens. Thus the queerness of Shahid's poem lies in its recognition that our vision is in fact always partial, subjective, incomplete, limited, fallible.[7] "Postcard from Kashmir" thus leaves us with an out-of-focus vision of home as a lost and longed-for region, a space where multiple temporalities (past, present, and future) collapse onto each other. Shahid suggests the ways in which, for *all* viewers, but perhaps particularly for those with an exilic or diasporic vision, this space of home is one that is multiply mediated and ungraspable in its "true" or authentic form. Ultimately, we the readers, like the speaker himself, are left to dwell within a disorienting landscape, caught between multiple times and spaces, and this may very well be where queerness lies.

Thus the queerness of Shahid's poetry lies not only in the ways in which it disorients our vision of "home-as-region" but also in the ways in which this disorientation of vision is occasioned by queer forms of intimacy. At one point in the writing of this chapter, I contacted the writer Amitav Ghosh, a close friend of the poet who was "commissioned" by Shahid in the months before his death to write what was in effect his eulogy. Ghosh published his remembrance of Shahid in a lyrical essay entitled "The Ghat of the Only World: Agha Shahid Ali in Brooklyn," upon Shahid's death in 2001. I asked Ghosh about the reason behind the curious silence regarding sexuality in relation to Shahid's work. Here is how he responded:

> As you will know from the piece ["The Ghat of the Only World"], I wrote it pretty much at Shahid's command. But I did speak to him at some length about it, and he made it clear that there were certain things he did not want to talk about. Since the piece was intended as a testament of friendship, as well as an expression of my admiration for his work, I felt I had to respect his wishes. But even if that were not the case I would not have had much to add. Shahid was not the kind of person

who talked about his private life much (at least to me). I really do think that the relationships he cared about most were his professional connections (i.e., with students, teachers, mentors, other poets, etc.) and his friendships—these were, in a way, also a part of his life's work and mission.[8]

To me, Ghosh's comment eloquently references the ways in which queerness emerges in Shahid's work, as it may have in his life, not as an overt declaration of homosexuality, nor as that which is ensconced safely within the realm of the private. He was neither a closeted homosexual nor an explicitly out, gay poet; indeed the dichotomy of closet versus outness, public versus private, are relatively meaningless categories in relation to both his life and work. Rather, the queerness of Shahid's work lies in the modes of relationality that it evinces and occasions: those forms of intimacy between friends, lovers, fellow artists, mentors, and students that, as Ghosh writes, were also "part of his life's work and mission."

The centrality of queer forms of intimacy to revisioning both time and space is particularly apparent in Shahid's 1991 collection, *A Nostalgist's Map of America*. One of Shahid's most beautiful poems here, an elegy entitled "In Search of Evanescence," was written at the height of the AIDS epidemic in the late 1980s and addressed to a friend (perhaps lover) who had died of the disease. The collection's title poem, in fact, is dedicated to Shahid's dead friend, Philip Paul Orlando. "In Search of Evanescence" is made up of eleven loosely connected poems that evoke what Shahid terms a "mythic terrain," one that traverses the Superstition Mountains of Arizona and the flat expanses of the U.S. Midwest, along with the Karakoram and the Hindu Kush mountain ranges of the Himalayas. In an interview a few years before his death, Shahid noted that it was the death of his friend that provided the connective tissue that combined poems that "originally had nothing to do with him." Here is an excerpt from one of them:

When on Route 80 in Ohio
I came across an exit
to Calcutta

the temptation to write a poem
led me past the exit
so I could say

> India always exists
> off the turnpikes
> of America . . .
>
> The warm rains have left
> many dead on the pavements
>
> The signs to Route 80
> all have disappeared
>
> And now the road is a river
> polished silver by cars
>
> The cars are urns
> carrying ashes to the sea

Route 80, queer scholar Scott Herring reminds us, is that straight line of superhighway that connects the metronormative centers of New York to San Francisco and that precludes any detours along the way. If compulsory heterosexuality is a kind of straightening device, as Sara Ahmed notes,[9] we can understand metronormativity as another kind of straightening device that disciplines bodies and desires into a singular, intelligible, homonormative mode of being gay.

Shahid's poem takes us off this metronormative grid: we journey through the byways and backroads off Route 80 that lead us into a different kind of queer territory, one where the Ganges and Calcutta exist alongside the small towns of the U.S. Midwest and the desert landscapes of Arizona. Shahid's *A Nostalgist's Map of America* radically disaggregates the borders of the U.S. nation. Instead, he invokes a queer regional imaginary that is both subnational and supranational simultaneously: the specificity of the U.S. Southwest and the expansiveness of the Himalayas occupy the same temporal and geographic frame. As Shahid himself comments on the poem, "it is not just the death of a friend, a simple elegy, but the death of tribes, the death of landscapes, and the death of language. All these things happen simultaneously to create a density."[10] Shahid's poem speaks precisely to this dense layering of multiple erasures and displacements, occasioned by various forms of historical violence: the AIDS epidemic, the colonial histories of South Asia, the displacement and attempted genocide of Native peoples in the U.S. Southwest.[11] Crucially, it is the queer body and queer relationality—the death of his friend from AIDS—that conjure this palimpsestic landscape into existence. Indeed, the HIV+ body—its blood, veins, and pain, its deterioration and its transformation—leaves an indelible imprint on this landscape. The poem thus enacts a queer optic: one through which we can see and sense the imbrication of various forms of erasure and dispossession that are typically obscured within dominant history. This capacious vision is in fact occasioned by queer forms of intimacy and friendship, love and loss.

But there is another level of queer intimacy evident in the poem: this is a queer intertextual intimacy with the poetry of Emily Dickinson on one hand, and the ghazal form on the other. Indeed, "In Search of Evanescence" can be read as an evocation of, and homage to, both Dickinson and the ghazal form. As such it makes apparent Shahid's own aesthetic genealogy that draws as much from the great Urdu singer Begum Akhtar as it does from Dickinson and other American poets. The poem's title itself, "In Search of Evanescence" is a direct reference to Dickinson's "A Route to Evanescence." The ninth section of Shahid's poem begins with an epigraph from Dickinson ("*I want to eat Evanescence slowly*"), and proceeds with twenty couplets that suggest the ghazal form. The repetition of the linguistic elements of Dickinson's poem in this section and in several others, along with the suggestion of the ghazal, gives a formal coherence to the different sections that they would otherwise lack. The ghazal, as Shahid himself noted, is a profoundly relational form: the lines are meant to be recited out loud, and the give and take between the poet and his audience is fundamental to the pleasure and enjoyment that the poem elicits. Indeed the relational aspect of the ghazal complements the queer relationality that provides "In Search of Evanescence" with its connective thread: many of the sections are addressed to "you," "Phil," the beloved friend who has disappeared from view.

In the poem that precedes "In Search of Evanescence," entitled "A Nostalgist's Map of America," Shahid writes: "I live in Evanescence / (I had to build it, for America / was without one)." To live in Evanescence is to live at the vanishing point. It is to learn to dwell in a state of permanent temporariness, in a space unimaginable within a nationalist cartography. Evanescence is a kind of utopian non-space that cannot be captured or identified on any conventional map. Shahid's citation of Dickinson's "evanescence" echoes the ways in which the queer scholars have theorized the fleeting, transitory nature of queer and racialized life-worlds, particularly at the height of the AIDS epidemic of the 1980s and 1990s. The queer scholar José Esteban Muñoz, in an early essay from 1996 that laid the grounds of what we now call queer of color critique, eloquently theorizes queerness as ephemera. In this essay, entitled "Ephemera as Evidence," Muñoz writes:

> I want to propose queerness as a possibility, a sense of self-knowing, a mode of sociality and relationality. Queerness is often transmitted covertly. This has everything to do with the fact that leaving too much of a trace has often meant that the queer subject has left herself open for attack. Instead of being clearly available as visible evidence, queerness has existed as innuendo, gossip, fleeting moments, and performances that are meant to be interacted with by those within its epistemological sphere—while evaporating at the touch of those who would eliminate queer possibility.[12]

For Muñoz, queer sociality, acts, and desires leave traces that cannot be codified within standard metrics of evidence, or contained within traditional archives. Instead he suggests other means of archiving, seeing, feeling, sensing, and knowing queerness that subsequent generations of queer scholars (myself included) have taken to heart. What Shahid gives us is precisely one method of archiving queer sociality and migrant existence, through a poetic idiom. We can glimpse in Shahid's routes to evanescence the queer life-worlds and forms of sociality that are lost to history, that leave no trace except in the lyrical landscapes he creates.

In short, Shahid's poetry gives us a queer optic that disarranges hetero- and homonormative sightlines so that other bodies, landscapes, and affiliations come into view. Through this queer optic, we can discern the outlines of a queer regional imaginary that produces region-to-region and diaspora-region connectivities that bypass the nation. Queerness in his work is a conduit for seeing and sensing the intimacies of disparate, apparently discrete histories. Thus Shahid's queer remappings of the region are profoundly disorienting: they palimpsestically layer multiple times and spaces atop one another and, in so doing, suggest different possibilities of relationality that may in fact reorient our vision toward more capacious and hospitable futures.

Notes

1. Portions of this essay are excerpted from a chapter entitled "Queer Disorientations, States of Suspension," in Gayatri Gopinath, *Unruly Visions: The*

Aesthetic Practices of Queer Diaspora (Durham, NC: Duke University Press, 2018). The chapter situates Shahid's poetry alongside the visual art of South Asian diasporic artists Chitra Ganesh and Seher Shah.

2. For queer scholarship that powerfully contests the ways in which both heteronormativity and homonormativity determine individual and collective temporalities, see Judith Halberstam, *In a Queer Time and Place: Transgender Bodies, Subcultural Lives*; Elizabeth Freeman, *Time Binds: Queer Temporalities, Queer Histories*; Sara Ahmed, *Queer Phenomenology: Orientations, Objects, Others*.

3. As Jack Halberstam writes, "we might consider getting lost over finding our way, and so we should conjure . . . an ambulatory journey through the unplanned, the unexpected, the improvised and the surprising." Judith Halberstam, *The Queer Art of Failure*, 15–16. Similarly Sara Ahmed suggests that if we "consider heterosexuality as a compulsory orientation," then "risking departure from the straight and narrow makes new futures possible, which might involve going astray, getting lost, or even becoming queer." Sara Ahmed, *Queer Phenomenology*, 84. And José Esteban Muñoz adds, "We can understand queerness itself as being filled with the intention to be lost. Queerness is illegible and therefore lost in relation to the straight minds' mapping of space. Queerness is lost in space or lost in relation to the space of heteronormativity . . . To be lost . . . is to veer away from heterosexuality's path." Muñoz, *Cruising Utopia*, 72–73.

4. Jack Halberstam coins the term "metronormativity" to refer to the dominant story of gay formation as "a migration from 'country' to 'town,'" where the urban is seen as the only viable space for queer worldmaking," while the non-urban is seen as the repository of homophobic backwardness. Judith Halberstam, *In a Queer Time and Place*, 36–37. Building on Halberstam's notion of metronormativity, Scott Herring takes to task what he terms "queer metronormativity" for sidelining and indeed erasing the richness and specificity of queer lives in the United States lived beyond the bi-coastal gay axis of San Francisco and New York, materially linked by Route 80. Herring demands that we disorient our metronormative vision and focus instead on those alternative routes off the superhighway to urban queerdom, that may initially appear as roads to nowhere, dead-ends, cul-de-sacs, far from Castro Street or Christopher Street; for Herring, it is these "countless other highways and byways that receive scant attention in an urbane queer topography," that are the "much needed detour[s]" that lead us to those queer topographies that remain unthought and unaccounted for within a metronormative gay imaginary. Scott Herring, *Another Country*, 181.

5. As Lavina Dhingra Shankar and Rajini Srikanth note, Shahid often referred to himself as a "Kashmiri-American-Kashmiri"; they write: "In the double hyphenation, Shahid reveals that the 'American' is not the endpoint of his identity, not the destination of his being . . . Cleverly, he suggests that America takes him back to Kashmir." Shankar and Srikanth, "South Asian American Literature: 'Off the Turnpike' of Asian America," 378.

6. A notable exception to this non-engagement with queerness in Agha Shahid Ali's work is found in the Introduction of Anjali Arondekar and Geeta Patel, eds., "Area Impossible," Special issue of *GLQ*, 151–171.

7. As Jacqueline Rose comments, "You can only start seeing—this was Freud's most basic insight—when you know that your vision is troubled, fallible, off-key. The only viable way of reading is not to find, but to disorient, oneself." Quoted in Stoler, *Along the Archival Grain*, 119.

8. Amitav Ghosh, personal e-mail communication, August 5, 2011.

9. Ahmed, *Queer Phenomenology*, 79.

10. Shahid quoted in interview with Rehan Ansari and Rajinderpal S. Pal, "Agha Shahid Ali: Calligraphy of coils," n.p.

11. However we could also read Shahid's elegiac rendering of the indigenous presence of Arizona as reiterating the settler colonial trope of situating indigeneity as always already past, as inevitably extinct. See Jodi Byrd, *The Transit of Empire* for an elaboration of the problematic rendering of the "pastness" of indigeneity within postcolonial studies.

12. José Esteban Muñoz, "Ephemera as Evidence: Introductory Notes to Queer Acts," *Women &Performance: A Journal of Feminist Theory* (London: Routledge, 2009) 8: 2, 5–16.

10

Beginnings

A Journey with Micronarratives

Amzed Hossein

Agha Shahid Ali (1949–2001) started his poetic journey with the fifteen poems of *Bone-Sculpture* published in 1972 in Calcutta by Writers Workshop. His second volume of poems, *In Memory of Begum Akhtar & Other Poems* (IMBA), was brought out by the same publisher in 1979. The poems in both these volumes trace the gradual estrangement of the poet from grand narratives of religion or constricting nationalist discourses. They also record his experiences of fragmentation of the cultural matrix of his ancestors. In the resultant circumstances, the poet is left with only micronarratives, independent of each other like the couplets of a ghazal, put together by the repetitions of iterative themes of memory and death functioning like the rhyme (*qafia*) and refrain (*radif*) of a ghazal in all the poems. This chapter attempts to approach the poems of these two books from the perspective of experiments in the vein of modernist ghazals that eschew traditional amorous or erotic themes and express the anguish of alienation and exile, of loss and death.

In his lecture "English in Its Tri-cultural Moment," Agha Shahid Ali clarifies that the three cultural moments he speaks of are Hindu, Islamic, and Western. He grew up in Kashmir, went to Irish Catholic school, and then as a teenager he attended Burris School in Muncie, Indiana. He completed his Master's in English Literature in 1970 at Delhi University and was teaching English in Hindu College there during the publication of his first book of poems. His family spoke English, Urdu, and Kashmiri. So for him to choose English as a literary medium was not a matter of great wonder. It is also predictable that in the first book of poems by a student as well as a teacher of English literature there would be "echoes of T. S. Eliot, W. H. Auden and others" (King, 260), but in hindsight, now it is also not difficult to decipher that Shahid drew upon the structure and character of the ghazal—although with different thematic preoccupations—even in his early poetry.

I

The genesis of the poet's sense of rootlessness lies in his choice of vocation: to be a poet in an "alien language," to be "a dealer in words / that mix cultures / and leave [him] rootless" ("Dear Editor") (BS 12). The burden of being a poet who writes in a language that "they" consider for him as "alien" entails the loneliness of a long-distance runner. Of course he has "hopes which assume shapes in / alien territories." But "in sunset horizons" these hopes are destroyed—"trains crash into them." So he has only the "dark room" to wake up in.

In "The Editor Revisited" (IMBA 47–48), almost seven years after the publication of "Dear Editor," he still feels that the language he employs in representing the Indian reality ("temples, beggars, and dust," the brutality of policemen beating children or the insensitivities toward the hermaphrodites, "their drums echoing a drought-rhythm") in his poetry is inadequate, his "faint British accents" sound "foreign" even to his own ears. He receives friendly advice from the Marxists to realize the obscenity of using English in Delhi and to replace it with Hindi or Bengali, so that "each word will burn / like hunger," because "A language must measure up to one's native dust." However, he remains unconvinced that the dictation to write poetry either in the cause of "Revolution" or in any language forced upon him would be any real service to his "hungry country." So he sticks to his choice of writing in English, for he feels his study of English literature helps him in discovering and articulating his own self: "Shakespeare feeds my alienation."

If we juxtapose the opening and concluding poems of *Bone-Sculpture*, we come across the same obsession with alienation and death. The setting of the former ("Bones," BS 11) is a "mosaic-world of silent graveyards" having only the "bones" of martyrs or ancestors of a "dying" generation;

the action in the latter poem ("Notes for the Unabandoned Stranger") is dramatized in "a city of stones" that is full of dead men, their graves and their skeletons being desecrated by a silent and dead man.

The speaker in the opening poem ("Bones") not only speaks of death, mourning, and loneliness but also the futility of complaining, of all-pervading sickness and lack of vitality: "In this mosaic-world of silent / graveyards the difference lies between / death and dying." For him "The years are dead. . . . Death filled the years, there was no time to mourn. No time to remember / slaughtered martyrs or ancestors / who knew a history of miracles." He participates in the ritual procession of Mohorrum that is a communal ritual of memory and mourning and empathizing with the martyrs of the community together with the other participants. Even in the procession he feels alienated ("I'm still alone"). There is a deep chasm that separates him from his past ("Grandfather still mocks me in my dream: did I light the oil-lamp at this tomb?"). The persona concludes: "It's / futile to light oil-lamps here / and search for grandfather or / forgotten ancestors." Their flesh has been reduced to dust with the irreducible bones lying in their graves. So he wonders: "how can one complain to the bones?" Does he suggest that the bones are unresponsive to our verbal complaints? Do the bones stand for some object-lesson, self-evident truth, beyond words? Are bones the bedrock of our existence? Are they the ones that remain when all pretensions, superfluities, trappings of civilizations, are stripped off? They are what remain even after death? Indeed, the title of the volume *Bone-Sculpture* may intend a poem to be a piece of artwork on the quintessence of our existence.

The concluding poem ("Notes for the Unabandoned Stranger," BS 31) has images of a silent man desecrating the "dream-ritual of dead men" as well as their skeletons. This silent man turns out to be a dead man: "he was dead having lived in a city of stones." The first-person speaker/persona "had died long ago," losing his identity "in this sacrilege of dreams." All the dead men from this "city of stones" are happy as they are stripped of their secret desires. Now they are searching for their dreaming eyes in their graves. They "undug" the graves to find their "eyes dreaming."

All these hallucinatory, surrealistic, apparently incoherent snippets of narratives constitute the human condition for an "unabandoned stranger" in a postmodern world. Who is this unabandoned stranger? The person is not abandoned by his chosen space where he has his residence, and yet he feels himself a "stranger" (he has lost his "identity") in this "city of stones." He has experienced the sacrilege of his dreams, his "dream-rituals."

These are the experiences and visions of a young man of twenty (BS 11) who has been uprooted from his native land, has moved back and forth from city to city and has lost his attachments to any particular city, being freed from his past ("ghost"): The "city of stones" and the "mosaic-world of silent graveyards" are identical places with different nomenclature.

Between these two poems of *Bone-Sculpture* are placed thirteen more micronarratives. In "After Seeing the Film *Who's Afraid of Virginia Woolf*?" (BS 14–15) the poet positions himself "somewhere between / truth and illusion." He realizes his barrenness as his "truths are untold." He feels he is "chilled in / a sweating illusion." His inability to articulate the truth reveals his helplessness: "truth stumbles / from my hands / and shatters / on tiles." He recognizes that these "fragments / are of broken / dreams." There are feelings of loneliness, barrenness, futility of tears, emptiness, a sense of "lingering death" and an experience or sensation of dying ("dying / i clutch thirst / an empty glass?").

"Lunerscape" (BS 16) presents a confrontation with the realization of loss of "home" and how to come to terms with this situation and invest meaning to this new space: the addressee, the stranger (because he has arrived in an unfamiliar location) must not only circle these naked rocks, but "add colour" to the "moon-wounds" carved in these thirsty rocks with his "bleeding feet." The stranger then certainly can hope that "Tomorrow on this hostile horizon / your silver earth will rise." The alliteration in "hostile horizon," softening the dread of the unknown, reveals the romantic appeal of the alien space. Similarly, "silver earth" reminds one of the effects of the lunar light indicated in the title: it is a world washed in silver moonlight; so how realistic will the world be? Frequent dislocating and relocating of place of residence (that cannot be identified/ equated with "home") brings into sight this "lunarscape"—not earthscape, not a home. The three couplets of the poem may suggest the form of a ghazal.

In "Autumn in Srinagar" (BS 20–22), the sunset is described with a few cosmic images: the sun dies, the day burns to ash "in the sky's funeral pyre"; the funeral pyre brings in the images of the smoke of burning incense, "the mute corpse," "the house of the dead." Death dominates over the stony land and the sky. In this country of death, in this "mosaic of graves" the persona says: "I design my tomb / and beat a prayer / on / the stone: / my hands / carving the stillness / of dead leaves." In section five, "a last image," there is a clear indication of hope, of transcendence: "i see your form coming for me / in this season not yours"; somewhere in a dusty room "a lamp burns." Still there is darkness and extreme coldness, but there is human presence: "in this / terrible darkness /i hear / bangles break / the measured / rhythm of / biting air." So finally there is prayer for transcendence, for release from this prison-house of death: "take me / far from here / of my own accord / on my own understanding / i have gathered the leaves for winter." Does "winter" signify another country? Or death? Is the speaker ready for a journey to the country of death, with the fuel ("leaves") required for surviving in the winter season? Will it be a final refuge? A sanctuary? A journey from autumn to winter—from death-in-life to actual death?

"Another Death" (BS 23) talks of "death of another / time" and a consequent deep existential void: "That stone we worshipped / long ago holds a savage emptiness." It is a death of a time of dreams. He accepts this death and asks his companion (another self? his alter ego?) to "bury the bones of dreams in a river." In this empty world there is a search for "A dream-skeleton counting / broken shells": this dream-skeleton is "stripped of all pretending flesh," stripped of all masks of wisdom, the forked bare creature or the unaccommodated man in *King Lear*, now belongs to the realm of death, and so must know the meaninglessness of "the false morning / of prayers echoing in the broken / distance of hills" and worthlessness of living life in a fragmentary manner ("dividing life by evenings"): so it must possess answer to the question "Is death worth dying?" Now the dilemma is to choose between death and the emptiness of the stony world: "Is death worth dying?" or "Will we return to find the emptiness?"

There are four "Fragments" numbered IV, V, VI, and IX (BS 27–30). Intriguingly, these titles are intended to indicate that they are merely a selection from a larger, perhaps abandoned, body of work. Since these are merely fragments, they lack any internal coherence. These are surrealistic dialogues conducted with his self or some figure from a surrealistic realm.

Fragment IV is titled "Diwali, 1971." He remembers the little boy who cut the flame into pieces of blue and red, half-blue and gold. Years later he realized that the illumination of the city had charred his secrets and had revealed his strange longings in "half-shadows." If the dismemberment of the flame was like "a pattern of death," this exposure of his desires was no less so. But he forgot the pain and kept on smiling to keep the world happy. So "he / rebuilt / the flame with his cluttered colours," his micronarratives.

Fragment V, entitled "You," is perhaps an ironical address to a critic or reader who does not like his poetry and says that they are merely ash and producing good poetry is like spitting out blood. The criticism leaves the poet strangely free and glad—perhaps because he does not have to write poetry to please anybody. This criticism spurred him to write more and more rapidly and there was "blood more blood." The critic arrested his smile in the mirror and so he became more severe: "you split my skull my words / were spattered on the cold cement." The poet was not unhappy: the critic's blows will help bring out more and better poems; so he prays: "please mutilate my / wounded poetry hands / i will not write again." But the implication is that more poetry will flow like blood.

Fragment VI begins with someone's comments that the persona is like his dead friend. The persona does not particularly dislike it: "This is then my / identity: a / kinship with tombs a smile borrowed from / a dead child." Unfortunately, this smile will be associated with a nightmare and "There'll / be no surprise only the nightmare / of his smile."

Fragment IX alludes to a helplessness, a breakdown on a cosmic level: "There / is no help, / not even in the stars. The stars / are breaking, they /do not guide our destiny." There is a sense of disillusionment: "Destiny is another matter" and not under the control of the stars. Destiny or anything in life cannot change "with our permanent disguises." Of course the persona "whores" himself to the "escapes of the times," which only "hide" his "permanent wounds." However, the sense of personal crisis, of horrifyingly macabre invasion from the surreal realm persists: "Your smile / eats into my flesh, it breaks my bones." The persona confesses: "I do not have cures nor do I protest."

II

In Memory of Begum Akhtar, Agha Shahid Ali's second volume of poems, largely continues the thematic preoccupations of *Bone-Sculpture*, though with a much greater range of resources. The first volume ended with a poem ("Notes for the Unabandoned Stranger") containing the macabre image of two dead men looking for their "eyes dreaming" in a "city of stones." *In Memory of Begum Akhtar* also is permeated with images of death, coffin, graves, loss, nostalgia, autumn, wars, "streets calligraphed with blood," "the rhythm / of a dying / dynasty" (IMBA 40)—the sad inexorable passing away of an era, a culture, a way of life.

It opens with the title poem, a four-part elegy on the death of a great icon of a particular cultural tradition. Begum Akhtar (1914–1974) was an exponent of a gharana of Hindustani classical vocal music, singing chiefly the genres like ghazals, dadras and thumris in an inimitable style and an unforgettably melodious voice. In a note, Shahid himself describes Begum Akhtar as "One of the Indian subcontinent's greatest singers and certainly the greatest ghazal singer of all time" (*The Veiled Suite*, 378).

The opening section of the poem contrasts the devastating news of her death in every newspaper and the calm, blue sky without a hint of calamity—unlike Nature mourning as in traditional elegies like Milton's "Lycidas." However, for the poet, the passing away of Begum Akhtar is "the end of the world." His anger and helpless frustration explode in the disguised couplet "no room for sobs, / even between the lines; / I wish to talk of the end of the world." The next section expresses the poet's disbelief that her fingers, instead of scaling the Bhairavi raga, are now perhaps scaling the "muddy shroud." Her death has put ghazal in "dingy archives" sobbing in grief. She added flavor ("seasoned") to the notes of the ragas with the beautiful words of the ghazals of poets like Ghalib, Mir, Faiz for decades. In his poem "Homage to Faiz Ahmed Faiz" in *The Half-Inch Himalayas* (1987) Shahid puts Begum Akhtar's relation to the ghazals of Faiz in a more felicitous way: "Begum Akhtar, who wove your couplets / into ragas: both language and music / were sharpened" (VS 58). With the demise of Begum Akhtar, the rich world of ghazal now lies in ruins, bereft of the well-knit structure of the ragas like Bhairavi and Malhar in which they were sung by Begum Akhtar; she made even "catastrophe" appreciable by the connoisseur of music: who will now put the ghazals to music in classical ragas and keep them alive? A unique world of music has vanished with the death of Begum Akhtar. Now the mourning poet has nothing to fall back on and draw on and he would perforce have to "innovate on a note-less raga."

The coffin, the grave, "the earth's claw" that attempt to obliterate the memory of the singer dominate the last two sections. The speaker's anger and anguish come out in his characterizing the coffin as "stupid" and ignorant, the grave as unresponsive and indifferent ("damp and cold"). Besides, he has also attempted to portray the Ghazal Queen with her "records, pictures, tapes" but the endeavor has turned out to be presenting merely a lifeless and incomplete portrait—"a careless testimony." These are "circumstantial evidence" that cannot bring back her warmth, her creativity, her hypnotic charm. Now the raga of the rain, the Megha Malhar absorbs her to the notes of the rain, and she has become inaccessible to a writer of obituary or to a professional music critic and she "elude[s] completely." The closing section acknowledges that now she has become part of nature—the source and final home of all life forms, all beauty, all creative energy; for nature, a small community of even disconsolate mourners is superfluous: "The rain doesn't speak, / and life, once again, closes in, / reasserting this earth where the air / meets in a season of grief." Death cannot put a full stop to the march of life. Loss, anguish, memory, nostalgia may dominate the duration of the "season of grief," but the irresistible call of life cannot be silenced.

Each group of the verses and each section of the elegy are apparently autonomous units, expressing diverse kinds of emotion, and yet these are interlinked, as we observe in a ghazal. Bruce King also comments that in structure and temperament the poem shows "how instinctively Ali writes English-language poetry with the music and pattern of the ghazal in his ear" (King, 261).

That "In Memory of Begum Akhtar" was reprinted in the next collection of Shahid's poems, *The Half-Inch Himalayas* (1987) demonstrates the importance that the poet accorded to it. There is another poem, "Begum Akhtar," in the 1979 volume. Begum Akhtar occupies a large space in "I Dream I Am the Only passenger on Flight 423 to Srinagar" in *The Country without a Post Office* (1997). Indeed, along with Begum Akhtar, great musicians and singers such as K. L. Saigal and Rasoolan Bai (IMBA 15, 16) and their music become for Shahid signifiers of his ancestor's culture. Closely linked with the music was Urdu poetry, an important component of this inheritance. It was not exactly Islamic culture; we may call it Indo-Muslim culture, because as Karen Leonard argues, Indo-Muslim "puts emphasis on the Indian location" and "Muslim rather than Islamic emphasizes a civilizational and not a religious culture" (Alka Patel and Karen Leonard, 165–166). Whether one observes evidence of a cultural synthesis or of a successful plural society, Shahid's poetry is replete with nostalgia for that slowly dwindling public culture of pre-partition India and is a recurrent subject in the lyrics of this second book of poems.

In "Note Autobiographical–1" and "Note Autobiographical–2" (IMBA 20, 21), Shahid attempts to narrativize the process of his alienation from the religion of his grandparents. His doubts about the existence of God could not be answered by his grandmother. The death of his grandfather, whom he "worshipped," intensified his doubts. But when the shoes of their servant were stolen at the mosque, he lost his faith in Islam: "the calligraphed dome gave way to the sky: / Autumn caved into me / with its script of flames / and ignited my dry garbage of God." However, this crumbling of institutional Islam did not make him follow his father, who "mouthed Freud or Marx"; even though he may take a quiet pride in his mother's embrace of modernity, as she "had long since discarded the veil," the tone of both the poems reveals his deep attachment, fondness, and warmth for his practicing grandparents. His grandmother's affectionate admonitions, "Kafir, you're no good" or "My grandson is lost to us," still haunt him. Islamic faith might recede for him, but the absence of godliness was replaced with a secular constituent of his grandfather's cultural capital—Urdu poetry, the poetry of Ghalib and, as he mentions elsewhere in the book, Khusro, Mir, Faiz: "My voice cracked on Ghalib / and my tongue forgot the texture of prayer."

Three poems in this book—"Learning Urdu," (27), its revision "After the Partition of India" (28), and "The Jama Masjid Butcher" (45)—are Shahid's meditations on the partition of the Indian subcontinent in 1947. We may also include in this group "A Butcher," published in *The Half-Inch Himalayas* (VS 47–48). Indeed, all four poems are marked by repetitions and echoes of phrases and images. In the first of these poems, the butcher—a "victim of a continent broken / in two"—recounts his personal tragedy: he has forgotten half of the name of his village; he has seen "Across a line of blood my friends dissolved / into bitter stanzas of some dead poet." He implies perhaps that the pain of the tragedy can be embodied and found in poetry only. But he who knew the poetry of Mir and Ghalib by heart now cannot remember any poetry: he saw their "poetry dissolve into letters of blood." However, the poet finds that ultimately political violence of Partition cannot permanently divide language and great poetry created in that language: "I find Ghalib / at the crossroads of language, refusing / to move to any side" ("Learning Urdu," IMBA 27).

Although the political violence and upheaval seemed to divide and destroy the cultural fabric—"History broke the back / of poetry"—("After the Partition of India") Urdu language, or rather poetry in Urdu by great poets like Ghalib and Mir, gradually succeeds in establishing a connect between the elite and the subaltern, or even the two broken halves of the subcontinent—India and Pakistan—because Ghalib cannot be partitioned. In "Jama Masjid Butcher" (45) the speaker with his "well-fed skin" finds that Urdu used by the butcher at work in his shop "is still fine, polished / smooth by the generations." So they "establish the bond of phrases, / dressed in the couplets of Ghalib."

The poem is still further revised in "A Butcher" in *The Half-Inch Himalayas*. Here the speaker meets the butcher—his knuckles smeared in blood—but his Urdu is still impeccable and they can communicate through Urdu poetry: "I smile and quote / a Ghalib line; he completes / the couplet, smiles, / quotes a Mir line. I complete / the couplet." Poetry transcends class barrier. Structurally, too, these different versions demonstrate how through their rewritings they gradually move toward acquiring a ghazal-like form: a sequence of interlinked couplets.

Delhi, as the center of Indo-Muslim art and culture, occupies a prominent space in several poems of this volume. In "At Jama Masjid, Delhi" (36), for example, the poet exercises his historical imagination and recreates the rise of the mosque: how the first brick was laid and how the minarets came up where there was nothing. He attempts to understand the spiritual aspiration of Shahjahan—the emperor who undertook to construct this grand mosque because he "knew the depth of stones, / how they turn smooth rubbed on a heart." Whenever one listens to the call to prayer, one will be reminded of the "scrolls of legend" revealing "how the prayers rose, brick by brick." Ironically, Shahjahan's reward in this world for this act of devotion was imprisonment in old age: the only consolation was the company of his virgin daughter Jahanara, who "dressed the cracked marble reign" and who is described in another poem as mumbling "Sufi quatrain" ("Qawwali at Nizamuddin Aulia's Dargah," 39), as Jahanara herself also wrote poetry.

"Qawwali at Nizamuddin Aulia's Dargah" (39–40) in its four sections encompasses a variety of micronarratives. Nizamuddin Aulia (1238–1325), the great Sufi saint, in his dargah or tomb draws many people: the poet imaginatively visualizes Jahanara, the Mughal princess who "garbed in the fakir's grass / mumbles a Sufi quatrain." A beggar woman weeps and prays on Khusro's pillars, another poet and mystic. There is also Muhammad Shah II (1719–1748), called Rangeele ("Colour"), the Mughal emperor who was a patron of painters, Urdu poets, musicians, dancers, scholars, and Sufi saints. Time, the great destroyer, obliterates everything: "Time has only its vagrant finger. / Knowing no equal, it paused for massacres." The last section refers to Nadir Shah's massacres of the people of Delhi in 1739, while the drunken emperor Muhammad Shah Rangeele was dancing with "hoofs of sorrow," presiding over "a dying / dynasty." The poem closes with a one-line verse: "We walk through streets calligraphed with blood," suggesting the long history of Delhi passing through many bloody phases.

"The Walled City: 7 Poems on Delhi" (29–35) is a loose sequence portraying the poet's varied mood. The first in the sequence is a search for creative inspiration: he roams from one tomb to another, chewing "the ash of prayers. / Won't poetry happen to me?" It is a temporal as well as spatial journey of the imagination: "Caught in the lanes of history, / don't I qualify now?" Poem 2 records how the bitter memory of the "Two-Nation Theory" still rankles the older generation and are "hoarder of regrets" and mistrust. But the younger generation is free from feeling the need for such cautions:

"My friend and I are rather simple: / We never saw the continent divide." Poem 5 talks of a bootblack of Delhi and the insensitivities of people toward their participation in enhancing the beauty of the city: "The bootblack brushes my shoes: / Does my heart beat in my feet? // His knuckles carry the memory / of this city. / My shoes shine like death." Poem 6 portrays an old man who may be taken to represent the ancient city of Delhi. Now nobody seems to care about the past of the city: although the old man sat there in all seasons, suddenly "This morning he wasn't there /with his ancient beard / and his stretched-out hand." The cleanliness drive of the modern city planners clears of those accretions of the past: "The sweeper said he took him away / with the morning garbage."

Shahid's occasional venture at writing slightly elaborate autobiographical or historical vignettes in several poems of *In Memory of Begum Akhtar*, such as "Profile" (22), "At Jama Masjid, Delhi" (36), and the two sections of "Legends of Kashmir" (43–44), lack the lyrical poignancy that marks what we call here micronarratives. "Qawwali at Nizamuddin Aulia's Dargah" (39–40), on the other hand, may be longer, but its structure, consisting of loose sections, gives it a lyrical appeal.

In "Ancestors" (41), which comprises only three lines, Shahid accepts with resignation the inexorable march of time the destroyer, and the inevitable disappearance of all things we hold dear in our life: "How can we ruin this distance of time? / I must agree / to let your bones rot." The last two lines clearly constitute the second line of a couplet fragmented into two, evoking the sense of the dismantling and slow annihilation of our cultural inheritance: the image of the bones rotting also suggests the painful awareness of the irreducibility of the ancestral bond deep within his consciousness.

Throughout his life Agha Shahid Ali experimented with many complex verse forms. However, his love for the ghazal, like a subterranean river, has always flowed in the substratum of his heart. This love led him to publish *Ravishing DisUnities: Real Ghazals in English*, and *Call Me Ishmael Tonight*. It is my contention that in most of the poems of the first two books of Agha Shahid Ali, though written in free verse, the trace of the ghazal's form and spirit can be discerned.

Works Cited

Ali, Agha Shahid. *Bone-Sculpture*. Calcutta: Writers Workshop, 1972.
———. *In Memory of Begum Akhtar & Other Poems*. Calcutta: Writers Workshop, 1979.
———. *The Veiled Suite: The Collected Poems*. Gurgaon: Penguin Books India, 2010.

———. "English in Its Tri-cultural Moment." Video. February 20, 1997. https://www.youtube.com/watch?v=6Iu3pkJQJOw&list=PLRYCUWu00g7R6NllTN96C4MSvQJZqcnZq&index=2&t=0s

Farooqi, Mehr Afshan, ed. *The Oxford India Anthology of Modern Urdu Literature: Poetry and Prose Miscellany*. New Delhi: Oxford University Press, 2008.

King, Bruce. *Modern Indian Poetry in English*. Revised ed. New Delhi: Oxford University Press, 2001.

Patel, Alka, and Karen Leonard (Eds). *Indo-Muslim Cultures in Transitions*. Brill's Indological Library, Vol. 38. Online publication date: December 7, 2011.

Russell, Ralph (Ed). *The Oxford India Ghalib: Life, Letters and Ghazals*. New Delhi: Oxford University Press, 2003.

11

Braiding Disparate Strands

Tracing the Arcs of Agha Shahid Ali's *The Half-Inch Himalayas*

JASON A. SCHNEIDERMAN

Two years after finishing his MFA at the University of Arizona, Agha Shahid Ali published his third book of poems, this one with Wesleyan University Press. *The Half-Inch Himalayas* is a short collection, only thirty-one poems long. The volume established the themes that would occupy Shahid for the rest of his writing life, although it does not contain any of the formal poems for which he later became known. The book is composed of four sections, with the poem "Postcard from Kashmir" preceding the first section. The first section is primarily about family and history; the second section traces encounters of East and West; the third focuses on Shahid's own sense of displacement and duality. The fourth section and the proem weave together the themes of the other three sections so that the book functions somewhat like a symphony. The proem establishes the major themes, each of which is explored in its own section, while the final section brings everything together for a crescendo.

The title of the book comes from the poem "Postcard from Kashmir," and refers to the image of the Himalayas reprinted on a postcard. The mountain range in the image is quite literally a half-inch high. The poem focuses on the way the postcard represents an idealized, processed, remembered—and therefore impossible—version of Shahid's homeland. "Kashmir shrinks into my mailbox" (1), the poem opens, treating the postcard as a metonym. This manageable version is in tension with the sense of displacement. Three times in the poem, Shahid calls the postcard "home." The poem considers the way leaving alters the self: "When I return, / the colors won't be so brilliant" (6–7), emphasizing the way that the nostalgia evoked by the postcard is a product of distance. The self grows and changes; home is a relation, as well as a location. The cover of the book has an image of a postcard of the Himalayas, and the image is also reproduced on the full title page, in a sort of centerfold spread. Interestingly, the poem emphasizes the saturated colors and vivid image of the postcard, while the cover is black and lavender, and the black-and-white image inside the book suggests a certain muted dullness. The contrast between the description and the image reproduces the contrast between reality and the postcard. The poem ends with the speaker having returned to Kashmir, but with his memory "out of focus" (12) and "undeveloped" (14). The poem enacts the arc of the book, with the journey's end already foretold. Although the poem is in irregular stanzas and unrhymed, choosing a fourteen-line poem to open his book suggests a nod to the sonnet tradition. However, while the sonnet tradition tends to dramatize the internal conflict of a Western, modern self, Shahid's poem focuses on the self divided by geography and shaped by migration.

The first section of the book explores Shahid's family history. Sufia and Ashraf, Shahid's parents, dominate this section. The opening poem, "A Lost Memory of Delhi," is a sort of love poem that mythologizes his parents' youth. Set in 1948, a year before Shahid's birth in 1949, and year after partition in 1947, the poem lets Shahid watch his parents like a sort of guardian angel. Unlike much of the poetry of the period—most notably Sharon Old's "I Go Back to May 1937," in which she wants to warn her parents of their impending abuse and argues against her own existence—Shahid is remarkably tender toward his parents. "I want to tell them I am their son / older much older than they are" (25–26). History and culture also loom over the persons and events Shahid recounts. Indian independence came in 1947, as did partition, which sparked the first Indo-Pakistani war over Kashmir. The brutalities of British occupation and the conflicts that followed decolonization are touched on frequently in the poems of this section, but always in a way that is evocative rather than didactic. The reader unacquainted with the region and its history may wish to consult a few sources to understand Shahid's references and allusions.

Later in the first section, the ekphrastic poem "Cracked Portraits" portrays four images of the paternal generations of Shahid's family. Opening with "My grandfather's painted grandfather"—depicting a "strange physician" (2) in robes and a turban, "the Koran lying open on a table beside him" (4), the speaker searches for "prayers / in his eyes" (5–6), but finds only a will and a burial place. Without the personal connection, he can find only a legacy and death, not a living person to receive affection. His great-grandfather "simply disappoints me," while grandfather is seductive in his youth, but philosophical in his old age. Tenderness is reserved for a youthful photograph of his father, "brilliance clinging to his shirt" (39). Another poem "Story of a Silence" continues the narrative of the grandfather, who had retreated into Plato as his wife "worked hard, harder/ than a man / to earn / her salary" (8–11). The poem moves toward dreamlike allegory as the religious grandmother goes in search of the grandfather with a Koran in one hand and a torch in the other—only for him to disappear when she discovers him. The final poem of the section evokes the mixture of cultures in Kashmir, mentioning iconography and lore that draws from Hindu and Muslim sources.

The second section moves from Shahid's relationship to his family's past in the subcontinent to his own experiences as a Muslim poet in Kashmir and India. The family become the platform from which his relationship to the landscape and figures becomes his own. The first section ends with the speaker's mother saying "The monsoons never cross / the mountains into Kashmir" (32–33), and the second section opens with "A Monsoon Note on Old Age," in which the speaker is alone and exhausted with his memories. As in the proem, the end is forecast before the story is told. In this section, the speaker becomes the vehicle who carries the lore of the first section, but he also carries the burden of not passing it on, expecting to die childless, and describing himself as "a tired eunuch" (4). This question of fertility and sterility tends to arise when the poems are contemplative or dreamlike; it disappears in moments of action and activity. The next poem tells of exchanging lines of poetry with a butcher while buying meat in Delhi, and one would never think to question the virility of the narrator. In "A Butcher," the speaker and the butcher complete the couplets of poetry the other begins. Muslims in a Hindu country, they share a love of poetry. The scene has the seductive quality of a Cavafy poem, although the intimacy between the two ends with the purchase. Shahid includes a note that explains that the shop is near a large mosque, though Hinduism's vegetarianism sets them apart even without the note. Throughout the second section, the poet mentions the ghazal a number of times, and invokes the form's masters: Ghalib, Mir, Faiz Ahmed Faiz, and Begum Akhtar (the ghazal singer). In the same way that the first section establishes Shahid's personal heritage, the second section establishes his poetic heritage.

The third section ends with "Homage to Faiz Ahmed Faiz," in which Shahid explores the senior poet's life, prosody, and the impact of his work. This is the longest poem in the book, and Faiz becomes a poetic father. Each of the three sections reduces the size of the stanza, so the first section is in quatrains, the second section is in tercets, and the last stanza is in couplets. This first section looks at Faiz's orientation to the political, and how his peripatetic life taught him to address injustice in all its forms and to feel it: "Sometimes it must flood the eyes, / surprise them by being clear as water" (19–20). The first section discusses political violence as an ongoing historical tragedy that poets—and Faiz, like Ghalib, in particular—respond to in language. The second section of the poem focuses on how Shahid first encountered Faiz's work: "I didn't listen when my father / recited your poems to us / by heart" (21–23). As a boy, Shahid cannot understand the importance of Faiz's reconfiguring "the cruel / beloved" (24–25) as "Revolution" (27). But through the beauty of Begum Akhtar's renditions of Faiz's poems, he comes to find Faiz "like memory, / necessary" (39–40). The third section of the poem describes Shahid's becoming Faiz's translator. He thinks of Faiz's life as a prisoner while his "hands turn to stone, / as must happen to a translator's hands" (45–46). Shahid quotes Faiz, and takes his poetic mantle, even as he is in obeisance to the demands of Faiz's work.

The third section contains a number of poems that lightly touch on Shahid's sexuality. These poems engage common tropes of gay identity including doppelgangers, melancholy isolation, distance from heterosexuality, connection to gay authors, and partners without names or pronouns. The vacated tenant becomes a version of himself, as well as a haunting presence, in "Vacating an Apartment." The couple moving in is strikingly fertile in contrast to Shahid's sterility: "the woman, her womb solid with the future" (18) is contrasted with "my love affair with the furniture" (21), which "they ignore" (21). In the following poem, "The Previous Occupant," the speaker sees his double through his absence, identifying a missing volume of Cavafy, and writing "I know he knew their poetry, by heart / the lines I love" (5–6). In placing the poems side by side, the speaker is on either side of time—leaving or arriving—but, in both, united by space and divided by time from himself and his idealized lover. In both poems, death is the only form of futurity available to the speaker, in contrast to the procreative possibility available to heterosexual couples. "I'm moving out holding tombstones in my hand" (30) ends "Vacating an Apartment" while, "He'll never, never, move out of here" (31) ends "The Previous Occupant." "Leaving the City" is more explicitly about a lover, and the speaker returns to the apartment of the lover, "balanced on / the tip of your smile" (3–4). But here as well, the relationship can lead only to further loneliness, everything happening on a trajectory toward death and late-night phone calls that may or may not be answered. "Philadelphia, 2:00 A.M." also posits the end of desire as mortality: "All routes to death / will open up, again, / as the bars close all over / Pennsylvania" (1–4).

Melancholic loneliness was a primary signifier of homosexuality for much of the twentieth century American and English poetry. Although Shahid did not locate himself exclusively in the Anglophone poetic tradition, his sensibility was largely molded by his reading of British and American poetry, and that might have consolidated the queerness of his sexual orientation, which is evident in many poems in this third section, lyrics that eroticize the trope of queer fatality. The poem "Philadelphia, 2:00 A.M.," for example, describes the disco as a place for "by-passing death" (12), and ends with "my skin tense with / the taxi-hour of loss" (13–14). The following poem, "The Jogger on Riverside Drive, 5:00 A.M.," opens three hours later, and even though the runner seeks to outrun himself, his eroticized body renews the cycle of desire ended by the lights going on at the club. "The dark scissors of his legs / cut the moon's / raw silk" (1–3). The queer sensibility at work here is subtle and coded, but equal parts mournful and erotic. Shahid's play with distance and desire in the third section of the book feels specific to the late 1980s, with its sense of the self as the ideal lover and the coding of gay desire. However, in refusing explicit or liberationist modes of gay expression, Shahid allies himself to earlier writers of sensuality like Cavafy and Gide, rather than to contemporaries such as Monette or Hemphill. AIDS is never mentioned, but it seems impossible to imagine that the epidemic is not a ghostly presence here, a contemporary avatar of the age-old bridge between sexual desire and death.

"Stationery" is one of Shahid's most impressive and accomplished poems. It closes the third section with incredible force. The pun in the title encapsulates Shahid's most common theme—connection across great distance, and all implied by the paradox of a wholeness through breaking. The spelling of the title suggests the paper one writes on, but the homophone suggests the stillness required to receive a letter. Writing before the Internet, Shahid explored the forms of intimacy contained in epistles, which were always received at a delay. The act of writing and reading literature also happens at a delay. A book published in 1987 was of course written earlier, and as a contemporary reader traverses over three decades to read this poem, the poem enacts the lag as it explores the gap with its reader. The sense of stillness and motion—that one travels, but that travels contain pauses and ends—pervades the poem. Even though the dominant mode of the poem is surreal: "the moon did not become the sun. / It just fell on the desert / in great sheets" (1–3), the ending is a stunningly clear demand for a return to connection and the loss that separation creates. "The world is full of paper. / Write to me" (7–8). With all the anxiety that artists in the West feel over the connective tissue between the personal and the universal, Shahid brings them together in an eight-line poem that has one of the best endings in poetry, rivaling Rilke's "You must change your life" (14).

The book's fourth section brings the themes of the first three together, with a renewed emphasis on the speaker's absence. The first poem, "Survivor," resumes the theme of the double: "Someone lives in my house" (1), a version of the poet who listens to "Radio Kashmir" (4) and "wears the cardigan / my mother knit for my return" (14–15). This persona sees "my face" (17) in the mirror. The poem ends, "He is breathless to tell her tales / in which I was never found," (20–21). "Survivor" brings out the roles that the poet had expected to play, and finds him slipping out of them. In the following poem, "I Dream It Is Afternoon When I Return to Delhi," the landscape continues to slip into the dreamscape. A ten-year gap recurs, as an image system of tickets, headlines, beggars, and movie theaters grounds the poem's dizzying motion. Identity is both stable and shifting in the dreamed landscape, but the theme of exile is clear: the remembered homeland is accessible only in dreams, if for no other reason than that time passes. "A Call" opens with the "cold moon of Kashmir" (2) entering the speaker's house, where it "steals my parents' love." (4). The poem explores a broken phone call, where the father's request to know when the speaker will "come home" (7) becomes unanswerable. The speaker asks his father, "Are you all happy?" (10) just before the disconnection. The poem ends with the word "Kashmir," (14) highlighting the sense of displacement and the gap that is both known but impossible to bridge.

Despite his untimely death in 2001, Shahid produced a significant and lasting body of work on the platform established in *The Half-Inch Himalayas*. I have written elsewhere about his turn to form, and particularly the way that his re-introduction of the formal ghazal to English language poetry became his most visible legacy. This slender volume served as his introduction to the American poetry scene, where he remained a beloved fixture until his death in 2001. His memory and his work continue to influence younger generations of writers, and the power of his work is holding up to the test of time. His themes of displacement, cultural hybridity, desire, memory, and belonging have become ever more relevant in U.S. politics, culture, and poetry. While Shahid's ghazals are often his most visible and celebrated legacy, his third collection remains a powerful anthology of poems that continue to reward its devoted readers.

Works Cited

Ali, Agha Shahid. *The Half-Inch Himalayas*. Middletown, CT: Wesleyan University Press, 1987.

Rilke, Rainer Maria. "Archaic Torso of Apollo." Translated by Stephen Mitchell. https://poets.org/poem/archaic-torso-apollo

12

Dialing a Joke

Agha Shahid Ali's Long-Distance Calls to Lands without a Post Office

VEDATRAYEE BANERJEE

"I am writing to you from your far-off country. Far even from us who live here. Where you no longer are. Everyone carries his address in his pocket so that at least his body will reach home."[1] Agha Shahid Ali's body did not reach his home. He lay far away from Kashmir, as Kashmir shrank only into his mailbox.[2] That would be the closest he would be to home, ever. Was it a mere coincidence that Shahid quoted Emily Dickinson when he said, "If I could bribe them by a Rose, / I'd bring them every flower that grows / from Amherst to Cashmere?"[3] Or did he know, somewhere deep within, that this would be his span, "Cashmere" his home and Amherst his resting place?

The anxiety that haunts almost all of Agha Shahid Ali's poems including his experimental forms, ghazals, villanelles, and canzones is the eternal anxiety of communication—the anxiety that quivers in the hearts of all Kashmiris perhaps, of losing touch with the rest of the world, of isolation and death, of death without a memory. In almost all his poems, Shahid talks about radios, post offices, postcards, telephones, or newspapers. One remembers that his "blood is news in the *Saffron Sun* setting on the waves."[4] One cannot think of Shahid without remembering Kashmir, without remembering Rizwan, whose letter might have been lost, without remembering death, rain and a deadly "saudade."[5] One cannot think of Shahid without thinking of music, Ghazals, Begum Akhtar, and love. One cannot think of Shahid without thinking of post boxes, letters, telegrams, radios, televisions, and telephones. And in most cases, when one thinks of them, these were radios and televisions that were "smashed"; these were post offices that had stopped delivering mail; these were telephones that received no calls; these were all attempts at communication that failed.

This failure in communication affects Shahid's poetry, not just because he was a Kashmiri, but also because he was a modernist at heart, a man with both a fear and a preference for anonymity, a silent man, whose love and music had been frozen in the wild snow of Kashmir, waiting to thaw, like so much rain in his hands wherever he went.[6] This strange psychic contradiction and impasse of a modernist estrangement perpetually urged by a desperate attempt to connect remind one of the recurrent image of the listeners in Walter de la Mare's poem, "The Listeners." In that poem, the traveler, without a name, with no address and no entity, repeatedly knocks on a "moonlit door," asking each time "Is there anybody there?," and receiving no answer, he addresses himself to nothingness, like Shahid's letters, and finally leaves, telling "them" that he "came and no one answered, that he kept his word."[7] Published in 1912, the poem reveals this strange tension between the allegiance of keeping a promise and lack of a means to communicate it, between the urgency to convey a message and the absence of someone at the other end to receive it. The words hit the "moonlit door" and vanished, and it is interesting to note how the poem is named after the listeners who do not answer, who do not recognize that the promise was kept. Through a thin layer of haunted haze comes a clean picture of communication that is lost, like the communication lost in Shakti Chattopadhyay's "Abani Bari Achho?" For those familiar with the famous Bengali poem, it will be easy to reckon the relevance of this reference. It is night time, and the neighborhood is wrapped in slumber, when piercing the somnolence one hears someone ask "Abani, are you home?"[8] The one image that controls the structure of the Bengali poem is the image of the shut door, the only means of entrance, of exit, of transit, of communication. One is sure that someone is listening, but never sure if the listener is Abani himself, and if the speaker is within the house or without. There is this desperation to find Abani out, and the failure to do so. And what is more bewildering is that "Abani" is a Bengali word for "the universe," our larger home. Some questions will haunt every reader of the poem: Is the poet seeking the world? Is he estranged from the world he was born in? Does the world listen to him and does not answer? Is the world not in a state to answer as yet?

This crisis of communication, of not being able to relate to a world one is born in, is starkly prominent in the poems of Agha Shahid Ali, especially those collected in *A Walk Through the Yellow Pages*, a collection less read than other Shahid books, and consequently less discussed. One reason for this could be the strangeness of the collection. The characteristic features that distinguish Agha Shahid Ali's works are not evident here. There is no mention of Kashmir, no mention of war, no mention of rain or songs or loss as such. The poems are in a different league altogether from Shahid's poetic oeuvre. There is humor, a very dark and morbid humor, like a suicide note kept on the wall of a house, to be read by the new tenants once Shahid has moved out.[9] There are in this collection about thirteen odd poems dealing with various subjects delineated mostly in a tongue-in-cheek manner. The only reminder that it is Shahid writing is the obsession with communication. There are poems that deal with telephone conversations addressed to the dead, poems dealing with advertisements and Christmas celebrations, and poems narrating fairy tales that are ghastlier than ghost stories and grimmer than Grimm's own. There is, in this collection, another trait, an interest that Shahid has shown in no other work, an interest in advertisements. The title of the volume itself reminds one of business communications. The "Yellow Pages" are directories of business interactions. And "the walk" is typically reminiscent of modernity. While business has an aim, a purpose, the modern man walks aimlessly. He is a "flaneur" with no purpose and no direction. This explains why Shahid names each poem that deals with telephone conversations after a television advertisement, a business call, but the poem itself is about a call to the land of the dead, or the sleeping, lying at a long distance, the longest one can call. This curious, quizzical business with the dead, urged by a purpose that is lost in the telephone poems is extremely remarkable.

The Kashmiri shawl-sellers often come to the other places of India on business, for selling home-spun shawls, and they always take some time to talk about Kashmir, the beauty of the valley, their homes and hearth. But, every time the subject of the conflict is broached, they grow tense, and respond with absolute silence, never blurting out what they feel and think. Possibly they believe that no language would transmit their views, their pains and sufferings, and that even if it did, it would be lost as it made its way to us. The telephone poems and the poems about the fairy tales in *A Walk Through the Yellow Pages* are likely to remind one of this. The storyteller in Shahid's poems is dead, as Walter Benjamin had predicted. There are no stories anymore. And the story of "Little Red Riding Hood" is gruesome and pathetic, as the wolf, the "Big Bad Wolf," falls on his belly so that "children could laugh at the noise of stones"[10] cutting through his stomach, and there is no happy ending, as filth oozes out, leaving a bad taste in the mouth. All the stories often read aloud to children are turned on their heads as Shahid compares a conflict-torn city to a wolf's belly. There is a strange retreat into the womb that marks the fairy-tale poems in the collection. The narrators in these poems prefer a journey from the womb to the tomb, and seek refuge in a comfortable warm darkness inside the wolf, rather than the threatening liberation into the world, the city, a city where Hansel would not be born unless bribed, where the wolf reverses the eternal tale of morals taught to children. The witch and the wolf appear better than the humans, as the wolf makes himself a butt of children's jokes and the witch suffers being fed to guests. The stories are like tales being read in a mirror, an inverted image of what has been taught and said so far. The stories end in awkward silences, like the Kashmiri shawl-sellers' reticence, and the transaction does not take place because it is business with the dead. It is a walk through the yellow pages from a sender to a receiver, anonymity engulfing both sides. There is no message that is sent, no message that is received. Communication theory of redundancy claims that "hello" is the most redundant of words, as it has high predictability. However, none of these poems begins with this highly predictable term that we speak into the telephone every time we use it.

The poems in this collection are highly entropic, the opposite of redundant, where meaning is sheathed in layers of business talks, meaning that conveys the uselessness of words, the point where language breaks, the point of silence. The poem "Language Games," for example, completely scrambles up the language and something as funny as objects like "cat" and "ass" and "trophy" are made to combine into a solution that reads "catastrophe." The implication that the redundant can convey the entropic, the funny can point to the morbid, the meaninglessness can indicate the meaning, guides us along this walk through the yellow pages. Above all, there is the constant anxiety of communication being lost in the attempt at communication. Melissa Dinsman in her book *Modernism at the Microphone: Radio, Propaganda and Literary Aesthetics during World War II* shows how this anxiety has affected poets and authors from war-ridden countries and how that has resulted in their obsession with the inadequacy of mass media. Dinsman says: "Writers act as radios—picking up signals, from their surroundings, translating them, and transmitting them through narration to a broader audience."[11] She refers to Rudyard Kipling's story "Wireless" and shows how Mr. Shaynor catches poetic signals from the air and reads them out. However, in Shahid's poems in this collection, one can discern this war-caused anxiety about communication, but instead of expressing a dependence on mass media to communicate, the poet's persona asserts his indifference about the existence of media and is sharply skeptical about their efficacy to communicate the truth. He predicts a dystopic future where mails will not be sent, and phone calls will be made to the dead; radios and televisions will be smashed so that no news is broadcast.

Shahid's poems in *A Walk Through the Yellow Pages* thus portray a grim prospect where lack of media detaches a person from the world, leaving him to incurable loneliness and an inevitably lonesome death. In fact, a chapter in Dinsman's book is titled "Can't get through to you please Mr. Postman," reminding one of a world depicted in *The Country without a Post Office*. Any discerning reader of these poems can perceive this fetal withdrawal within the walls of one's own placental silence, walls of the wolf's belly. Also, as Dinsman observes, "communications technologies stem from war," and one might note that the war leading to the brutalities in Kashmir led Shahid not only to destroy all modes of communication, but also, more interestingly, to indicate how modes of mass communication do not appeal to him at all. While he smashes the radio and television, he does not do the same with the mailbox or the telephone. The latter means of private communication still remain, and the poet dials repeatedly, and he writes letters, hoping that there might be a promise of rain, a promise that the message will be delivered. Unlike the dominant examples of literature that resort to messages conveyed over broadcasts and other modes of reaching out to a large audience, the narrator in Agha Shahid Ali's poems of this collection, like a soldier who fights knowing that defeat is at hand, tries not to reach to many, but to someone, through a private communication system like a letter or a telephone call. He has an unwavering faith in the yellowed fringes of perpetually prospective letters running "Dear Shahid," a very private address, from a beloved, or a call from a distant land. And all he gets back is resounding silence. To this silence he adds the tang of a gradual commercialization: the colors of billboards, and advertisements, the catchphrases, that sound so flashy, but talk of dumbness, a numbness within. This is the silence of the commercial world, a world portrayed in the poem "Advertisement," where food from the exotic "Orient" is advertised on the streets of America and can be tasted only in a "Chinatown tea house," the "freshly frozen food" requiring only "15 minutes of steaming to eat."[12]

A Walk Through the Yellow Pages illustrates how the capitalist economy encroaches upon private lives, how it affects human communications, and how it plays a crucial role in the lives of Kashmiris too, as people engage in business with them for the exotic works of Kashmir, hang Kashmiri drapes in houses, but remain strategically and conveniently silent on the issues of the eternal Kashmiri war. The human communications are reduced to communications with the dead, and therefore in the first telephone poem the speaker calls the living, in the second he addresses the rich, and in the third he calls the dead. The growing capitalism and market trends have destroyed human emotions. As Shahid walks through the yellow pages, he walks over the bones of humanity once alive, reaching out to the dead, over a long-distance telephone call, redirected to Necropolis, USA, the heart of capitalist economy. Necropolis, the cemetery for the living, is the receiver of the message that Shahid has to deliver. This silence in communication is strangely reminiscent of Simon and Garfunkel's "The Sound of Silence," a 1966 song about another aimless walk through a neon-lit city, advertising men and goods as consumerism has engulfed man's existence. It is a walk at a night lit with neon bulbs, but the walk is a very bleak stroll in darkness with an old friend, on cobbled streets, with "people talking without speaking, people hearing without listening . . . and no one dared to disturb the sound of silence."[13] This is the point that Shahid has reached, a state of existence in which he dials numbers not to talk but to find out if anybody is there on the other side, for a consumerist market does not listen, and all communication has become so redundant or predictable that communication itself has collapsed. Poets write on bathroom walls, because poetry is reduced to graffiti, and pray for madness to find a cure, in order to build an asylum,[14] as the rich bow and pray "to the neon god they made,"[15] while Shahid keeps dialing numbers. It is a state somewhat similar to the last scene in Tom Twyker's film *Perfume*, where Jean-Baptiste baptizes himself in the middle of a marketplace with a bottle of perfume made from the essence of all beautiful women, and the consumers in the market, who had hated him all through and had gathered there to see him hanged until death, go and devour him, all humanity dissolving in a basic consumerist carnival, a carnivorous carnival, in the name of baptism. In the first poem of *A Walk Through the Yellow Pages* Shahid dials "The living . . . only the living," but "no one call[s] back," as he calls "for years till their lids beg[i]n to ring" and he gets only "busy signals of their nightmares."[16] In the second poem he gives "annoyance calls"[17] to the rich, and no one answers. In the third, he calls the dead, the "longest distance"[18] he had ever called, and the operators are too busy with the bones. This walk from life, to riches, to death, without being able to connect with anything, a lonely walk, leads him to ask for freedom, freedom of unfrozen seas, and he dials the seas in the fourth, and says, "get me the sea when there's no ice, / when the water is pure, absolutely / free."[19] He feels claustrophobic and suffers from a sense of being trapped in others' eyelids, in others' nightmares that he desperately wants release from. And, finally, he tries to call God, when Eros and Thanatos get mixed up like jumbled telephone wires and cause cross-connections. He asks for the "Angel of Love," but ironically it is the "Angel of Death" who picks up his call and pronounces the verdict of ultimate impenetrable silence, saying that God never answers the living and has no answer for the dead either. In the following poem, "Christmas, 1980s," the time for celebration of the birth of the son of God becomes reversed, as carols prove "lethal" and the Christmas trees light up in shops, with high-voltage security, an economy for consumption, and Shahid calls the Cops for Christ, calls Reverend Moon, and as it borders on blasphemy, he dismisses them all as jokes, ending with an obscene call to the White House, the final address. All these calls remain unanswered, and the joke is on him, proving that Shahid "dials a joke," a cruel joke.

Notes

1. Agha Shahid Ali, "Dear Shahid," *The Country without a Post Office*. Mumbai: Penguin, 2013, 29.
2. https://dusttalks.wordpress.com/2017/08/10/poetry-analysis-postcard
3. Agha Shahid Ali, "Some Vision of the World Cashmere," *The Country without a Post Office*, 21.
4. Agha Shahid Ali, "The Last Saffron," *The Country without a Post Office*, 13.
5. A Portuguese word for a melancholic longing for someone, a nostalgia. This could be someone who is physically absent, or someone who is present but is missed.
6. Agha Shahid Ali, "Dear Shahid," *The Country without a Post Office*, 29.
7. https://www.poetryfoundation.org/poems/47546/the-listeners
8. Translation for "Abani Bari Achho?," a poem by Bengali poet Shakti Chattopadhyay.
9. Reference to his poem "Vacating an Apartment" in his collection *The Half-Inch Himalayas*.

10. Agha Shahid Ali, "The Wolf's Postscript to Little Red Riding Hood," *A Walk Through the Yellow Pages*. Tucson, AZ: Gemini Press, 1987.

11. Melissa Dinsman, "Introduction," *Modernism at the Microphone: Radio, Propaganda and Literary Aesthetics during World War II* (London: Bloomsbury, 2015)

12. Agha Shahid Ali, "Advertisement," *A Walk Through the Yellow Pages*.

13. https://www.google.co.in/search?ei=uIAIWqnOISOvQSiioKACg&q=sounds +of+silence+lyrics&oq=sounds+of+silence&gs_l=psy-ab.1.0.0l10.89963.95316.0.976 99.26.19.0. Accessed on 2.10.2017

14. Agha Shahid Ali, "Poets on Bathroom Walls," *A Walk Through the Yellow Pages*.

15. https://www.google.co.in/search?ei=uIAIWqOnOISOvQSiioKACg&q= sounds+of+silence+lyrics&oq=sounds+of+silence&gs_l=psy-ab.1.0.0l10.89963.95316. 0.97699.26.19.0

16. Agha Shahid Ali, *A Walk Through the Yellow Pages*.

17. Agha Shahid Ali, "Poets on Bathroom Walls," *A Walk Through the Yellow Pages*.

18. "Bell Telephone Hours," *A Walk Through the Yellow Pages*.

19. "Bell Telephone Hours," *A Walk Through the Yellow Pages*.

Works Cited

Ali, Agha Shahid. *The Country without a Post Office*. Mumbai: Penguin, 2013.
Ali, Agha Shahid. *A Walk Through the Yellow Pages*. Tucson, AZ: Gemini Press, 1987.
Ali, Mohammed Kazim. *Mad Heart Be Brave*. Ann Arbor: University of Michigan Press, 2017.
Chattopadhyay, Shakti. *Sreshtha Kabita*. Kolkata: Dey's Publishing, 2002.
Dinsman, Melissa. *Modernism at the Microphone: Radio, Propaganda and Literary Aesthetics during World War II*. London: Bloomsbury, 2015.
Twyker, Tom. *Perfume*. Film. Munich, 2006.

13

Archiving Absences

Charting Chronotopes in Agha Shahid Ali's Cartography of Desire

DEEPTESH SEN

Born in New Delhi and brought up in Kashmir during the politically tumultuous years in the aftermath of Partition, Agha Shahid Ali could never forget his hometown and kept coming back to it throughout his poetry. As a poet doubly displaced—first from New Delhi to Kashmir and subsequently to the United States—Shahid was acutely conscious of what he had left behind even as he continued to live in a self-imposed exile. The term "exile" is of his own choosing because even when he acknowledged that he was an "expatriate" owing to the voluntary nature of his movements, his mind continued to dwell in a state of permanent exile, longing for the homeland he had left behind.

The desire for the past haunted him, and even when he began returning to India regularly on vacations, the changes he witnessed in his homeland drove him to grieve for the loss. Like in the works of many South Asian writers living in a state of diaspora, memory and nostalgia, thus, became the thematic fulcrum of Shahid's poetic world dominated by elegies.

Jahan Ramazani, while discussing the modern elegy, writes:

> Loss, grief, mourning: death is indeed the mother of beauty, uniting poets of our time who have little else in common—traditionalists and experimentalists, confessionalists and avant-gardists, poets of ethnic identity and anti-identitarian formalists. At a time when genre tends to divide poets—say, those who write sonnets and love poems, e.g., Seamus Heaney, and those who refuse traditional forms, e.g., Lyn Hejinian—the call of elegy overrides differences in school, nationality, style, and technique.[1]

In Shahid, the impulse for mourning always emphasizes the ephemerality of the moment and precipitates a modern elegiac consciousness. But in *A Nostalgist's Map of America*, remembrance and nostalgia work in a different register, making it difficult to classify the volume as a canonical work of postcolonial exile. This is because Shahid, with his life and poetry, quite consciously contests this classification. He gladly accepts America as his second home even while remaining sensitive to an exiled poetic consciousness that compels him to write in a foreign tongue. In an oft-quoted poem, Shahid talks about his multicultural rootlessness as he is ready to accept all the places he has lived in as his own:

> call me a poet
> dear editor
> they call this my alien language
> i am a dealer in words
> that mix cultures
> and leave me rootless

Shahid completed his graduation from the University of Kashmir before returning to New Delhi to work toward and earn his MA at Hindu College. Afterward, he earned a scholarship for a PhD from Penn State University in College Park, Pennsylvania. He fondly remembers his time at Penn State University, acknowledging the way it had enriched him: "I grew as a reader, I grew as a poet, I grew as a lover." In the United States, he formed new acquaintances with graduate students, many of whom were Indian.

What Gertrude Stein once wrote about her many homes can be said of Shahid as well: "America is my country, and Paris is my home town." As Jahan Ramazani points out, this translocal identity is common to many contemporary modern poets who subscribe to transnational affiliations, moving between "the spectral context of one nation and the lived metropolis of another."² Such identifications, necessitated by the "cross-national mobility of the modern" essentially challenge the pre-Romantic notion of literature as an expression of national identity further rigidified in Cold War America. Shahid's poetry, as best exemplified by *A Nostalgist's Map of America*, posits a transcultural sensibility with his nostalgic mapping of America accepting the country as his second home.

Despite having a modernist, cosmopolitan sensibility, there is a great deal of discomfort in Shahid's verses about modernism's relation with history. He is of course aware of the disruptive lineage of modernism, as its very existence often makes it imperative to deny the past. One may recall at this instance the famous saying of Stephen Dedalus in Joyce's *Ulysses*: "History is a nightmare from which I am trying to awake."³

Nowhere else than in Shahid's verses can one find a better explication of the figure of Angelus Novus that Walter Benjamin refers to as a metaphor for modernism in his essay "Theses on the Philosophy of History."⁴ The angel, as Benjamin states, stares ruefully at the rubble of the past as the winds of modernism fill its wings and hurtle it along at great speed, backward into the future.

Drawing on Bakhtin's idea of space-time, I would like to argue that Shahid's mourning for history in these verses is always a grieving for a lost chronotope as he remembers with fondness the physiognomy of spaces from the past. The poems in this collection are a "rehearsal of loss" and mourning, remembering his friend, Philip Paul Orlando (Phil), who died of AIDS. Shahid draws on the memory of their homosocial bonding to map out a nostalgic cartography of America.

The spaces on his map carry intense histories of loss and desire, assuming meaning only as sites of accumulated heaps of personal memory. His greatest fear is modernism's refusal to acknowledge history and his mourning becomes, therefore, an act of reminder and remembrance. An interesting example of this is his reference to the "desert" that refuses to acknowledge history:

When the desert refused my history,
refused to acknowledge that I had lived
there, with you (NMA 110)⁵

The imagery of the desert, which keeps recurring in these verses, represents a barren wasteland that has managed to bury the history of the landscape.

Once again, in another poem in the volume, the desert heat is presented as being so torturous that one must look for the shadows for some respite:

> Certain landscapes insist on fidelity.
> Why else would a poet of this desert
> go deep inside himself for shade? (116)

The desert here stands for a liminal space of forgetting; it paints a picture of utter desolation and loss where the past has vanished without a trace. With an essence of magic realism, Shahid paints a beautiful picture of these moments of disappearance—beyond the city limits, a woman who has climbed the steps "vanished into the sky" and ghost towns house tribes who speak in "desert voices" the last traces of a dying language. Even the train takes passengers to "a twilight with no water," where one encounters at every turn the "cadence of dead seas." The desert here functions as the black hole of history, gobbling up memory and nostalgia. Even when there is the fantasy of encountering a mirage, as the moon melts the sand into water, the search for history turns out to be futile as the poet finds only a dried ocean floor with no trace of the past:

> The moon turned the desert to water
> For a moment I saw islands
> as they began to sink
> The ocean was a dried floor
> Below me is a world without footprints
> I am alone I'm still alone
> and there's no trace anywhere of the drowned. (117)

Even the moon's efforts to throw light on the past is met with violent resistance as "ash-throated men in the desert," like the agents of apocalypse, leave behind "broken glasses" and remnants of "the moon splashed everywhere." It is this very burial of history and process of forgetting that Shahid fights against in his project of archiving memory. A powerful sense of *carpe diem* informs these poems as the poet as an archivist of memory battles against the ravages of time which destroys everything that "within his bending sickle's compass come."[6] A somewhat Shakespearean hubris perhaps motivates Shahid in his project as he hopes that his verses will outlive the materiality of desire to leave behind an indestructible poetry of remembrance:

Not marble nor the gilded monuments
Of princes shall outlive this powerful rhyme,
But you shall shine more bright in these contents
Than unswept stone besmeared with sluttish time.[7]

The desert in Shahid's poems is therefore lonely as it destroys the memory of the beloved and the rivers lined with skeletal bones in the landscape run dry in the desert of oblivion:

Cries Majnoon:

Beloved
you are not here

It is a strange spring
Rivers lined with skeletons (139)

It is these very bones, or the blood on the desert sand in the Ghalib couplet that the poet refers to in "From Another Desert," where the traces are left behind as the rem(a)inders of the past. If the desert in these poems functions as the river Lethe, these traces are the *aletheia* (ἀλήθεια) that makes the poet embark on a Heideggerian journey of unconcealing and documenting the truth of the past.

Shahid's verses in *A Nostalgist's Map of America* exude the same elegiac sensibility as Tennyson's grieving for Arthur Hallam or T. S. Eliot's remembering Jean Verdenal as the drowned Phoenician sailor in *The Waste Land*. Eliot too, in his poem, is faced with the problem of the incomplete burial of history that always threatens to return—the corpse is buried in the garden but the dog can at any time dig up the bones.

In his poem titled "In Search for Evanescence," Shahid maps out the body of his friend Phil on the landscape of America to etch out a personal map of loss and remembrance. All of it is precipitated by the refrain "Phil was afraid of being forgotten." Shahid's poems in this volume are essentially a recording of his friend's memory, perhaps following the unarticulated desire to keep his memory alive. He clearly recalls the moment when his friend had called him and informed him of his imminent death:

For a moment you were silent, and then,
"Shahid, I'm dying." I kept speaking to you

> after I hung up, my voice the quickest
> mail, a cracked disc with many endings (119)

Strangely, Amitav Ghosh in a famous essay would write many years later about the time when Shahid, his friend, first informed him of his death:

> The first time that Agha Shahid Ali spoke to me about his approaching death was on April 25, 2001. The conversation began routinely. I had telephoned to remind him that we had been invited to a friend's house for lunch and that I was going to come by his apartment to pick him up. Although he had been under treatment for cancer for some fourteen months, Shahid was still on his feet and perfectly lucid, except for occasional lapses of memory. I heard him thumbing through his engagement book and then suddenly he said: "Oh dear. I can't see a thing." There was a brief pause and then he added: "I hope this doesn't mean that I'm dying . . ."
>
> Although Shahid and I had talked a great deal over the last many weeks, I had never before heard him touch on the subject of death. I did not know how to respond: his voice was completely at odds with the content of what he had just said, light to the point of jocularity. I mumbled something innocuous: "No Shahid—of course not. You'll be fine." He cut me short. In a tone of voice that was at once quizzical and direct, he said: "When it happens I hope you'll write something about me."[8]

It is this fear of being forgotten that haunted Shahid when he was on his deathbed, and he gave Ghosh the responsibility of recording his memory, as Shahid had done for Phil earlier. As the news of the poet's death began to sink in, Ghosh understood the gravity of the responsibility he had been entrusted with. He wrote: "He wanted me to remember him not through the spoken recitatives of memory and friendship, but through the written word." "You must write about me" were Shahid's exact words to Ghosh.

Every contour on Shahid's map of America is charged with the nostalgia of loss as he maps out Phil's body on the cartography of the nation. It is not a linear movement of time, backward into history, but the highlighting of the scraps of some particular moments—each space laden with the *kairos* of the memories he shared with his friend becomes chronotopic in its representation in the poems of this volume.[9]

In the eponymous poem of the collection, the poet moves from the remembrance of an expedition of driving to Phil's home in Philadelphia to the "dead centre of Pennsylvania" and finally to sunny California. Speaking about the volume in an interview to Stacey Chase, he had said, "most of the poems are set in United States, particularly in the American Southwest, the desert. I think one very good thing that happened to me by moving to Arizona was that I suddenly found a landscape that could somehow bear my concerns and my themes of exile, loss, nostalgia."[10]

And later on in the interview, he added, "the homesickness in many of my poems is for what has vanished," with poetry being an act of both mourning and remembering the past. Shahid in the poems of *A Nostalgist's Map of America* represents his memories of Phil through flashbacks of the times they spent together. After one such flashback, he remembers the time he was driving in Ohio and came across a small town called Calcutta:

When on Route 80 in Ohio
I came across an exit
to Calcutta

the temptation to write a poem
led me past the exit
so I could say

India always exists
off the turnpikes
of America (123)

The juxtaposition of two Calcuttas opens up a whole new vista of meaning. The reference is obviously to the Indian city of Calcutta, the capital city of the British Raj until 1912. The cultural violence of renaming and hence claiming the space, as perpetrated by the colonizers, was undone when the Anglicized spelling was changed back to its Bengali original, Kolkata, in 2001. Xiwen Mai writes:

> The Indian city's name—Calcutta is loaded with the colonial history of South Asia. In 2001, the city changed its official English name to Kolkata to restore its Bengali pronunciation and largely, to eliminate the legacy of British colonialism. It is ironic to see while the Indian city struggled to erase the name—Calcutta—because

of the history it carries, the name has taken roots in America. It remains a question whether the small town in Ohio was familiar with the complicated history of the Indian city when it picked the name for itself in the early twentieth century.[11]

Throughout the poems in this volume, Shahid is concerned with the hegemonic cultural appropriations that led to the violent erasure of indigenous histories. The unmapped tribal hinterlands have "no map/but it has histories most/of them forgotten/scraps of folklore." He is also concerned about their fast disappearing oral cultures and the fate of their language when the community is left with its last speaker:

> a woman climbed the steps to Acoma,
> vanished into the sky. In the ghost towns
> of Arizona, there were charcoal tribes
>
> with desert voices, among their faces
> always the last speaker of a language.
> And there was always thirst: a train taking me
>
> From Bisbee, that copper landscape with bones,
> into a twilight with no water. . . . (130)

As Shahid dreads a future when these indigenous cultures will no longer exist, he is anxious to archive the last traces of the tribes who are living in a state of exile in their own land. Remembering the "ghosts," "desert voices," and "last speaker" of a vanishing language, the poet is already archiving the ephemerality of an indigenous culture at its moment of disappearance:

> But even
> when I pass—in Ohio—the one exit
> to Calcutta, I don't know I've begun
> mapping America, the city limits
> of Evanescence now everywhere. (122)

What disturbs the poet, however is, as Dipesh Chakraborty would say, the dread of being consigned to "the waiting-room of history"[12] where the past is eventually hushed up and deleted to impose violently a monolithic notion of cultural modernity:

departed, erasing
their names. Some
of those streets,
lost at junctions, were
run over by trains.
At stations

where you waited, history
was too late:
those trains

rushed by and disappeared
into mirrors
in which

massacres were hushed.
No reporters
were allowed (133–134)

While driving along Sedona, Arizona, on the Schuylkill Expressway in Pennsylvania, it is the rear-view mirror that keeps the "entire hemisphere" in view, as he looks back at the South American countries that had been similarly consigned to this waiting room of history when the bloody massacres had erased their past. Judith Rauscher writes:

> By describing the night in Uruguay as "black salt," Columbia as "vermilion," Brazil as "blue tar," and Peru as "titanium white," while the colours of Argentina and Paraguay are "breaking, like oil" and other countries are "wiped clean of colour" (Ali 96), Ali produces a rich tableau of Middle and South America in several senses of the word: his description not only sketches a portrait that hints at economic exploitation, violence, war, political unrest, and even genocide; it also conjures up a brightly coloured map, which relates these histories to the colonial project and its aftermath. At the same time, the continent reflected in the poet-speaker's mirror (of language) is presented as a painting, drawing attention to the artistic process of representation and the poem as text.[13]

The bloody history of neocolonial subjugation of the Latin American countries as also the colonial history of the American Indians reminds the poet of the colonial history of India. Yet the American Indians produce a sense of alienation in him, as he cannot fully identify with them. To them, he is "a stranger in your own house," a line that the poet also dedicates to his friend Phil, as it is *his* desire for remembrance and fear of being forgotten that holds the poems in this volume together. His project of mourning and archiving his friend's memory necessitates the articulation of a modern elegiac consciousness—it assumes importance because of his larger project to sketch out a map of cultural histories lost due to the ravages of colonialism.

Shahid's archival project thus maps out the nostalgic cartography of indigenous histories onto the body of his friend Phil. Each place on this landscape is filled with the nostalgia of memory as he maps out the absences into an imagined cartography of desire. His map-making project, impelled as it was by his transnationalist philosophy, is also a subtle critique of national boundaries which essentialize physical territorialization based on arbitrary decision making and imagined community building. Shahid's map of desire is thus a critique of such nationalist grand narratives.

If his map is interested in the de-territorialization of physical boundaries, it also brings about the re-territorialization of desire, archiving the chronotopes of Phil's traces onto the map of America. As the poet writes about his friend:

> I have no house only
> a shadow but whenever you are in need
> of a shadow my shadow is yours (128)

Map-making is not just an act of nostalgic reminiscing here; it also becomes an act of articulating unfulfilled wishes because of unattained futures as the bodies of the colonized nation-state and the male friend are both consigned to the waiting-room of history. It is the powerful ontological absence of Phil that governs the logic of the poems in *A Nostalgist's Map of America*, as memories of the deferred past carry the unrealized possibilities of a future that never came to be. What has been becomes as important as what could have been, and what was also necessitates mediations on what will never be. Agha Shahid Ali, therefore, is not just archiving absences here; he is also documenting a hauntology of desire.

Notes

1. Jahan Ramazani, "Can Poetry Console a Grieving Public?" *Poetry Foundation*. https://www.poetryfoundation.org/articles/68676/can-poetry-console-a-grieving-public-56d248486a430

2. Jahan Ramazani, *A Transnational Poetics* (Chicago & London: University of Chicago Press, 2009), 23.

3. See James Joyce, *Ulysses* (New York: Penguin, 1972).

4. Walter Benjamin. "Theses on the Philosophy of History," *Illuminations* (New York: Schocken Books, 1968).

5. All quotations in this article are from Agha Shahid Ali's *A Nostalgist's Map of America* (New York: W. W. Norton & Company, 1991). The in-text citations for this book will refer to only the page numbers hereafter.

6. William Shakespeare, Sonnet 116, *Poetry Foundation*. https://www.poetryfoundation.org/poems/45106/sonnet

7. William Shakespeare, Sonnet 55, *Poetry Foundation*, https//www.poetryfoundation.org/poems46455/sonnet-55-not-marble-nor-the-gilded-monuments.

8. Amitav, Ghosh. "'The Ghat of the only World': Agha Shahid Ali in Brooklyn." *Amitav Ghosh* [blog]. https://www.amitavghosh.com/aghashahidali.html

9. "History is the subject of a structure whose site is not homogeneous, empty time, but time filled by the presence of the now. Thus, to Robespierre ancient Rome was a past charged with the time of the now which he blasted out of the continuum of history. The French Revolution viewed itself as Rome reincarnate. It evoked ancient Rome the way fashion evokes costumes of the past. Fashion has a flair for the topical, no matter where it stirs in the thickets of long ago; it is a tiger's leap into the past. This jump, however, takes place in an arena where the ruling class gives the commands. The same leap in the open air of history is the dialectical one, which is how Marx understood the revolution." (See Benjamin, "Theses on the Philosophy of History," op. cit.)

10. "Agha Shahid Ali: The Lost Interview," interview by Stacey Chase, *Café Review*, March 3–4, 1990. http://www.thecafereview.com/spring-2011-interview-agha-shahid-ali-the-lost-interview

11. Xiwen Mai, "Mapping America, Re-mapping the World: The Cosmopolitanism of Agha Shahid Ali's *A Nostalgist's Map of America*," (2007). Graduate English Association New Voices Conference 2007. Paper 2. http://scholarworks.gsu.edu/english_conf_newvoice_2007/2

12. See Dipesh Chakraborty, *Provincializing Europe: Postcolonial Thought and Historical Difference* (Princeton, NJ: Princeton University Press, 2008).

13. Judith Rauscher, "On Common Ground: Translocal Attachments and Transethnic Affiliations in Agha Shahid Ali's and Arthur Sze's Poetry of the American Southwest." *European Journal of American Studies* (2014). https://ejas.revues.org/10434

Works Cited

Ali, Agha Shahid. *A Nostalgist's Map of America*. New York: W. W. Norton, 1991.
———. *The Country without a Post Office*. New York: W. W. Norton, 1997.
Bakhtin, Mikhail. *The Dialogic Imagination: Four Essays by M.M.*, translated by Caryl Emerson & Michael Holquist. Austin: University of Texas Press, 1981.
Benjamin, Walter. "Theses on the Philosophy of History," *Illuminations*. New York: Schocken Books, 1968.
Chakraborty, Dipesh. *Provincializing Europe: Postcolonial Thought and Historical Difference*. Princeton, NJ: Princeton University Press, 2008.
Derrida, Jacques. *Spectres of Marx: The State of Debt, the Work of Mourning & the New International*. New York: Routledge, 1994.
Mai, Xiwen. "Mapping America, Re-mapping the World: The Cosmopolitanism of Agha Shahid Ali's *A Nostalgist's Map of America*." *Graduate English Association New Voices Conference 2007*. Paper 2. http://scholarworks.gsu.edu/english_conf_newvoice_2007/2
Ramazani, Jahan. *A Transnational Poetics*. Chicago & London: University of Chicago Press, 2009.
———. "Can Poetry Console a Grieving Public?" *Poetry Foundation*. https://www.poetryfoundation.org/articles/68676/can-poetry-console-a-grieving-public-56d248486a430

14

Tradition, Home, and Exile in Agha Shahid Ali's *The Beloved Witness*

CHRISTINE KITANO

In "Tradition and the Individual Talent," T. S. Eliot famously criticizes the tendency to praise a poet "upon those aspects of his work in which he least resembles anyone else," and instead offers that the "best" and most "individual" aspects of a poet's work will often be those that are most rooted in tradition (111–112). Originality, then, is not the absence of tradition, but instead the development or expansion of the preconceived limits of the tradition. When considering a poet like Agha Shahid Ali, who wrote from multiple experiences and traditions, it is particularly necessary to consider how his poems work to expand our understanding of these various traditions. An understanding of Shahid's "individuality," then, requires an understanding of the multiple traditions from which he writes.

This chapter provides a brief overview of the major themes in *The Beloved Witness*, a collection of selected poems by Agha Shahid Ali. The collection, published in India in 1992, spans the earlier part of Shahid's career, with poems selected from *Bone-Sculpture* (1972), *In Memory of Begum Akhtar* (1979), *The Half-Inch Himalayas* (1987), *A Walk Through the Yellow Pages* (1987), and *A Nostalgist's Map of America* (1991). This chapter will focus on how Shahid weaves together various traditions, and how this act also incorporates the themes of "home" and "exile."

Seeing Shahid's work in a condensed book like this draws attention to some of the main themes the poet was working with throughout his life, but especially in his earlier poems. Shahid strikes out to make poetry in a language that does not always accommodate him and his experiences. He imbibes the Western tradition and aims to braid it with his own unique perspective. Though it would be easy to argue that his embrace of the Western tradition implies a certain type of assimilation (and therefore a neglect of his Kashmiri heritage), his project is more complex. Instead, Shahid works to braid the multiple traditions together, to create a new fabric of language and structure.

The first few poems that open the collection are selected from *Bone-Sculpture*, and initiate the reader into Shahid's project to embrace the Western tradition while simultaneously inscribing it with his own, non-Western experience. Though the first poems make no specific allusion to *The Waste Land*, Eliot's influence is clear. Compare the opening stanza of "Bones" to that of Eliot's poem. Shahid writes:

> The years are dead. I'm twenty,
> A mourner in the Mohorrum
> Procession, mixing blood with mud,
> memory with memory.
> I'm still alone.

The opening lines from *The Waste Land* read:

> April is the cruelest month, breeding
> Lilacs out of the dead land, mixing
> Memory and desire, stirring
> Dull roots with spring rain.

Shahid's lines serve as a re-envisioning of Eliot, a contemporary voice finding relevance in an older canonical text. Shahid calls himself a "mourner in the Mohorrum / Procession," which recalls the moment in *The Waste Land* when the ghosts of soldiers "flo[w] over London Bridge." For Eliot, World War I imposed a break on Western civilization; "The Waste Land" attempts to salvage what remains, and questions whether ritual or tradition can again make reality cohere. Of course, much of Eliot's project can be read from a Eurocentric view. In describing Eliot in a craft lecture given at the Warren Wilson College Master of Fine Arts Program for Writers, and later reprinted in *Poet's Work, Poet's Play*, Shahid writes, ". . . I can use *shantih* without being exotic, as Eliot clearly was in *The Waste Land*, a use that strikes one as full of irony when one remembers his customary fuss over the mind of Europe. Wasn't *The Waste Land* supposed to serve an exclusively European tradition?" (151). Still, this doesn't prevent Shahid from using Eliot as a reference point for his own poem. Like Eliot, Shahid takes issue with the belief in tradition and ritual, but is more forthcoming with his skepticism. The second stanza of "Bones" reads:

> Death filled the years, there
> was no time to mourn. No time to remember
> slaughtered martyrs or ancestors
> who knew a history of miracles . . .

When Shahid writes there was no "time to remember / slaughtered martyrs or ancestors / who knew a history of miracles," he seems to outright reject the relevance of tradition or ritual. He confirms this stance when he continues, "It's / futile to light oil lamps here / and search for grandfather or / forgotten ancestors." Still, Shahid ends the poem on a question, indicating, perhaps, a level of optimism: "Their // flesh must have turned soft as dust / and how can one complain to bones?" The use of the question as the poem's ending line, in addition to Shahid's gestures toward Eliot, indicates a stance that is not entirely accusatory of tradition. Instead, Shahid indicates a simultaneous skepticism and openness toward tradition. This opening poem invites the reader into *The Beloved Witness*, and prepares us for a dialogue about multiple traditions (even those that have been exclusionary) in his approaches to writing poetry.

In the appropriately titled "Introducing," a poem selected from the collection *In Memory of Begum Akhtar*, Shahid comments explicitly on the various traditions he was introduced to as a young writer. He details his beginnings with the Western Romantic tradition. The poem opens:

> At fifteen it was easy
> to write poetry: Shelley
> the prophet, Winter here
> and Spring round the corner.
> And when the narcissi
> came, Truth was Beauty,
> Beauty simply Truth, and I,
> sitting by the river.

Shahid describes his early encounters with the Western tradition as "easy," his willingness to accept the eminence of Shelley and Keats, and the expected rhythms of nature. His description of this moment as "easy" obscures the political contexts of a young Kashmiri Muslim poet finding models in the British Romantics, but it is, in fact, this attitude that makes his work particularly resonant. In the same lecture reprinted in *Poet's Work, Poet's Play*, Shahid speaks of the diverse influences he learns from:

> Because of my background, the culture of the West was and is automatically available to me. I listened to Grieg and Chopin, to Elvis Presley, the Beatles—ever since I can remember . . . I read British and European history. My grandmother read Keats, Shakespeare, and Hardy, quoting them often by heart in English. I read English/American/European literatures . . . The Hepburns, both Katharine and Audrey, were a part of my imaginative life, as were Madhubala, Meena Kumari, and Suchitra Sen. (150)

The ease with which Shahid straddles cultural influences mitigates the colonial critique in this poem. Still, he does present his young self as someone simple and unquestioning. This naiveté follows into the next stanza:

> This made sense, at sixteen, in Kashmir
> where Mahjoor sang of the gul
> (its thorn piercing the bulbul).
> Our teachers taught poetry
> under chinars, their eyes misty
> with odes to autumn. And we
> responded to this Urdu game
> of moths, their everbeaten flame.

In the same tone Shahid describes his readings of the Kashmiri poet, Mahjoor. Notably, in this stanza and the stanza that precedes it, he makes no explicit mention of the fact that he was navigating multiple traditions and languages in his early life. Instead, he presents his early poetic education as a natural reflection of the world around him ("This made sense," he writes). In the fourth line, he writes that his teachers taught him poetry "under chinars, their eyes misty / with odes to autumn." In these lines, Shahid successfully merges two cultural strains, that of the Kashmiri (represented by the word "chinar," a maple tree local to the Kashmir valley) and that of the British

Romantics with direct allusion to Keats's "To Autumn." He then brings in a third cultural reference, the Urdu story of the moth and the flame. He positions himself as a student whose attraction to poetry mirrors that of the moth to the flame. Even a small stanza such as this demonstrates his commitment, not only to revealing the sources of his poetic tradition, but in refusing to privilege one over the other.

The sources of his poetic tradition shift in the next stanza:

> At eighteen I was surprised
> by vers-libre. A Ph.D. from Leeds
> mentioned discipline, casually
> brought the waste-land.
> Unawares I was caught in wars
> and wars, Vietnam pulling me
> towards suppleness of language.
> Death punctuated all my poems.

Here, the poet describes the movement from a more formal tradition (interesting to think that Keats, Shelley, and Mahjoor might be grouped under one descriptive term) to "vers-libre" (free verse). After reading Eliot, Shahid's sense of poetry becomes both more personal and political. The "wars" in "Unawares I was caught in wars" may refer to World War I as referenced in *The Waste Land*, but the repeated phrase "and wars" after the line break seems to refer to more personal, and contemporary, wars. As a witness to Vietnam, for example, the poet finds his language changed, his poetic tradition directly responsive to and impacted by the world in which he writes.

A parallel idea, and directly related to Shahid's concern with presenting the multiple traditions from which he writes, the tension surrounding the concept of "home" pervades the poems in *The Beloved Witness*. A self-proclaimed "exile," he is in constant transit from tradition to tradition, form to form, home to home. "Postcard from Kashmir," the first poem selected from *The Half-Inch Himalayas*, presents this tension and movement:

> Kashmir shrinks into my mailbox,
> my home a neat four by six inches.
>
> I always loved neatness. Now I hold
> the half-inch Himalayas in my hand.

> This is home. And this the closest
> I'll ever be to home.

The insufficiency of memory, language, and image are all common postmodern tropes, but with Shahid as both an exile and ambassador, this lack takes on a new urgency. The first verb, "shrinks," immediately sets the stakes for this poem. To write about a place is to "shrink" it, and the image of the majestic Himalayas reduced to a "half-inch" highlights the violence of such an act. In this poem, the poet posits memory as a reduction, a rendering of reality as only an approximation. He recognizes that the idea of "home" will always be idealized, and therefore, always untrue. Paradoxically, the "half-inch Himalayas" on the postcard are "the closest" the speaker will "ever be" to this idealized version of home.

In a poem like "Survivor," also selected from *The Half-Inch Himalayas*, Shahid presents a surrealist scene in which he imagines someone lives in a house he has vacated. The title "Survivor" might imply that the speaker has died, and is viewing this scene from beyond the grave, but another possible interpretation is that the "survivor" is a version of the speaker himself. Both readings underscore the strange relationships we hold with the objects that surround us, and comment on the poet's larger questionings of "home." As an exile and immigrant, we understand that, in addition to idealized visions of a mythic homeland as seen in "Postcard from Kashmir," Shahid will also find trouble feeling "at home" in his new, adopted homeland. Such a tension is clear in "Survivor," where he details the acts of this "survivor" with notable objective distance:

> In my room
> he sits at the table
> practices my signature answers my mail
>
> He wears the cardigan
> my mother knit for my return

The survivor performs these perfunctory acts, and the speaker maintains his distance. If interpreted as a poem about disassociated selves, the latter couplet comments explicitly on the impossibility of returning "home." The mother assumes the son's return, but the "survivor" wears the cardigan in this new land, with no indication of a "return." To take the logic of this one step further, even if one version of the speaker were to "return" to Kashmir, to the mother, another version of him (the "survivor") would still exist in this other realm. Home then, is always a space of fracture and multiplicity. Once the exile leaves, the intact home can only ever exist in memory. In this way, the poem's final lines demonstrate the erasure of the self as example of what it would literally mean to return home. The poem concludes:

> He calls to my mother in my voice
>
> She turns
>
> He is breathless to tell her tales
> in which I was never found

For the son to return, the speaker himself vanishes, gives himself over to this "survivor." This surreal move demonstrates the impossibility of the exile's return.

These troubled relationships between person and home, person and memory, appear elsewhere in this collection, as in the poem "Houses," also selected from *The Half-Inch Himalayas*. In this poem, the poet presents an almost fabulist situation, in which the speaker imagines that the fates of his parents and his hometown impinge on his waking life. If "Survivor" demonstrates Shahid's disconnect from his family and the notion that "home" exists only in memory, "Houses" demonstrates the strength and power of that memory. The speaker's sleep, in this poem, depends on his notion of his parents' safety:

> My parents sleep like children in the dark.
> I am too far to hear them breathe
>
> but I remember their house is safe
> and I can sleep, the night's hair
> black and thick in my hands.
>
> My parents sleep in the dark.
> When the moon rises, the night's hair
> turns white in my arms.
>
> I am thirteen thousand miles from home.
> I comb the moon out of the night,
> and my parents are sleeping like children.

The repeated images of the parents sleeping "like children" or "in the dark" position the parents as static. The interspersed surreal images of the "night's hair" demonstrate the speaker's attempts to reach his parents, if only through imagination and metaphor. Though they remain out of reach (painfully so, as the speaker asserts, at "thirteen thousand miles"), the speaker is convinced of his implication in their lives. When he receives a letter from an old neighbor, he tries to will himself into agency back home:

> "My father is dead," Vidur writes,
> and a house in my neighbourhood, next
> to my parents', has burned down.
>
> I keep reading the letter.
> If I wake up,
> my body will be water, reflecting the fire.

The poem ends on a note of mystery. Still, the speaker clearly senses a connection between his active engagement (through metaphor and memory) with his parents and their hometown, and he can only hope that this engagement somehow serves to keep them safe. In his dream, he transforms his body into water to protect their house against fire, an image of sacrifice. This poem gains resonance from its placement alongside "Survivor," in that both poems uphold the tension between the son who stays and the son who leaves, underscoring the complex guilt of the son who can never fully return.

These themes, of exile, of weaving multiple traditions, of the longing and inability to find a "home" in space or in language, coalesce in the later poems in this collection. The poem "Snow on the Desert," selected from *A Nostalgist's Map of America*, opens with a question of the past's relation to the present. The poet writes:

> "Each ray of sunshine is seven minutes old,"
> Serge told me in New York one December night.
> "So when I look at the sky, I see the past?"
> "Yes, Yes," he said, "Especially on a clear day."

The present moment is already past, which places us in a perpetual state of nostalgia. This sense of perpetual distance widens Shahid's scope in relation to the themes previously discussed. Here, the poet moves away from highlighting the tension (and therefore, division) between past and present, home and adopted home, current self and past self. Instead, he works to merge these moments and selves together, just as he worked earlier to merge various traditions. The effect is an almost dizzying catalog of times and spaces. The narrative loosely follows the speaker's driving his sister to the airport in Tucson, during which he muses on various topics inspired by the passing landscape. The saguaro cacti, for example, prompt this:

> The syrup from which sacred wine is made
>
> is extracted from the saguaros each
> summer. The Papagos place it in jars,
>
> where the last of it softens, then darkens
> into a colour of blood though it tastes
>
> strangely sweet, almost white, like a dry wine.
> As I tell Sameetah this, we are still
> seven miles away.

Such a declaration demonstrates the speaker's attention to the connection between people and place, how culture and tradition evolve around landscape. Though left unstated, the reader must wonder then about the culture and tradition of exile—what is the relationship between person and place when "place" is always in flux? Shahid seems to answer this with the unexpected interjection of the fact of their location, "seven miles away." Though this presumably refers to the airport, it recalls the "seven minutes" phrase from the earlier stanza, and reminds us that the relationship between person and place, past and present, is *always* in flux. The fact that he is driving his sister to the airport, a concrete act of departure, further dramatizes this point.

After leaving his sister at the airport, his attention turns again to the landscape, and the imagery turns mythic: "I breathed the dried seas / the earth had lost, / their forsaken shores." This prompts a flashback to a time in New Delhi at a Begum Akhtar concert. Shahid writes:

> It was perhaps during the Bangladesh War,
> perhaps there were sirens,
>
> air-raid warnings.
> But the audience, hushed, did not stir.

> The microphone was dead, but she went on
> singing, and her voice
> was coming from far
> away, as if she had already died.

The images of stillness that occur earlier in the poem on the drive to the airport ("wine frozen in the veins of the cactus," "the road is glass," "the past now happening so quickly that each / stoplight hurts us into memory") return here, with the hushed audience. Such images contrast the perpetual movement of time and space. In this case, the ghostly moment of Begum Akhtar's *a capella* voice transcends time and space, so that it seems she is singing from beyond the grave. Of this poem, Rajini Srikanth writes:

> Four nations are linked in the poem—the United States, India, Bangladesh, and Pakistan.
> Perhaps two peoples are linked as well: the Native Americans in their beleaguered fight against the United States government and their long claim on the land, and the people of East Pakistan who sought independence from West Pakistan so that they could pursue their own destiny. The act of remembering allows him to meditate on loss and his ability to cope with it. (70)

"Snow on the Desert" is the penultimate poem, and concludes *The Beloved Witness*. The final poem, "Ghazal," in which Shahid reveals the genesis for the collection's title ("They ask me to tell them what 'Shahid' means— / Listen: It means 'The Beloved' in Persian, 'witness' in Arabic"), serves as a kind of postscript. "Snow on the Desert" makes an effective conclusion. While earlier poems serve to delineate the ideas of exile, tradition, and home, this poem works to bring them together, thereby working to transcend the limits of time and space.

And, as Srikanth notes, Shahid effectively weaves his multiple worlds and traditions into a single community, most notably by drawing alliance between the United States and the wider world.

The poem ends, hauntingly, with the speaker's return to the natural world and the reminder of time's incessant movement:

> . . . a moment when only a lost sea
> can be heard, a time
> to recollect

every shadow, everything the earth was losing,
a time to think of everything the earth
and I had lost, of all
that I would lose,
of all that I was losing.

Shahid presents his closing poem as a collision, of time and space, of past and present. In the final two lines, the repetition of the verb "to lose," from the future conditional tense ("all / that I would lose") to the past progressive ("all that I was losing") enacts this perpetual movement and ongoing state of loss. And yet, the exile experience teaches us that we are all connected—divisions of time and space, past and present, are illusory. Shahid, as the "beloved witness," demonstrates that these divisions, instead of presenting us with insurmountable differences, in fact indicate connection.

Works Cited

Ali, Agha Shahid. *The Beloved Witness*. New Delhi: Penguin Books India, 1992.
"A Darkly Defense of Dead White Males." *Poet's Work, Poet's Play: Essays on the Practice and the Art*, edited by Daniel Tobin and Pimone Triplett. Ann Arbor: University of Michigan Press, 2008.
Eliot, T. S. *The Waste Land. The Waste Land and Other Poems*. New York: Penguin, 1998.
Eliot, T. S. "Tradition and the Individual Talent." *Twentieth-Century American Poetics*, edited by Dana Gioia, David Mason, and Meg Schoerke. Boston: McGraw Hill, 2004.
Srikanth, Rajini. *The World Next Door: South Asian American Literature and the Idea of America*. Philadelphia: Temple University Press, 2004.

15

"It Is This"

Agha Shahid Ali's Representation of Kashmir in *The Country without a Post Office*

CLAIRE CHAMBERS

Nineteen years have passed since the death of Agha Shahid Ali. In this chapter of a volume on this peerless poet, I focus on his 1997 book, *The Country without a Post Office*, in many ways his signature collection.[1] I discuss its themes and imagery alongside the poet's biography and legacy, and the wider history of his troubled place of birth, Kashmir. Shahid had a striking and firm commitment to literary aesthetics, and he is often analyzed in relation to form. While this is undoubtedly important, and his efforts to popularize *ghazal* poetry in the English language have been particularly effective,[2] literary form is not my primary concern here. Instead, I want to foreground Shahid's political message, which has sometimes been posthumously soft-pedaled by critics.

As is true of many of the greatest contemporary writers, it is not easy to define Shahid's nationality. He has a hyphenated identity and a transnational background as a Kashmiri-(Indian)-American. Born in Delhi in 1949 into a rich, influential, educated Kashmiri family, Shahid grew up in Srinagar. Although a Shia Muslim, he went to a Catholic convent school because it offered the best education. He had a cosmopolitan upbringing, spending years in Indiana as a boy when his father was a PhD student there. The young Shahid went through phases of professing belief in both Christianity and Hinduism, and his liberal family was relaxed about this. Shahid disliked being pigeonholed according to any one aspect of his identity:

> Critics, interviewers and newspaper writers always want to put you into a slot: you are an Indian writing in English, therefore, you should write about India, Kashmir, Pakistan or whatever. The point is, you are a universe, you are the product of immense historical forces. There is the Muslim in me, there is the Hindu in me, there is the Western in me . . . I have grown up . . . with various permutations of these cultures.[3]

He argues that his identity is created by the interweaving of many historical strands, and that multiple personalities are reflected in his writing through references to Hindu, Christian, and Muslim myths and imagery. Kashmiri Muslims have a reputation for being tolerant of other religions. This standing partly derives from unusually close historical interchange between Muslims and Hindus in the region, which resulted in the composite brand of Sufism that is popular there. However, this syncretism can be overstated or sentimentalized, as I have previously suggested in a reading of Amitav Ghosh's treatment of the theft of the Hazratbal relic in *The Shadow Lines*.[4] Ultimately, even though the Islam of Kashmiri shrines is syncretic, it is still recognizably *Islam*, and Shahid does not shy away from acknowledging this. Reportedly, he used to introduce himself as a Muslim to his American students in order that through getting to know him they would begin to see through Orientalist stereotypes.

Shahid returned to the United States to pursue postgraduate study, and in 1984 he successfully completed a doctorate on T. S. Eliot at Pennsylvania State University. An awareness of this interest in Eliot contributes to a richer understanding of his writing. Like Eliot, Shahid is interested in poetry's form and evinces wide-ranging literary allusion and respect for his literary antecedents, while also experimenting with and bending the formal boundaries of the tradition he inherits. After his studies, he embarked on a dual career of creative writing and teaching in the United States, living in various places, including Arizona and New York State, before settling in Amherst, Massachusetts. Nonetheless, he continued to visit Kashmir on an annual basis. He had a very close relationship with his mother, who died of a brain tumour in the late 1990s. A few years later, Shahid was diagnosed with the same condition, and in 2001 he too died of brain cancer, at just fifty-two years of age.

There is an autobiographical, even confessional, aspect to many, though not all, of the poems collected in *The Country without a Post Office*. Shahid incorporates references to Amherst, where he was then living, and to Begum

Akhtar, a *ghazal* singer whom he idolized and counted among his friends. However, several of the poems are entirely imaginary inventions that have nothing to do with his life. "A Fate's Brief Memoir," for example, is narrated by Clotho, one of the three mythological Fates.

As well as the personal, however, it would be extremely limiting to read *The Country without a Post Office* without reflecting on its political dimensions and agonizing representations of the darkness of 1990s Kashmir. To give a sense of the background, Kashmir in 1947 was a princely state outside of the British Raj, ruled by a Hindu maharajah, but with a predominantly Muslim population. At Partition, Maharajah Hari Singh was given the choice as to whether he wanted Kashmir to become part of India or Pakistan, but with the split between his own heritage and that of his subjects, he could not make up his mind. Pakhtun invaders, from what is now Pakistan's Khyber Pakhtunkhwa province, tried to speed up his decision making through violence, and in alarm Singh jumped to the conclusion that Kashmir should belong to India. A war was fought in 1947–1948 between the new nation-states of Pakistan and India, which resulted in Pakistan taking approximately one-third of the region, which became known as *Azad* (free) Kashmir. India held the majority touristic and strategically important area across the Line of Control, the *de facto* borderline that both sides dispute. There have been at least two subsequent wars between India and Pakistan over Kashmir, and countless unofficial "skirmishes," but the problem is growing rather than abating.

In the late 1980s, Kashmiris vented their anger over longstanding issues. These included the corruption of local government, with Kashmir's "disco chief minister" living a lavish lifestyle while most locals struggled with extreme poverty.[5] An unfairly steep electricity price rise and, more significantly, a disputed election in 1987 became the catalysts for insurgency. Many young Kashmiris began disappearing over the border to Pakistan for weapons and combat training. In July 1988, bombs went off in the heart of the Srinagar political establishment, marking the start of a new phase of insurgency in Kashmir. From this point on, it is Kashmiris who "'have done [much of] the fighting'—and most of the dying'" in the region.[6] Different guerilla groups continue to fight either to join Pakistan, or in support of full independence (*azadi*) for Kashmir. The collection portrays many of the atrocities that have been committed on both sides.

Kashmiris carried out targeted killings against Indian government representatives, but some high-caste Hindu Kashmiris, known as Pandits, also became victims in the valley. Assassinations and fear campaigns led to an almost complete exodus of Pandits from the valley, after residing there for centuries. Despite the region's tolerant, interdependent history, noted earlier, Kashmir is now witnessing interreligious and interethnic hatred, with few Hindus still living in Kashmir because of their vulnerable minority position. Shahid's poem "Farewell," which he describes as a "plaintive love letter from a Kashmiri Muslim to a Kashmiri Pandit,"[7] addresses this issue. The poem speaks eloquently about the "othering" of the two sides in the Kashmiri conflict: "You needed me. You needed to perfect me: / In your absence you polished me into the Enemy."[8] In elliptical fashion, the poet suggests that in the bitterness of their exile the Pandits who had been forced to leave the valley viewed Kashmiri Muslims as the enemy and encouraged Indians to share this perception. Perhaps this also hints at the attitudes of and toward the most famous member of the Kashmiri Pandit community, India's first prime minister, Jawaharlal Nehru. Shahid also paints an evocative picture of the "polishing up" of the enemy. He shows that Kashmir is now "a society under daily siege."[9] As was inherent in his evocation of "the various permutations of . . . cultures" that exist within his own identity, Shahid is even-handed in his recognition that both Hindus and Muslims have suffered in the valley, but there is no doubting whose side he comes down on.

By the mid-1990s, there was "demoralization and atrophy" in the valley.[10] People still wanted independence from India, but there had been so much suffering that, by the late 1990s, many of them were beginning to give up hope. The streets of Srinagar became temporarily quieter, and fewer popular demonstrations took place. However, guerrilla warfare and terrorist activity continued, especially in the rural and border areas. This is the historical backdrop against which Shahid writes *The Country without a Post Office*. He felt the early 1990s to be a personal turning point, after which he became increasingly preoccupied with the *de facto* war taking place in his distant homeland.

The Country without a Post Office is notable for its recurring themes. Events are described from various points of view in order to shed broad light on the Kashmir situation. For example, the death of the young Kashmiri Rizwan at the hands of the Indian security forces is related from the perspectives of family members, friends, and mysteriously intangible narrators. Certain images repeated several times in the text are illustrative of the poet's political interests. I will explore some of these in what is by no means a comprehensive inventorization of the patterned motifs.

First, there are repeated evocations of a return to Kashmir as a paradise lost. Before the violence, Kashmir was frequently represented almost as an earthly heaven. The region is extremely mountainous and its capital, Srinagar, boasts of the beautiful Dal Lake. There the British loved to holiday, staying in houseboats in order to avoid paying tax on landed accommodation. The British were not the first to find in Kashmir a summertime refuge from the searing heat of the plains. The earlier Mughal rulers were also highly appreciative of the valley. The Mughal Emperor, Jehangir, is said to have written a couplet that echoed older verses on Kashmir and loosely translates as: "If on earth there is a garden of bliss / It is this, it is this, it is this." He adored Kashmir so much that he built the Shalimar Gardens there, and was rumored to have died with the words "Only Kashmir" on his lips.

However, it is important to realize that while Kashmir's landscape may have resembled an earthly paradise, its social and political conditions were far from rosy. For centuries, Kashmir was not independent but ruled by a series of invaders. These included the previously mentioned Mughals, a cruel and rapacious Sikh group who lasted only one generation, and the princely Dogra dynasty of Hari Singh's ancestors who bought Kashmir from the British for a mere seven million rupees. Many of these rulers cared little for the Kashmiri locals except for the tax and land the latter could offer. Succeeding generations of visitors to the region have commented on the contrast between the beauty of the area and the destitution and poor education of its inhabitants. For example, Allama Iqbal wrote a disapproving couplet:

"In the bitter chill of winter shivers his naked body
Whose skill wraps the rich in royal shawls."[11]

Kashmir has long been noted for its handicrafts, especially papier-mâché and shawls, but the quotation indicates that these beautiful goods often come out of inequality and oppression. Put simply, the rich benefit from the cheap labor borne out of poverty.

Agha Shahid Ali echoes well-established literary representations of Kashmir as a paradise on earth. For example, the final lines of "The Last Saffron" quote Jehangir's couplet on Kashmir as a blissful, Edenic garden, "If there is a paradise on earth, / It is this, it is this, it is this,"[12] although the words seem hollow in the light of the blood-drenched images that have come before. In the volume's final poem, "After the August Wedding in Lahore, Pakistan," Shahid uses mythology common to the Jewish, Christian, and Muslim traditions when he compares Kashmir to the Garden of Eden.[13] In the context from which he writes of a Kashmir torn apart by interreligious violence, the references to Kashmir as a paradise are ironic. However, it is worth remembering that in both the Judeo-Christian and Qur'anic story, Adam and Eve were banished from the Garden of Eden and were forced to live in a world of sin and suffering. Shahid takes up the Miltonic theme of *Paradise Lost*, and many of these poems deal with a Kashmiri's return, after many years away, to the paradise of his childhood—only to find that it has been irrevocably damaged. Frequent contrasts are drawn between the heaven of memory and the present-day hell.

Shahid often uses two further images as miniature emblems for Kashmir, the earthly paradise: saffron and paisley. Saffron is a spice produced by pounding flower petals to make an orange paste more valuable by weight than gold. As Shahid explains in the notes, the best saffron comes from Kashmir but, ironically, in light of the region's troubled history, the color saffron is also associated with the Hindu religion, since *sadhus* and other holy men wear robes of this color. The spice saffron has also acted as a symbol of Kashmir itself, given its "exquisite" qualities despite its creation through violence (in the smashing of fragile flower petals).[14] Paisley is cloth covered in abstract, fossil-like shapes. Again, this has often been associated with Kashmir, particularly as the region's highly prized shawls tend to be adorned with this print, and Western companies such as Liberty's have adapted curved paisley designs. These two delicate, beautiful images recur in such poems as "Farewell," "The Last Saffron," and "The Country without a Post Office," reinforcing the sense of a Kashmir of rare beauty. In his essay about the loss of paradise felt by children and uprooted peoples, "The Greatest Sorrow: Times of Joy Recalled in Wretchedness," Amitav Ghosh argues:

> If the twin terrors of insurgency and repression could be said to have engendered any single literary leitmotif, it is surely the narrative of the loss of Paradise. . . . The reason why there is no greater sorrow than the recalling of times of joy, is . . . that this is a grief beyond consolation.[15]

Agha Shahid Ali is one of the writers that Ghosh cites as exemplifying this use of the motif of a lost utopia, which trope is easily apparent in close readings of many of the individual poems in *The Country without a Post Office*.

Another concern that Shahid exhibits is to bring an international dimension to the Kashmir situation. As a Kashmiri-American, he wants to look at Kashmir from a broader perspective than the local politics of South Asia. He achieves this by drawing comparisons with conflicts elsewhere in the world—Bosnia, Chechnya, and Palestine—in an approach that is humanist, but also alert to the sufferings of Muslim people in recent global history. He takes a longer view of Empire than simply focusing on the situation of states hurriedly carved up in the post-war period out of bits and pieces of nationalism by hard-up and harried ex-colonizers. Many of the poems' epigraphs connect the Kashmir conflict with earlier anti-colonial struggles elsewhere. For example, Shahid quotes W. B. Yeats's lines, "Wherever green is worn / A terrible beauty is born."[16] Yeats employs green, the color associated with the "emerald isle" as a device in his poem "Easter, 1916" to argue for Irish independence from Britain in the early twentieth century. However, green is also the color associated with Islam, so Shahid neatly draws comparisons between Ireland and Kashmir's troubles—both in large part deriving from colonization by British. He takes an even longer view of Empire, reminiscent of the sweeping argument of Ashcroft et al. in *The Empire Writes Back*, when he quotes Tacitus at the beginning of part I of the collection. In his writings, the Roman historian Tacitus reports a British chieftain's speech, which includes the line *Solitudinam faciunt et pacem appellant*, meaning "They [the Romans] make a desolation and call it peace."[17] Thus, like the Caribbean poet Derek Walcott, Shahid gives us a broad view of history, showing that European empires are not the only ones to have existed, and showing its impermanence as this too shall pass. Many societies have had cruel systems of control over others, and Shahid demonstrates that even Britain was once so afflicted, under the Roman Empire.

Shahid is not content only to survey Kashmir alongside warzones and colonies. He scrutinizes the region from relatively peaceful vantage points, such as India's capital in "I See Kashmir from New Delhi at Midnight." Moreover, his poetry oscillates between Kashmir and his other home in Amherst. He exhibits a dazzling ability to cross national frontiers. The freedom of poetry allows him to do this even more easily than his friend and admirer, Amitav Ghosh, whose fiction has a similarly international purview. Shahid refuses to respect the artificial construction of the nation-state, which has caused such problems in the multiply partitioned region of Jammu and Kashmir.

This repudiation of the sanctity of national frontiers is reflected in Shahid's representations of letters, correspondence, and the postal service. This preoccupation with communication is highlighted by the collection's very title and the poem of the same name, "The Country without a Post Office." In a prose poem that begins "Dear Shahid," the mysterious reference to the country without a post office is to some extent explained. An unnamed friend of Shahid's family writes to the poet to explain that during the Kashmiri fighting, a pile of undelivered mail had begun to stack up.

The friend had wandered over and by chance picked up a letter for Shahid from one of his loved ones—perhaps someone who is now dead. The post office malfunction is a suggestive and yet economical image, in that it simultaneously evokes politics and love between people. Communication between families and friends is disrupted by conflict, phone lines are dead and mail is lost, so people wait desperately for news of their loved ones.

There is a poem entitled "The Correspondent,"[18] and one expects it to be about one of the collection's letter writers—either the writer of "Dear Shahid" or the earlier correspondent who penned the letter found by that writer. Instead, the poem centers on a second meaning of the word "correspondent": a journalist who has come to Kashmir on an assignment. This war correspondent draws parallels between the Kashmir conflict and the Sarajevo/Bosnian war, reminding the reader of a third connotation: "correspondence" as "similarity" or "analogy." The poet is interested in all three nuances: communication between people, the media's view of violence, and parallels that can be drawn between different countries' struggles.

Moreover, the volume is punctuated by journeys and crossings. Shahid shows an interest in the transition and transgression of travel. In "I Dream I Am the Only Passenger on Flight 423 to Srinagar," he uses the resonant location of the night-time flight, in which the narrator exists between two countries in a provisional, liminal space. What Peter Adey calls the aerial gaze[19] gives Shahid a wide-angled lens on both the migrant, nonresident Kashmiri's errant position and Kashmir's no-man's-land vulnerability caught as it is between India and Pakistan's animosity. In "The Last Saffron" (and several other poems), the narrator makes a journey. In this dreamlike poem, he is taken on a taxi ride and is then rowed on a boat to an island where a keeper guards the "world's last saffron"—a metaphor for fast-fading Kashmir. As well as these physical crossings and the letters and correspondence already discussed, there are recurring depictions of long-distance telephone calls. Different worlds collide when the phone rings, as in "Some Vision of the World Cashmere," in which the poet's milieu in Amherst is interrupted by the news that his grandmother is dying in Srinagar.

Additionally, *The Country without a Post Office* is replete with images of shadows, mirrors, and doubles. The shadow is especially noticeable in discussion of the death of an 18-year old, Rizwan, who is mentioned in many of the poems. His death is portrayed as being emblematic of Kashmiri deaths at large, as he is one of many promising youths killed in conflict without his family's knowledge. In "I See Kashmir from New Delhi at Midnight," Rizwan is depicted as a phantom roaming the streets of Srinagar, searching for his body. The boy's troubled ghost bears witness to further atrocities, such as the torturing of a prisoner by dripping molten tyre on his back. Intimations are provided that Rizwan is the poet's double, or Other, who stayed in Kashmir and was killed. Shadows also intimate menace and threat, as with penumbrous figures from the Indian security forces and the shadows of boys "disappeared" from their homes, their bodies never found.

A further image of doubling is found in the trope of looking into a dusty mirror in an abandoned house. A mirror implies the closeness and yet separateness of the two sides in the Kashmir conflict—to adapt Ashis Nandy, the intimacy of hatred[20]—like the perfect enemy described in "Farewell." Amitav Ghosh uses this leitmotif in his novel *The Shadow Lines* when he laments the "looking-glass border" that exists between Calcutta and Dhaka.[21] Shahid similarly writes, "Upstairs, the window, too, is a mirror; if I jump through it I / will fall into my arms."[22] The mirror of course separates two similar-looking figures by means of a two-dimensional divide. So it neatly reflects the nature of national borders. Just as geographical boundaries signify proximity to one's neighbors while at the same time emphasizing difference, so too the mirror is a dividing line that also replicates. Ghosh and Shahid use the "mirror image" partly to suggest the underlying similarities between Hindus and Muslims. However, it is also worth recalling psychoanalysis's mirror stage, which heralds the child's moment of separation from the mother. Judith Butler argues that the mirror stage marks "the genesis of bodily boundaries,"[23] and the realization that one's identity is unique and differentiated from other people's. As well as signifying closeness, it can also more pessimistically denote separation.

A final image of doubleness and yet separation comes in Shahid's frequent pairing of snow and ash. Snow is a regular feature of Kashmir's climate, which is dazzling but cruel. There are many references in the text to cold weather being used as a weapon, as when prisoners are made to stand in icy water in an inventive method of torture.[24] Snow is described as falling like ash, an incongruous motif that juxtaposes liquid with aridity, cold against hot. The inference once more is of a beautiful thing gone wrong: the fertile paradise is now barren. Yet, through the legend of the phoenix, ash is also associated with optimistic connotations of rebirth; the poet makes reference to this when he writes, "and when we—as if from ash—ascend / into the cold."[25]

Shahid's legacy is assured, with the past decade seeing an upsurge in quality Kashmiri writing in English, most of it influenced, even inspired, by his poetry. References to *The Country without a Post Office* are extensive:

for example, Basharat Peer uses Shahid's depiction of a shadow searching for its body in his memoir about the valley, *Curfewed Night*, Mirza Waheed's *The Collaborator* begins with "I See Kashmir from New Delhi at Midnight," while Salman Rushdie depoliticizes "The Country without a Post Office" by quoting the poem alongside Shakespeare's epigram "A plague on both your houses" in his unconvincing novel about the Kashmir conflict, *Shalimar the Clown*.[26]

To examine just one of Shahid's literary inheritors, Mirza Waheed was born and brought up in Srinagar, moved to Delhi for his studies and subsequent journalism work, and in 2001 came to London to join the BBC's Urdu Service, where until recently he worked as an editor. *The Collaborator* is his debut novel, published by the prestigious house of Viking/Penguin, and Waheed recently followed it up with the love story *The Book of Gold Leaves*.[27] *The Collaborator* was mostly reviewed in a positive way, aside from political difficulties that some Indian writers (such as the author and politician Shashi Tharoor[28]) had with it.

The Collaborator is set in Kashmir in the early 1990s, when the war in Kashmir has finally reached the isolated village of Nowgam close to the Pakistan border. Shahid is an influence on *The Collaborator*, and provides one of the novel's epigraphs, about the murdered Rizwan: "the body / of which unburied boy in the mountains."[29] The novel centers on a group of five teenage friends. One by one, four of them cross the border into Pakistan to join the insurgency. The story is narrated by the fifth, the son of a headman, who is left behind near the Line of Control, with only his memories of cricket matches, shared music, and banter about budding romances with the friends who have disappeared. The headman has forbidden his family to leave, so the son has little choice but to become the titular "collaborator." Picking possessions off the dead bodies of "militants" in the "sad paradise on earth" in Kashmir's borderlands,[30] he dreads the day that he will see the corpse of one of his friends. Like Shahid, Waheed makes demands on his readers, presenting them with a challenging intermixture of violence and beauty. Yet he manages to find a balance in writing about the violence of Kashmir without either aestheticizing it or being gratuitous. The novel is focalized throughout by the young narrator, whose name we never learn (another Rizwan?). He thinks, as he watches his employer, the vicious Captain, binge-drinking: "I'm beginning to get used to this. That's worrying."[31] In a dark take on the *Bildungsroman*, the novel charts the boy's "progress" from shock and revulsion at the dead bodies to communing with the dead people, even lying beside them, to not really noticing them as he becomes inured to the work. We see other characters, such as the Captain's peon, only from the boy's perspective, as unmitigated embodiments of evil.

Echoing the foreign journalist in "The Correspondent" cynically demanding "exclusive rights / to this dream,"[32] Waheed too examines the language of the media when reporting the war. He satirizes the language of propaganda: "an encounter, a skirmish, whatever they choose to call it."[33] When a film crew from Delhi comes to broadcast the conflict, the Captain boasts that "the stupid hacks want to film foreign militants . . . I can make any maderchod look like an Afghan."[34] This statement reveals that war is staged through the media and that news bulletins do not reflect what is occurring "on the ground." Perhaps the most extraordinary paragraph in the novel comes near the end, where an Indian politician lectures uncomfortable, captive Kashmiris under curfew with a eulogy about

> the two-nation theory and the Crown of Mother India and proxy war and . . . Nehru and General Douglas MacArthur and the history of failure and "too late" and "too late," and Article 370, and *Namaste Saradadevi, Kasmira Mandala Vasini* and Kashmir's ineradicable place in the Indian vision![35]

Both Shahid and Waheed take an unflinching look at the brutality of the Indian army. But they are also pessimistic about Pakistan, which Waheed describes as "that goddamn country a few kilometres across the border which is never at rest and will never let anyone else rest in peace either."[36] And the Kashmiri separatist or Islamist groups do not come off lightly in *The Collaborator* either; for example, a woman has her tongue cut out and her son's arm is maimed because they are seen to have betrayed the *azadi* movement. Tariq Ali rightly calls the Islamists and the Indian army the "neither-nor" of Kashmiri politics.[37]

What future can there be for Kashmir, caught in this triple bind between India, Pakistan, and the separatists? One problem is that the conflict is little understood or publicized outside of South Asia, as is painfully evoked in an Amnesty petition against the "Thousands lost in Kashmir mass graves," which garnered a paltry 617 signatures in three years.[38] Basharat Peer recognizes that Shahid's poetry was "foremost" among the "few literary responses" to the Kashmir conflict that existed when he was growing up, and argues that this younger generation "had to find the words to save [memories and stories] from the callous varnish of time. I had to write."[39] Through writing of all sorts—letters, journalism, fiction, and poetry—such authors as Peer, Waheed, and their forebear Shahid (as well as many other writers working in the Kashmiri language whom my linguistic shortcomings prevent me from reading) are ensuring that Kashmir's post office is once again open for correspondence of all kinds.

Notes

1. An early version of this essay with a different title was published in *Contemporary World Literature*, 7 (May/June) 2011. Here it is reprinted with the permission of the author.

2. Agha Shahid Ali and Sarah Suleri Goodyear, *Ravishing DisUnities: Real Ghazals in English*. Middletown, CT: Wesleyan University Press, 2004.

3. Rehan Ansari and Rajinderpal S. Pal, "Agha Shahid Ali: Calligraphy of Coils," *Himalmag*, March 1998, http://old.himalmag.com/component/content/article/2385--agha-shahid-ali-calligraphy

4. Claire Chambers, "Riots, Rumours, and Relics: Amitav Ghosh's *The Shadow Lines*," in *Amitav Ghosh's* The Shadow Lines: *A Critical Companion*, ed. Murari Prasad. New Delhi: Pencraft, 2008, 37–55.

5. Sumantra Bose, *Kashmir: Roots of Conflict, Paths to Peace*. Cambridge, MA: Harvard University Press, 2005 [2003], 95.

6. Bose, *Kashmir*, 3.

7. CWPO 93.

8. CWPO 22.

9. Bose, *Kashmir*, 4.

10. Bose, *Kashmir*, 135.

11. Quoted in Tariq Ali, "Bitter Chill of Winter," *London Review of Books* 23.8 (2001): np.

12. CWPO 29.

13. CWPO 91.

14. Ananya Jahanara Kabir, "A Story of Saffron," *Kashmir Monitor*, 15 August 2003, www.countercurrents.org/kashmir-kabir150803.htm.

15. Amitav Ghosh, "The Greatest Sorrow: Times of Joy Recalled in Wretchedness," *The Imam and the Indian: Prose Pieces*. Delhi: Permanent Black, 2002, 305–325, 308, 313.

16. W. B. Yeats, "Easter, 1916," in *Selected Poems*. London: Penguin, 2000 [1916], 24.

17. Stephen Howe, *Empire: A Very Short Introduction*. Oxford: Oxford University Press, 2002, 43.

18. CWPO 54.
19. Peter Adey, *Aerial Life: Spaces, Mobilities, Affects*. Chichester: Wiley-Blackwell, 2010, 86–88.
20. Ashis Nandy, *The Intimate Enemy: Loss and Recovery of Self Under Colonialism*. New Delhi: Oxford University Press, 2010 [1983].
21. Ghosh, *Shadow*, 233.
22. CWPO 47.
23. Judith Butler, *Bodies That Matter: On the Discursive Limits of "Sex."* London: Routledge, 1993, 71.
24, CWPO 43.
25. CWPO 30.
26. Basharat Peer, *Curfewed Night: A Frontline Memoir of Life, Love and War in Kashmir*. London: Harper, 2010, np. Mirza Waheed, *The Collaborator*. London: Viking, 2011, vii. Salman Rushdie, *Shalimar the Clown*. London: Jonathan Cape, 2005, vii.
27. Mirza Waheed, *The Book of Gold Leaves*. London: Viking, 2014.
28. Shashi Tharoor, "What the Brook Saw: A Need for Pathetic Fallacy." *Outlook India*, 7 March 2011, http://www.outlookindia.com/magazine/story/what-the-brook-saw-a-need-for-pathetic-fallacy/270612
29. Waheed, *The Collaborator*, vii.
30. Waheed, *The Collaborator*, 19.
31. Waheed, *The Collaborator*, 9.
32. CWPO 55.
33. Waheed, *The Collaborator*, 5.
34. Waheed, *The Collaborator*, 9.
35. Waheed, *The Collaborator*, 233.
36. Waheed, *The Collaborator*, 152.
37. Tariq Ali, "The Story of Kashmir," *Kashmir: The Case for Freedom*, Tariq Ali et al. London: Verso, 2011, 7–56.
38. Amnesty, "Appeal for Action: Kashmir." http://www.amnesty.org/en/appeals-for-action/thousandslost-kashmir-mass-graves
39. Peer, *Curfewed*, 95.

Works Cited

Adey, Peter. *Aerial Life: Spaces, Mobilities, Affects*. Chichester: Wiley-Blackwell, 2010.
Ali, Agha Shahid. *The Country without a Post Office*. New York: Norton, 1998.
Ali, Agha Shahid, and Sara Suleri Goodyear. *Ravishing DisUnities: Real Ghazals in English*. Middletown, CT: Wesleyan University Press, 2004.
Ali, Tariq. "Bitter Chill of Winter." *London Review of Books* 23.8 (2001): 18–27. http://www.lrb.co.uk/v23/n08/tariq-ali/bitter-chill-of-winter

"The Story of Kashmir." *Kashmir: The Case for Freedom*, ed. Tariq Ali et al. London: Verso, 2011, 7–56.

Ansari Rehan, and Rajinderpal S. Pal. "Agha Shahid Ali: Calligraphy of Coils." *Himalmag*. March 1998. http://old.himalmag.com/component/content/article/2385--agha-shahid-ali-calligraphy-of-coils.html

Ashcroft, Bill, Gareth Griffiths, and Helen Tiffin. *The Empire Writes Back: The Theory and Practice of Post-Colonial Literatures*. London: Routledge, 2002.

Bose, Sumantra. *Kashmir: Roots of Conflict, Paths to Peace*. Cambridge, MA: Harvard University Press, 2005.

Butler, Judith. *Bodies That Matter: On the Discursive Limits of "Sex."* London: Routledge, 1993.

Chambers, Claire. "Riots, Rumours, and Relics: Amitav Ghosh's *The Shadow Lines*." In *Amitav Ghosh's* The Shadow Lines: *A Critical Companion*, ed. Murari Prasad, 37–55. New Delhi: Pencraft, 2008.

Ghosh, Amitav. *The Shadow Lines*. Delhi: Oxford University Press, 1995.

Ghosh, Amitav. "The Greatest Sorrow: Times of Joy Recalled in Wretchedness." *The Imam and the Indian: Prose Pieces*, 305–325. Delhi: Permanent Black, 2002.

Howe, Stephen. *Empire: A Very Short Introduction*. Oxford: Oxford University Press, 2002.

Kabir, Ananya Jahanara. "A Story of Saffron." *Kashmir Monitor*. August 15, 2003. http://www.countercurrents.org/kashmir-kabir150803.htm

Nandy, Ashis. *The Intimate Enemy: Loss and Recovery of Self Under Colonialism*. New Delhi: Oxford University Press, 2010.

Peer, Basharat. *Curfewed Night: A Frontline Memoir of Life, Love and War in Kashmir*. London: Harper, 2010, Print.

Rushdie, Salman. *Shalimar the Clown*. London: Jonathan Cape, 2005.

"The Story of Kashmir." *Kashmir: The Case for Freedom*, ed. Tariq Ali et al. London: Verso, 2011, 7–56.

Tharoor, Shashi. "What the Brook Saw: A Need for Pathetic Fallacy." Review of Mirza Waheed's *The Collaborator*. *Outlook India*. March 7, 2011. http://www.outlookindia.com/magazine/story/what-the-brook-saw-a-need-for-pathetic-fallacy/270612

Waheed, Mirza. *The Collaborator*. London: Viking, 2011.

Yeats, W. B. "Easter, 1916." In *Selected Poems*, 119–121. London: Penguin, 2000.

16

Epistemology of Mourning

A Reading of *Rooms Are Never Finished*

SISIR KUMAR CHATTERJEE
SINCHAN CHATTERJEE

What you never lose, you must forever mourn.

—Goethe[1]

Mourning is regularly the reaction to the loss of a loved person, or to the loss of some abstraction which has taken the place of one, such as one's country, liberty, an ideal, and so on.

—Freud[2]

There comes a point in the life, and therefore in the art, of every artist, when all his work becomes a form of lamentation—a monument to the whole philosophy of mourning, of grieving over the loss of what he once believed was his own and unlosable—a deeply personal dirge through which the artist, mourning the object of loss, is in effect mourning for his own self, and for the sake of collective humanity. And the graver the elegy, the louder the tormented wail, the more effective the work of art grows, for then it becomes sublimated from the demented cry of an agonized individual venting his personal bereavement to an expression of pain and suffering, of loss and despair, of the whole of mankind.

Agha Shahid Ali's poems in *Rooms Are Never Finished*, expressing a kind of grief that wells up from the deepest recesses of his soul, rise above the level of a solitary son lamenting the demise of his mother, or an individual weeping his displacement from his home, his natural habitat, his motherland, to the height of a powerful and stirring poetic act that brings into the world of poetry a magical ability hitherto touched upon but never explored in all its depth—the ability to cry and scream and shout and wail and still make it sound beautiful, the ability to make the cosmic universal energy partake of one's sorrow, to shake the mountains and make the earth rumble, and to cry out with the mourner, sharing the trauma of his pain. Shahid's poems thus become a form of tacit rebellion, endowing the act of mourning, which is the inescapable fate of all men, with a sense of dignity in its wildness, a kind of rare pride in all its helplessness, a strength in the honesty that it takes to even break down.

Shahid's poetic sensibility was shaped up by the techniques of impressionism, surrealism, symbolism, a combination of Eliotian intellectualism and Dylan Thomasish bardic emotionalism, and a ghazal-like repetitiveness and incantatory modulation of voice. It was also steeped in an acute global consciousness of the contemporary reality of insurgence and counter-insurgence, of rebellion and subjugation, of the rise of terror and the control of a repressive, authoritative power, of the battle for life and the state machinery bent on crushing lives, the likes of which had been devastating the human world in places such as modern Bosnia, Chechnya, Sarajevo, Armania, Palestine, Granada, Chile, Deir Yassein, Sabra-Shatila, and Kashmir. Being densely allusive and laden with images from the contemporary reality, which coalesce with those from the world of myths and legends recorded mostly in scriptures and history, in a network of highly complex associational matrix, almost every Shahid poem in this collection reads like a poetic transcript of his consciousness that was molded by the deep impact of the teachings of Hinduism, Islam, Buddhism, Sufism, and Christianity. The temporal as well as spatial planes are mixed up. In his poems, the narratives sacrifice linearity for the sake of translating the complexity of emotion, so that they break in the middle, change their course, and indulge in cinematic jump cuts and ellipses. And it is by employing these techniques that Shahid forged a new poetics to ventilate his grief over loss, separation, exile, rootlessness—all caused mostly by the use of religions as weapons to tear humanity asunder, and to annihilate lives for narrow, short-sighted material profit or for assertion of power and control over territories. All this gives birth to a voice of acutely complicated poetic psyche that bursts out into a strain of excruciating pain that sounds like the throttled but protracted inward-moving howl[3] of an individual grown delirious with grief, a lamentation too layered to simplify, and yet too profound and affective to hear and pass by. No wonder, then, that a Shahid poem is too wild a cry for any reader to paraphrase, too labyrinthine to come out of it with a sense of critical victory. In this chapter we will make a humble attempt to capture the spirit and the tone of that lamentation through a poem-by-poem reading.

In a brief prefatory note to *Rooms Are Never Finished*, Shahid explains the background in which this volume was written: it was composed during and after the time he, along with his father and siblings, brought his "mother's body for burial" from Amherst (where she went to his brother's home for treatment of brain cancer, which took her life in 1997, in a Northampton hospital in Massachusetts) to Kashmir, because "she had longed for home throughout her illness." By 1990, Kashmir had been reduced to "a home at war," a place that had "erupted into a full-scale uprising for self-determination" and large-scale atrocities perpetrated on the Kashmiris by the Indian army on one hand and the conflicting militant outfits on the other. This led to a state of "despair and rage, then only rage, then only despair" (*The Veiled Suite*, 245; hereafter VS). Consequently, Kashmir caused "international anxiety" as it was feared that it might have been "the flashpoint of a nuclear war" (VS 245). Shahid claims that the "ongoing catastrophe" in Kashmir provides the backdrop to *Rooms Are Never Finished*. So we need to take a brief look at *The Country without a Post Office*, which depicts the dark, agonizing sociopolitical reality plaguing the Kashmir of 1990s. The very epigraph to the volume shows the poet's agony that is shared by the elemental, cosmic presences, as he quotes from the *Quran* a line to indicate that the human plight in Kashmir has reached such a pathetic height that even "the moon is rent asunder" on witnessing the daily reports of "mass rapes in the villages, towns left in cinders, neighbourhoods torched," carrying on the same story of "Power [that's] hideous / like a barber's hands,"[4] (CWPO 2).

The social atmosphere in Kashmir was so much vitiated that the minority Hindu Kashmiris called Pandits, gripped by a feeling of terror and suspicion issuing in mutual animosity, more imagined than real, fled from the valley. This phenomenon is captured in the poem called "Farewell," in which the speaker, a Kashmiri Muslim, writes a letter to a Kashmiri Pandit with an emotion of anguished regret: "You needed me. You needed to perfect me: / In your absence you polished me into the Enemy. / Your history gets in the way of my memory. / I am everything you lost. You can't forgive me; / I am everything you lost. Your perfect enemy." (CWPO 8) But, the situation in Kashmir is far worsened by Indian army's barbaric handling of the Muslims' armed insurgency in the valley. As a consequence, Kashmir witnessed rampant violations of human rights, "suspension of civil liberties, institution of martial law, widespread police killings, brutalization, and the automatic equation of Kashmiris with 'terrorists.'"[5] In the beginning of section II of the book, Shahid is informed by one of his acquaintances through a letter to him that in Kashmir, "Everyone carries his address in his pocket so that at least his body will reach home . . . Men are forced to stand barefoot in snow waters all night. The women are alone inside. Soldiers smash radios and televisions. With bare hands they tear our houses to pieces" (CWPO 29). In "I See Kashmir from New Delhi at Midnight," Shahid shows the inhuman torture perpetrated on the Kashmiris: "Drippings from a suspended burning tire / are falling on the back of a prisoner, / the naked boy screaming, "I know nothing" (CWPO 10). In "After the August Wedding in Lahore, Pakistan," a sadist brigadier says, "The boys of Kashmir / break so quickly, we make their bodies sing, / on the rack, till no song is left to sing." (CWPO 81) The heart-rending suffering of the Kashmiris is recounted also through the unnerving narrative of the killing of a young eighteen-year-old Kashmiri named Rizwan by Indian security forces:

"Don't tell my father I have died," he says,
and I follow him through blood on the road
. . .
From windows we hear
grieving mothers . . .
Kashmir is burning." . . . (CWPO 11)

"There is curfew everywhere . . . There is panic on the roads" (CWPO 21). In Kashmir, "Everything is finished, nothing remains" (CWPO 38). It has been reduced to a world where the poet's lament (which evokes the tone of a sense of spiritual void and despondency as it reminds us of the lines from one of Hopkins's terrible sonnets[6]) "is cries countless, cries like dead letters sent / to this world whose end was near, always near" (CWPO 40). The story of desperate insurgence and brutal repression had thus reduced Kashmir, once looked upon as a paradise on earth—both for its natural beauties and the ambiance of peaceful human existence—to an inferno, a "bleeding piece of earth" (CWPO 47). The metonymic image that depicts the place now is that of saffron, a spice costlier than even gold but produced through a violent process of crushing the petals of numerous fragile flowers. *The Country without a Post Office* thus depicts an infernal, dystopian world of barbaric violence that forms the backdrop for *Rooms Are Never Finished*, which deals with the themes of loss (of beauty and love as well as of faith in the existence of a benevolent God) and separation (of a community from their homeland and of an individual from his emotional refuge), both feelings painfully augmented and protracted by memory and exile (of self from its roots and from identity), and of an inconsolable grief resulting from these experiences.

In *Rooms Are Never Finished*, the speaker restlessly straddles History (both remote and contemporary), Myth, Religion, and Literature to mourn the death of his mother who is elevated to the level of a galaxy that dares to defy the Master of the Universe. In the epigraph to the very first poem "Lenox Hill," the sound of wailing shoots out of the pages of distant history, "across fifteen centuries," of Kashmir during the Hun invasion of this land of peace. Mihiragula, son of Toramana, the Hun invader from Sialkot, was a sadistic tyrant who delighted in monstrous acts of cruelty. "Once, while crossing the Pir Panjal Pass, one of the elephants in Mihiragula's train slipped and fell. The cry of the animal was so pleasing to Mihiragula's ears that he subsequently drove one hundred elephants over the precipice, caused their fall down the hill and relished hearing the terrified shrieks of the dying elephants."[7] This traumatizing sound of the elephants falling off the cliffs of the mountains in the Pir Panjal Range rent the ears of Shahid's mother, as she was reminded by this of the sound of the sirens of ambulances coming to and going from the Lenox Hill Hospital in Manhattan, which in turn brought back to her mind the nightmarish sound of sirens of the army jeeps in Kashmir hunting for the Kashmiri youths:

> The Hun so loved the cry, one falling elephant's,
> he wished to hear it again. At dawn, my mother
> heard, in her hospital-dream of elephants,
> sirens wail through Manhattan like elephants
> forced off Pir Panjal's rock cliffs in Kashmir:
> the soldiers, so ruled, had rushed the elephants. (VS 247)

Shahid remembers what Buddha said: "*The greatest of all footprints is the elephant's*," and laments that even "those prints vanished forever into the universe." His lamentation for the wanton killing of the elephants merges with his agony caused by the death of his mother. Thus, the historical pain seeps into the personal agony, and the past sorrow blends with the present crisis.

Shahid then remembers his mother's nightmare (of "being stoned to death") in Amherst, which shows that she was agonized not only by the pain of the elephants but of the suffering of all those mythological and historical men and women who were subjected to "lapidation" or "rajam."[8] Shahid realized that his mother had grown delirious with pain, and prayed to the Saints to "let her die," although initially, when he found it difficult to reconcile to the thought that she would die, he resisted the very idea by praying that "If she must die, / let it only be some dream." When, however, he realized that her death was inevitable, he expressed his anguish by swearing "not to forgive the universe / that would let [him] get used to a universe / without [her]." He takes refuge in memories to avoid looking pain in the face: he recalls his mother telling him that as he sat there in the hospital bed by her side, he was just like her mother, and this made Shahid imagine her in the immediate post-marital past of her life in Kashmir: "a bride in Kashmir, / she's watching, at the Regal, her first film with Father." Kashmir is robbed of all its rights; but, at least, he prays, his mother should not be denied the right that "she gave its earth to cover her." He claims, like a child, that he could have saved her from God, the "Destroyer," "if only [he] could gather [her] in [his] arms." And now that his mother had become his daughter, and he her mother, he cried in despair: "How helpless was God's mother!" Mary could not save her son, who was also God's son. He apprehends that his mother might hear the cries he had once held back from her when she was alive: "Do you hear what I once held back, in one elephant's / cry, by his mother's bones, the cries of those elephants / that stunned the abyss?" Shahid's grief over his mother's death is inconsolable and he bursts out: ". . . compared to my grief for you, what are those of Kashmir, / and what (I close the ledger) are the griefs of the universe / when I remember you—beyond all accounting—O my mother?" (VS 249) "Lenox Hill" thus reminds one of Ginsberg's "Kaddish" written to mourn the death of his mother Naomi Ginsberg, and reads like a "specif."[9]

In "From Amherst to Kashmir," a poem comprising twelve sections, Shahid proceeds to place his grief in a wider historical-mythological perspective of one of the most grievous stories in the history of human civilization, the story of Hussain's martyrdom in Karbala. The poem is a *marsiya*, which is an Urdu elegy used for long as a medium of religious mourning. Section 1, "Karbala: A History of the 'House of Sorrow,'" written in prose, recounts the entire story of Hussain's death, with Christianity and Islam interlinked, which they originally are. Fourteen hundred years before the Karbala incident had taken place in AD 680, Jesus, while passing through the plain of Karbala along with his disciples, spoke to them: "'At this site the grandson of Prophet Muhammad . . . will one day be killed.' And Jesus wept. *Oh, that my head were waters, and mine eyes a fountain of tears, that I might weep day and night for the slain* . . . And Jesus wept" (VS 250). Hussain, the prince among martyrs, the grandson of the Prophet and son of Ali ("Father of Clay") and Fatima ("the Prophet's only surviving child"), died like Jesus: "For just 'as Jesus went to Jerusalem to die on the cross,' Hussain 'went to Karbala to accept the passion that had been meant for him from the beginning of time'" (VS 250). The poet glides to the present scenario of Kashmir, which is no better than that of Karbala. "For two years," he writes during his act of reminiscing a *majlis* (a gathering of people to mourn Karbala), "Death had turned every day in Kashmir into some family's Karbala" (VS 253). He remembers his mother identifying herself with Hussain's sister Zainab with a feeling of absorbed empathy: "Since she was a girl she had felt Zainab's grief as her own" (VS 253). At his mother's funeral, a mourner sang an elegy put in the mouth of Zainab, and Shahid says that the words in that requiem "now are my mother's, for she too was tired, fighting death, from hospital to hospital, from city to city" (VS 253). As Zainab wept for her brother, the poet's mother wept for Zainab, for Hussain, for the Kashmiri young men and women, and for all the suffering creatures on earth, like the elephants falling off the cliffs of hills at Pir Panjal Range. And the poet weeps for his mother and for all those for whom she weeps, suggesting thereby that all contemporary Zainabs should weep for every Kashmiri Hussain martyred for the cause of freedom.

Shahid's lamentation assumes a more poignantly touching dimension in section 3, "Summers of Translation," in which his present grief is augmented by his memory of the past. His inability to verbalize his memory leads him only to "desolation's desert," and he seeks comfort in his memory of his hearing a "*bhajan*" (a Hindu devotional song) in which Radha helplessly and desperately holds on to the sleeve of Krishna, the "Dark blue god," and entreats Him: "Don't cast me into oblivion"—a memory that has sustained him through "so many summers, so many monsoons, dimmed on Time's shelf," like the memory of his mother reading all of Faiz Ahmed Faiz aloud to him, with the mother and the son choosing the Faiz poems "that would translate best." His grief is also alleviated to some extent by his memory of hearing Begum Akhtar singing "Raga Jogia," a ghazal that held him completely under its spell. But his memory is also troubled by "the wound-cry of the gazelle,"[10] by some words of the ghazal: "Not all, no, only a few return as the rose / or the tulip," and by his memory of every Newspaper headline that read "PARADISE ON EARTH BECOMES HELL" when he had visited his mother in Kashmir in "later summers," because, he remembers, "In every home, although Muharram was not yet here, / Zainab wailed. Only Karbala could frame our grief: / The wail rose: *How could such a night fall on Hussain?*" (VS 258). Shahid's memory of what Kashmir once was and what now seems to have been irrevocably lost takes away his belief in the existence of a benevolent God, and brings back to his mind the memory of the *bhajan* in which Lord Krishna is described as "a thief." Radha's appeal to her God—"Dark Krishna, don't let your Radha die in the rain"—merges with Zainab's grief heard "from Karbala to Kufa to Damascus" and with the "cry of the gazelle" filling the night. Zainab cried for her brother, and Begum Akhtar cried for all who suffer(ed) loss, and the legendary singer with her melodious voice cried "so purely that even in memory it lets memory cease," which implies that her doleful rendering of the song had the power to stop the flow of time and memory and to dissolve "even terrible pain" in "wonder."

Section 4, "Above the Cities," shows Shahid continuing his airborne journey along with the coffin of his mother, and crossing Boston and Frankfurt before arriving at Delhi, and from there at Kashmir. His mother is with them, but they are without her. The poet's mind slides into memory again. He remembers the hour in which she died, the hour, which to him was equivalent to "Doomsday's very / first breath," for ever since her decease he has been "piling Doomsday on Doomsday / over oceans, continents, deserts, cities," and he re-suffers the agony of "Karbala's slaughter / through [his] mother's eyes" (VS 260), which resembled "two candles / lit above the cities she'll never visit." Shahid is hurled back from the memory of a distant past to that of a nearer one by the words of the nurse: "*She is / gone!*" when the ICU light was still green, and the monitor's pulse was throbbing mildly like the heart in pain for being unable "to empty itself." This section ends with a consolatory universalization and eternalization of lamentation, of a son's expression of grief over the death of his mother: "And where there's a son, in any / language saying *Adieu* to his mother, she is / you and that son . . . is me, that / son is me. Always" (VS 263).

In section 5, "Memory," Shahid seems to find a healing touch in the power of memory that enables him to visualize a reunion with his mother: "Memory's placed its hand so on Time's face, touched it / so caressingly that although it's still our / parting's morning, it's as if night's come, bringing / you to my bare arms" (VS 263). Section 6, "New Delhi Airport," begins with an epigraph taken from a Bombay film song, which shows a reversal of the natural process, as it speaks of the flame searching for the moth instead of the other way round: "When the flame itself has gone searching for, / that moth—just imagine!" This reversal prepares us for an ironical situation that comes soon: Shahid's mother longed intensely to come back to Kashmir, come back alive, to her home, to light up with candles the shrines of Kashmir, "the broken idols in temples" and the "Scripture" containing God's words that would bring light to the world. But with her death, all the flames of all the candles seem to have been extinguished in Kashmir, as if they have gone searching for "God the Moth" and God's "wings have caught fire." Once again, Shahid is pained by the sound of Zainab's wailing as they climb the ramp to board another plane in Delhi airport, the flight that would take them to Kashmir, and once their plane takes off, "the sky is empty."

In the next Section, "Film Bhajan Found on a 78 RPM," Shahid identifies himself with Radha, who is the speaker of the whole piece, and laments in her voice as she appeals to her lover and God, Krishna, never to break her heart, never to abandon her, because

> your eyes are my refuge hide me from the world
> dark god Dark Krishna you are all I have
> do not hide yourself merely to break my heart
> . . .
> take my hand place your hands in mine in yours
> I'm yours dark god do not abandon me
> . . .
> dark god you are all you are all I have
> swear only swear I am yours I am yours (VS 266–267)

The absence of all kinds of punctuation marks in Radha's irresistible surge of longing to remain perpetually united with Krishna enables the poet to give vent to his own raw, uncensored emotion for his dead mother in a ceaseless flow.

In section 8, "Srinagar Airport," the speaker has reached Srinagar. As his mother's shrine is brought out of the plane, the people waiting there to receive her are heard weeping *silently*, because they have "never made a holocaust" of their passion. They hold Shahid in their arms, and unable to absorb the unexpected shock, ask him, "*How could this have happened, /*

Bhaiya, how could it?" They carry her on their shoulders to the waiting van. Shahid's mother "rivals God today" in respect of the veneration she receives. People in every street that the van speeds through bid her "farewell" with heavy hearts. Although she is "unable to say goodbye," Shahid visualizes her waving back to them "with such pity" that they melt, because by waving to them, she is "just waving herself goodbye." There is not a single soul who "doesn't owe her tears." And, as the doors of "*her* house" are opened "with her keys," Shahid sees her everywhere. When the poet thinks of starting the ceremony of "FAREWELL" from the "quiet centre" of what was her room, "Outside, a man says, / Soon it will be dark. We must reach the graveyard." Shahid ruminates on the significance of the nonexistence of his mother: "She is / farther than any / god today," because she is absent in her presence as she is no longer alive, and "nearer than any god," because she is present in her absence, because no god can enjoy so much of warmth and love and closeness from his devotees even after death. And the God spoken of in the *Koran* seems to have an utterly insignificant and inconsequential existence for Shahid: "He's farther, farther from us, forever / far." His mother's shrine is lifted, and the women break into the ritual of prayer, the only thing they can offer to the dead woman as a farewell gift to accompany her in her journey away from this world.

Shahid's accusative irreverence to God caused by his overwhelming pain due to the loss of his mother is more articulate in section 9 ("God"), which is written in the form of a *shikwa* (meaning complaint or grievance), where God is described as "only the final assassin," not the savior, but the killer. When the prayers end, and "emptiness" of the grave "waits to take her in," he finds all his laments lost on his lips, and resigns himself "to His every Name," and lets night begin in the name not of God but of his mother, who is thus made to replace and triumph over God in his belief system.

In section 10 ("Ghalib's Ghazal"), the poet remembers Begum Akhtar's song saying that "only a few— / disguised as tulips, as roses— / return from ashes," and bursts out: "Let me weep, let this blood / flow from my eyes. / She is leaving." He does not want to stop weeping because the tears he has shed to mourn the death of his mother have "lit" his eyes and made them into "two candles / for love's darkest spaces," so that he is now able to confront his pain, to dare to search for the end of pain in pain itself:

> Man is numbed to pain
> when he's sorrow-beaten.
> Sorrows, piled up, ease pain.

> Grief crushed me so
> again and again it became
> the pain that pain erases. (VS 271)

The next section, "The Fourth Day," shows that four days have passed after the death of Shahid's mother, which means that the first active period of mourning has ended, but Shahid's mourning continues unabated, although the howl of the mourning seems to have been reduced to a moaning sob now. The poet speaks of those "who have come from shrines after breaking their heads on the / threshold-stones of God," and "have arrived with wings, as burning moths, to put themselves / out" on his mother's grave. Time seems to Shahid to have "so quickly slowed down" in four days, that for him it marks the beginning of "Doomsday." He remembers the time when he "stood weeping in the desert and the sun rose" and visualized "Hussain's blood" streaming the desert sands. Thus historically distant time commingles in Shahid's mind with the present in the recent past of his life, as he sees the people gathering "in the courtyard" with "only Karbala in their hearts," and hears: "Abraham weeps. And God's angels weep . . . And Jesus weeps."

In the last section of "From Amherst to Kashmir," section 12, "By the Waters of the Sind," Shahid turns inward and sounds overtly philosophical. He becomes introspective and probes into the epistemology of mourning over loss and separation: "So what is separation's geography? / Everything is just that mystery, / everything is this roar that deafens." Two months pass after his mother's departure; the pangs of separation in his mind intensify, and he perceives an answer to his own groping:

> So this
> Is separation? Sharpened against
> rocks, the stream, rapid-cutting the night,
> finds its steel a little stained
> with the beginning light,
>
> and the moon must rise now from behind
> that one pine-topped mountain to find
> us without you.

Separation, Shahid implies by forging the images in the lines quoted above, is passing through a state of psychic laceration with time flowing like a knife cutting the silence of the mind's night, its blade sharpened by a clash against rough-edged rocks of memory and stained by the invisible fluid of the tissues of bruised emotion caused by the absence of the loved one while the world of Nature remains pitiless and indifferent. The moon, an elemental entity representing the cosmic world, rises "completely" and "silvers the world / so ruthlessly, shining on / [him] a terror so pearled" that he once again bursts into lamentation:

> *How dare the moon*—I want to cry out,
> Mother—*shine so hauntingly out*
> *here when I've sentenced it to black waves*
> *inside me? Why has it not perished?*
> *How dare it shine on an earth*
> *from which you have vanished?* (VS 278)

Thus, Shahid's mourning becomes a protest, an answerless complaint, against the indifference of the cosmic presences to his personal bereavement.

From the lyric that follows, which is the title poem of *Rooms Are Never Finished*, the poet's lamentation begins to be transmuted into an intellectualized expression of his emotion of loss, so that wailing starts dying down to give way to subdued internalization of his grief. In this poem, the speaker talks to a "rare guest" whom he has invited to visit his house. He welcomes the guest and explains why he was sitting in a room that is kept deliberately dark: because here he can "sigh in peace." He also explains to his guest, who has been to "everywhere" with hardly any city left unvisited, the interior design of his house. When the guest had come to his house earlier, Shahid had led him "through all the spare rooms" he "was to die in." But now "each room's been refurbished," although, he bleakly utters, rooms are places "where one plots only to die." He asks the guest to "come to the window," for he will show him how "panes plot the earth apart," which implicitly reveals his reaction to the man-made division of the earth into plots, houses and rooms that splinter oneness into anti-humanist multiplicities. Memory of some pathetic past incident makes the guest weep, and the speaker consoles him by describing what he has learnt from his own horrific experience: "Out there it's poison." And he shows how dismissive he has grown, after what has happened to Kashmir and after the death of his mother, about the existence of God: "Now that God / is news, what's left but prayer . . . ?" He further shares with his guest his thought that a house "is a work in progress, always." This brings out the literal significance of the title *Rooms Are Never Finished*. A "room" in Italian means "stanza."

So, "rooms" are also synecdochal signifiers for "poems." And Shahid's poetry of mourning is never "finished."[11] Thus, the word "rooms" in the title of the volume may suggest an inner, private space that remains perpetually in the process of being built and perpetually unfinished, because the world is always inadequate. In "By the Waters of the Sind," Shahid had asked, "What is separation's geography?," and the answer to this epistemological question is found buried in the last lines of the title poem of this collection: "My world would be / mere mirrors cut to multiply, then multiply / in. But for small hands. Invisible. Quick" (VS 281). The implication here is that the "invisible" and "quick" hands of the self-aggrandizing, manipulative and scheming politicians have constructed the "geography" of "separation" by raising "thick walls" between races, nation-states and ethnic groups, preventing one human being from multiplying into many through a humanistic identification with all the suffering members of humanity all over the world. These are walls, which, when raised, build "rooms," and when demolished can create a world, undivided and indivisible, holding up before us true, uncontaminated, transnationalist selves in clear "mirrors" of universal humanism. The elliptical, incomplete one-word sentences halting in a way as to show the poet pausing and contemplating and then uttering only one word (deliberately omitting or suppressing the other ones that might be naturally coming to his mind) after each stop (there are four full-stop marks in the last line of the poem) reveal the poet's unwillingness or inability to end the poem and the helplessness that impels him to end it still.

Thus, from the title poem onward, *Rooms Are Never Finished* begins to take on an intellectual and spiritual dimension, which shows how the vision of Shahid, an Eliot scholar, has begun to be objective. His objectivity finds expression in his sense of humor discernible in the very beginning of the poem that follows, "Barcelona Airport." The epigraph to this poem (which is spoken by the hostess of the flight the poet is traveling by) asks the passengers: *"Are you carrying anything that could / be dangerous for the other passengers?"* Shahid mutters his answer to himself: "O just my heart first terrorist." Shahid here deconstructs the word "terrorist" in order to counteract the white, non-Muslim world suffering from Islamophobia (suspecting every Muslim and bearded man as a terrorist), by positing his "heart" as the "first terrorist," as a weapon that "could / be dangerous for the other passengers," because his "heart" is essentially humanist, transnationalist, multiculturalist, anti-separatist, and therefore a veritable ideational threat to the majoritarian world that has empowered itself by promoting the policies of racism, nationalism, parochialism, and the hegemonic dominance of privileged singularity. The spiritual intent of the poem is tangible, when he speaks of his heart being "relit each time it tries to exit / this body for another's in another century," and defines the soul as "its own blood-filled crystal / ruby refuge for a fugitive angel," suggesting thereby that every soul is destined to migrate eternally from one state of exile to another unless and until it attains salvation. But, that Shahid's spiritual vision is evidently postmodern is brought out by his impish couching of his inner-directed contemplation in the language of modern technology (the words like "profile," "exit," "skipped," "track," "delete," "uncut" and "ENTER" are all chosen from the computer vocabulary).

In "A Secular Comedy," Shahid subverts the concepts of the Christian and Islamic religious-mythical paradigms to build up a spiritual world inhabited by an anthropomorphized God, as contradistinguished from a religious world dominated by a punishing or a benevolent Almighty. In the poem's first section, "Heaven," the pervasive sights of fragmentation and destruction—broken windows, "clouds in cobwebs on ceilings," "shredded wings in the corners"—reveal that God "has learned nothing from His / errors," that "God is voiceless, / missing passion. All of His hands lie broken." Shahid dismisses the doubt as to whether this "separation" of Satan from God or of himself from his mother is the state of "death," and entertains another positive, pro-life doubt as to whether this does not necessitate the assertion of the will for "survival." Without his mother, even in heaven he finds himself burdened by an "unfinished pain," as if he is left to carry out an "unfinished business." He finds himself "empty," with "no shadow" to take refuge under, not even the shadow of God, who expelled Satan from His abode out of animosity ("poison") but Himself suffered from "grief" when "he fell through Chaos," and His "mad," "raging" wings "deafened the soundproof / halls of Heaven." When Shahid enquires God about the secret "apart from legend," "He doesn't answer. He lets His Light go / out completely," turning Heaven at once into Hell, and the poet is "left without a / chance of a shadow."

After Shahid leaves the dark Heaven, and comes down to "Earth" (section 2), he feels that God is "pulling down Heaven" over him. The earth he finds himself on is Kashmir, where "Every door awaits a returning lover, / corridors caught gleaming with wounds," and the story of "violence," which no one dares to tell, is "going on and on," where "Grief's the question asked" and "Grief is the answer" (VS 288). From this hellish "Earth," Shahid shifts to "Hell" (section 3) itself. He finds hell a place where "We who lost our lovers on earth are welcome; / all are welcome, mirrored among the angels

/ lonely with pity." The speaker's feeling of pity is aroused "for love's first story": the story of love between God and Satan, and for God who is "so lonely," bereft of love, estranged that he is from his lover, Satan / Iblis, whom He has himself banished from Heaven, but who like a faithful lover, keeps on guarding "God's secrets," without bothering whether his act would be called "perverse." Satan then takes a short break to drink the wine that he had hidden under his wings just before he was hurled "through exits," because this wine will remind him of the "passion" of his "Beloved Tyrant."

Toward the later phase of his mourning for the death of his mother, Shahid extends his self and identifies himself with the baby elephant (wailing for its mother), Zainab (mourning the death of her brother), with Satan (pining for the loss of the company of his beloved God), with Magdalene, Jesus's wife, and Virgin Mary, His mother (lamenting the killing of Jesus, her son), and thus elevates his act of mourning to the level of "epic griefs." The next poem ("The Nature of Temporal Order") enacts the scene of the crucifixion of Jesus, His head crowned with thorns. On seeing "their one God nailed to / Life" and "His slow torment," Mary Magdalene and Virgin Mary, unable to bear the traumatizing sight, "vanish" from the scene "unseen" and two "ruthless" sentries take their place, "stand at the Cross's foot, as / if they guard the gates of the Viceroy's mansion." The scene implies that "even God" with "His sacred / blood" is subjected to the tyranny of philistine and brutal political power, so that "the king of kings" becomes "Caesar's captive." This extension of his suffering self enables the poet to confront and accept his mother's demise, as in the first "Ghazal" of the volume, the poem that follows, he says, "I felt my heart growing so old in real time," and also realizes that his mother's "heart must be ash where her body lies burned," and, in the second and last "Ghazal" of this collection, he contemplates total surrender, and welcomes even absolute extinction of his own self to present it as a gift to his enemy: "If my enemy's alone and his arms are empty, / give him my heart silk-wrapped like a child by exiles" (VS 298). In the next poem ("The Purse-Seiner Atlantis"), Shahid still desires to be filled with longing, "with the longing to long," but now he is longing "to be / flame, and moth, and ash," that is, to be the cause, the object and the consequence of destruction, all at once, which is the other way to express a longing for absolute self-effacement. This helps him attain a state of relative calm, so that he no longer mourns the loss of his mother alone but also for all sufferers in all the "lost continents," for all exiles who have experienced loss, rootlessness, uncertainty, estrangement from their loved ones and separation from their home, and have been inconsolably shattered.

This identification of the poet with the suffering souls in all the countries of the contemporary world, in History, Myths and Legends, and with the suffering creatures even in the subhuman world effects a dissipation and diffusion of his own pain, so that the trauma caused by the death of his mother and the infernalization of his motherland now enables him to sublimate his personal sorrow through empathic act of feeling the pity underlying the more painful losses. In "Eleven Stars Over Andalusia" (which is Shahid's adaptation and translation of the Palestinian poet Mahmoud Darwish's "Quasida" or "Mouwashah" about the expulsion of the Moors from fifteenth-century Spain), the poet plumbs the depth of the agony of an Arab exiled from Andalusia, a region in Southern Spain. Andalusia was a place inhabited by adherents of many different religions and ethnicities—Arabians, Muslims, Berbers, Christians, Jews, Gypsies—interacting with one another, and upholding thereby a rich humanistic heritage of a multicultural, pluralistic, tolerant and peaceful coexistence. But with the passage of time they began to be disintegrated by internal conflicts and civil wars. Initially, the Moors invaded Spain, and exiled the native Spanish. Eight centuries later, the Christians became united, and began the Granada war, wherein Granada was defeated and annexed to Spain, putting an end to the Muslim control. The Christians forced the Jews and the Muslims either to be converted to Christianity or to be exiled, or else to become their slaves. Even the descendants of the converts were expelled. Shahid's choice of including this moving piece of elegy in *Rooms Are Never Finished* clearly brings out his anti-separatist worldview, and the eleven pearl-like lyrics of lamentation that twinkle, like stars, in the sky of loneliness and isolation caused by distance and banishment, express the loss of a glorious and exemplary human civilization, a loss the contemplation on which leads the poet to a state of melancholy, languish, and fatalism. The very title of this Mouwashah contains an allusion to the *Quran*, which betrays a sense of mutual hostility between nations, races, and ethnic groups, the members of which should look upon one another just as brothers, because they all belong to only one race, the race of mankind.

The speaker of the first elegiac lyric, "On our last evening on this land," as already mentioned, is an Arabian Muslim exiled from his native land Granada, from Andalusia, and throughout the eleven verses that constitute "Eleven Stars Over Andalusia,"[12] Shahid empathically depicts the plight of this representative individual, and through his identification with this hapless exile, the poet gives vent to his own anguish, his lamentation now assuming a deeper philosophical and universal significance in the perspectives of exile and memory. The speaker remembers their "last evening" in their homeland, when they looked "closely at the mountains besieging the clouds: a conquest . . . and a counter-conquest, / and an old time handing this new time the key to" the doors of houses that once were theirs. Caught in a diaspora, he asks the conquerors, who have pushed him to "the margins" of their history, to "Enter them" so that they themselves "may exit completely" in search of their lost history in a distant land where they will be strangers. In the second verse, "How can I write above the clouds?," the speaker laments his state of being exiled, of being abandoned by his own people, who have engaged themselves in a game of destroying what their ancestors had built and building their own "tent" on its ruins. In the third part of the elegy, "There is a sky beyond the sky for me," exile is placed in a wider cosmic and spiritual perspective and is depicted as a universal, inevitable state of all human beings, as the speaker says: "I am Adam of the two Edens, I who lost / paradise twice" (VS 303). Thus, in the banished, diasporic individual's perception, the concept of exile transcends the immediate geopolitical barriers of history and reaches the eternal history of myth and archetype.

Describing himself as "the last gasp of an Arab," the speaker, in the lyrics that follow, laments on the loss of his identity in a profoundly spiritual-philosophical vein. In the fourth verse ("I am one of the kings of the end"), for example, he mourns: "there is no land in this land / since time broke around me, shard by shard." An exile from time immemorial, he bids his own historicized, logocentric existence adieu: "Farewell to our history!" In the fifth lyric ("One day I will sit on the pavement"), the speaker asserts how as an exile he can communicate with all exiles of recorded human history: "Five hundred years have passed" (after the armed Muslim revolt was crushed by the Christian "Reconquista"), "but our breakup wasn't final, / and the messages between us never stopped." He says in the sixth verse ("Truth has two faces and the snow is black") that despite the flux of history, "Everything is fixed for us," because every war fought in the battleground of history is only an "unending conclusion." The speaker imagines himself to be an eternal exile, destined forever to lose his original (?) identity, as he begins the seventh verse ("Who am I after the night of the estranged?") by questioning his identity after he is separated from his race, and visualizes himself as destined to travel without any destination: "Where is the road to anything?" The eighth verse ("O water, be a string to my guitar") lends a more intense and more poignant urgency to his desire to lose his Andalusian / Granadian Muslim identity, and seeks to drown his search for self in the tide of a greater cosmic consciousness of existence of the elemental world, the only relatively permanent entity. Since time does not let him salvage his past from a moment (of the victory of the enemy conquerors) that has led him to this state of exile, he will never know "In which Andalusia do I end? Here / or there?" Since, by implication, every part of this world is an Andalusia eternally caught in the process of being built and ruined and re-built—a place where old conquerors will be conquered and exiled by the new conquerors who will with the passage of time be old as rulers—he realizes that "Nothing remains but my guitar," the instrument of non-verbal, and non-logocentric medium of communication with self and the others, and, therefore, he appeals to water, the symbol of flux, fluidity and evanescence: "Then be to my guitar a string."

In the ninth verse ("In the exodus I love you more"), the speaker turns inward, becomes less philosophical, more personal, and yet psychologically stronger in his mourning. "In the exodus," he says, he loves his homeland more. Now that there is "no / road anywhere for my journey," he finds everything in and around him—the palm trees, the hills, the streets, the earth, words, stories—"weightless," and, he mourns, "My heart alone is heavy . . . / barking, howling for a golden time." It is from his pain and suffering that he attains a spiritual enlightenment, as he realizes that "In departure / we become only the birds' equals." He attains, in other words, the wisdom that freedom (symbolized by the birds) can be attained only in migration, in exile, in departure, and not in attachment. This leads him to assert unequivocally: "nothing hurts me after this departure." After this realization, the speaker, in the tenth verse, yearns for "only the beginning" of the end, because that is enough to start a journey afresh, and the end being uncertain yet inevitable—only the form may vary—he no longer longs for a whole world of space to let his love flourish: "A little land will suffice for us to meet, a little land will be enough for peace." In the last, eleventh, lyric ("Violins") of "Eleven Stars Over Andalusia," the exiled Granadian Arab stops his own mourning, and hears instead "Violins weep for Arabs leaving Andalusia / Violins weep for a time that does not return / Violins weep for a homeland that might return" (VS 311).

Shahid's identification with characters lamenting their loss, separation and exile, with their suffering aggravated by memory—cutting across the boundaries of space and time, the barriers of geography and politics, the vast and ever-wakeful knowledge of which has molded his sensibility right from the beginning of its growth—and even with the subhuman creatures and elemental presences wailing in their own plight, effects a dissipation of his own pain through sharing, and brings about a cathartic effect. It enables him to attain some "calm of mind" after his "passions" are assuaged to a large extent, though not "spent," and to adopt an intellectually negotiated stance of objectivity to his own sorrow, to "salve" his dirge. This explains why in the last poem of *Rooms Are Never Finished*, entitled "I Dream I Am at the Ghat of the Only World," his earlier excruciatingly painful, elegiac tone turns into a sublimated, visionary narrative of an imagined voyage, and a poised and sobered discourse on the limitations, mysteries and significance of life in this world, "the only world" he believes he has all to inhabit, however troubled that world may be. Shahid begins this poem by reminiscing "A Night of Ghazals" coming to an end and his feeling after the departure of the singer (Begum Akhtar) that he has once "again lost everyone." Then with the memory of James Merrill, Eqbal Ahmed, and of his deceased mother seething in his mind, he steps onto a boat waiting for him. The oarsman, whom the poet knows he knows not "from which time," tells him: *"Don't you know me? You were a mere boy. For no money / I—I was a young man then—I always rowed you across / the Jhelum . . ."* (VS 313). When he seems to hear the voice of James Merrill, and asks the oarsman, "Whose voice was that . . . ?," he is told that it is the voice of *"One who forsook you by dying, the way you forsook / me, and so many, by not dying."* The poet finds, from the rower, the book left for him by Merrill and clutches it in fear that it will disappear, and reads something written in "austere black": "Before his untimely death, James Merrill / requested that a copy of A SCATTERING OF SALTS, / now his last book,[13] be sent to you with his compliments" (VS 314). The speaker wonders whether Gula, an affectionate name for Ghulam Mohommad (the "SLAVE OF THE PROPHET"), who is now rowing his boat "Upstream," will take him to his mother waiting to meet him on the other shore of the river of life. The boatman promises to take Shahid to the shrine of his mother. But when Shahid steps off the boat, he finds not a shrine but "a house, the one in Amherst, the one / where my mother fought death." Shahid dreams that "Eqbal Ahmad / opens the door," embraces him, and says, "There's only news of blood / out there in Kashmir." Eqbal Ahmad talks to Shahid affectionately:

Shahid, when you smile,

it seems your mother has returned to life. We all know
how you—you all—miss her.

. . .
for even here a voyager,
I always move in my heart between sad countries.
But let it not end" IT WON'T "this grief for your mother.

She is on the shrine-island where the Kashmiris,
from martyred voices, salve their every dirge, sublime
till the end. (VS 317–318)

Meanwhile, Gula, the boatman, comes back, and informs him: "*We have time / left for only one destination.*" Gula then rows Shahid to "the saint's grave," where he sits on his knees before his mother, who ties around his wrist "the saint's thread" as a talisman, and prays: "May this always keep you safe from the flames of Hell." Darkness sets in, and "curtains descend / on all sides of the boat." Time for bidding farewell to his mother arrives even in his dream, and he cries: "Mother, will I lose you again, and in this, / the only world left?" (VS 320). Shahid visualizes his mother entering the boat, leaving him alone on the awakened, disconcerted shore of the river of life. He runs out in the rain, and laments again, for the last time and evidently with a tone of resigned acceptance and endurance: "Will I wait here, alone, by this ebony abyss, / abandoned by you, alone?" His mother departs, but before she leaves, she does not forget to utter her prayerful wish for her son with the words universally said by all mothers when they bid farewell to their sons: "Son, live long, I've died to wait for you all your life. / So you won't weep night and day for me, or the slain, / I will tighten this thread" (VS 320). Gula, the oarsman, leaves Shahid by saying: "*This is farewell I have rowed you this is farewell.*" The absence of punctuation marks in Gula's last few words indicates not only that this journey of the poet was merely a dream but also that this journey is endless, as Gula himself so succinctly had said with a proverbial-philosophical profundity a little earlier: "*To be rowed forever is the last afterlife.*" Shahid's dream breaks to hurl him back into reality, and he realizes: "He is Death . . . His is the moving finger . . ." His mother's "boat enters fog," and soon it disappears from Shahid's sight, and he hears the affectionate but authoritative voice of James Merrill: "WEEPING? YOU MUST NOT." He asks Merrill, "Which world will bring her / back, or will he who wears his heart on his sleeve eaves- / drop always, in his inmost depths, on a cruel harbinger?" (VS 321). And the poem ends, and so does the volume, with Merrill's words uttered in a tone, which is as reverberating as the sea, as grave as the mountain, as profound as the apothegmatic asseveration of a sage, and as "cruel" as Truth: "SHAHID, HUSH. THIS IS ME, JAMES. THE LOVED ONE / ALWAYS LEAVES" (VS 321).

To sum up, *Rooms Are Never Finished* begins with the poet mourning with a heart laden with an overwhelming sense of personal loss and separation. But, gradually, as the volume progresses, Agha Shahid Ali, a disciplined Eliot scholar, invokes the entire "Tradition" of mourning in human history in order to blend his "Individual" suffering with it, and thus "depersonalizes" his own pain through a process of diffusion, by multiplying and extending his self, and by merging it with the self of all the suffering members of the human, subhuman, and the nonhuman world. Shahid himself said to Christine Benvenuto, "When you're dealing with a painful subject matter . . . I would say definitely you need . . . a formal distancing device because otherwise you might end up sounding simply hysterical."[14] He justifies his point by citing the example of Sylvia Plath: "Even someone like Sylvia Plath . . . is on the verge sometimes of [saying] something that may sound like hysteria. . . . but everything is so finely tuned. Like it's on the edge, but there is also distance being maintained by that."[15]

Shahid's lamentation for the death of his mother merges with the baby elephant's dumb pain for its mother that died at Pir Panjal Range, with the wail of the wounded gazelle, with the weeping of Zainab for her brother Hussain martyred in Karbala, with Begum Akhtar's doleful rendering of Ghalib's ghazals, with the suffering of Radha estranged from her "dark-blue God" Krishna, with the anguish of Satan or Iblis when he is separated from his "Beloved Tyrant," with the prolonged lamentation of the homeless Arab Muslim exiled from his homeland, with the deeply rueful and agonized voice of Eqbal Ahmad mourning for Kashmir and the Kashmiris, with the placid but melancholy voice of Ghulam Mohommad asking Shahid to weep at the time of bidding farewell to his mother in his dream, with the weeping violins, and the strings of his guitar plaintively melting in pain, with the grief-stricken, solemn silence of the stars that are "shredded" and of the "oceans, continents, deserts, cities" suffocating under the burden of the pile of Doomsdays. This is how Shahid impersonalizes his own grief and transcends the heaviness of his personal mourning, so that it goes past the narrow limit of self-obsessed and self-centered insularity to assume a universal and cosmic dimension. The poet has indeed "made a holocaust" of his passion of sorrow to register his complaint against the universe—the human, subhuman, nonhuman, and the elemental presences all marching in a procession behind him—that forces him to live without his mother.

To put it in other words, Shahid mourns his personal loss by universalizing it with the sensibility and consciousness of one of the greatest humanists.

But, although Shahid articulates his grief in his epical elegy *Rooms Are Never Finished* in an evidently humanistic vein, it is covertly tempered by his postmodern sensibility and his multicultural, transnationalist consciousness. This is borne out by a number of features and devices that have unobtrusively gone into the making of this collection. For example, most of the poems individually, and the collection as a whole, are "polyphonic,"[16] with a multitude of characters mourning their loss and suffering. We hear the voices of mythical and historical characters—like Zainab, Satan, Gabriel, Jesus, Mohammed, Buddha, Radha—interspersed and commingled with the voices of the Muezzin's "Call to Prayer," of the ghazals of Ghalib, with the poetry of Faiz Ahmed Faiz, the melodious voice of Begum Akhtar, the anguished wailing of the exiled Granadian, the guiding voice of Ghulam Mohommad, the voice of the poet's mother permeating the volume from the beginning to the end, and the voice of James Merrill, Shahid's predecessor in American poetry, who had exerted an indelibly significant and formative impact on the younger poet.[17] These human voices blend with the cry of the dying elephants and of the wounded gazelle, and are attuned with the poignant music of the guitars and the violins. The harmony of these voices produces an effect of congregated mourning for all losses, separations, exiles, and sufferings that human civilization has experienced due to social, religious, cultural, economic, and political conflicts that have very often shaken the foundation of humanity. The ventriloquistic use of this multiplicity of voices indicates Shahid's new-historicist approach of utilizing the textuality of not only histories but also of mythologies, and underscoring the historicity of the texts like *the Quran* and *the Bible*. All this—in combination with his inverted (de)construction of the story of God and Satan, which for him is the "first story" of love, presented in a mythological parallelism on almost the same plane as the love story between Krishna and Radha—enables the poet to design a complex matrix of loss, lamentation, exile, and memory, to give vent to a "collective grief."[18]

The postmodern aspect of Shahid's mourning is also discernible in his pervasively paradoxical phrasing that points to semantic or conceptual contradictions, which are related to his consciousness of the post-structuralist theory of deconstruction. The most glaring example of this is the expression of Shahid's feeling that his mother who is dead may be "somewhere alive," which implies the deconstructivist idea of "trace," the concept that absence includes the sense of presence. It is also noticeable in Shahid's assertion that his mother is present in his poetry, "even in lines in which [she] can't be found." It is further perceptible in Shahid's ambivalent articulation of the state of his deceased mother: "She is farther than any / god today and nearer than any god." These ideational paradoxicalities are quite in tune with the basic premise of the theory of deconstruction which, to quote Terry Eagleton, "detect[s] in each sign . . . traces of the other words which it has excluded in order to be itself,"[19] and claims that "one term of an antithesis secretly inheres within the other," and that "what is outside is also somehow inside, what is alien also intimate,"[20] which is to say that contrariety subsumes complementarity.

The postmodernist dimension of Shahid's mourning can also be perceived in his transnationalist wish that all "seas and continents"—with reference to which only "the shadow lines"[21] are drawn for anti-humanist partition—be "erased from every map," as the speaker in "The Purse-Seiner Atlantis" asserts. Shahid's worldview as expressed here echoes Amitav Ghosh's. In an interview with John C. Hawley, Amitav Ghosh, like Agha Shahid Ali, contends: ". . . lines are drawn in order to manipulate our ways of thought: that is why they must be disregarded" (Hawley 9).[22] Shahid's postmodernist sensibility is further perceptible in his longing for a complete erasure of identity through obliteration of names ("Who will tear our names from our identity?," as the exiled Granadain in the sixth lyric of "Eleven Stars Over Andalusia" asks), because names are only illusory, logocentric determinants of a person's race, sex, nationality, religion, ethnicity, communitarian allegiance, historical background, geographical roots—all of which merely serve as tools in the hands of the separatist forces, who form the powerful majority, to conveniently construct for a minority individual his or her identity, an abstract, polemical idea that prepares the ground for any measure of violence that can be perpetrated on him or her. The whole world has been witnessing this for centuries in places like Bosnia, Chechnya, Sarajevo, Armania, Palestine, Granada, Chile, Deir Yassein, Sabra-Shatila, and Kashmir. Amartya Sen insightfully illustrates this concept in his discourse on the relation between identity and violence.[23] The Caribbean poet Derek Walcott in his poem "A Far Cry from Africa" condemns the violence of man on man in a tone of scathing satire and biting irony, when he says: "The violence of beast on beast is read / As natural law, but upright man / Seeks his divinity by inflicting pain."[24] Closely related to this is Shahid's equally postmodernist angst about the concept of the self, and his wish to obliterate it from his mind, as put in the mouth of the wailing Arab in the seventh lyric of "Eleven Stars Over Andalusia": "Through others I once walked toward myself, and here I am, / losing that self, those others."[25]

Again, it is Shahid's postmodern consciousness that impels him to refuse to believe in the existence of any absolutist, essentialist notion of Truth or any originary idea of the Real. When, for example, he writes in the second ghazal of the collection, "Even things that are true can be proved," his reflection implies the provisionality of Truth. The poet's perception of the nonoriginary concept of Real is also proved by the exiled Granadian's question: "Was Andalusia here or there? On the land . . . or in the poem?" This question points to the unspecificity and uncertainty about the geographical location of the place called Andalusia, or, for that matter, any place in the world, because one can never be certain as to whether it is prehistorically located in some unalterably specified area of land or whether it is a geopolitical or linguistic-literary construct, and can, therefore, be perpetually altered or deconstructed. Again, when, for instance, the banished Arab Muslim in the seventh lyric of "Eleven Stars Over Andalusia" invokes "Death" as "a blessing on the stranger who sees the unseen more clearly than / a reality that is no longer real" (VS 307), his perception, enunciated in a memorably paradoxical language, undermines the notion of the Real and clearly reminds one of Baudrillard's theory of "simulacra" and of the "hyperreal."[26]

The postmodern texture of Shahid's mourning is further brought out by another related notion of his ontological perception of the permanence of evanescence ("Nothing lasts"), of the absence of any unalterably and indestructibly built up presence ("there is no land in this land"), of the certainty of uncertainty ("on which unknown future—or past—does all depend?"), and of the nowhereness of the voyage of life which has no destination ("Where is the road to anything?") But, the postmodern condition of Shahid's lamentation in *Rooms Are Never Finished* is most conspicuously discernible in his belief in the impossibility of transcending the bounds of logocentricism ("How can I write my people's testament above the clouds . . . ?"), which stems from his conviction that "the sky is empty," and the unknown is unknowable. His predicament, however, is that he cannot derive any solace from the logocentric world, which is testified by his inability to cling on even to the apparently most reliable of the logoses—namely, God. He refuses to believe in the existence of God (the god of elephants cannot save His creatures from the brutality of Mihiragula). "God is missed in his ruined temples" and what the poet sees are only "the sky-sized posters of God." "God is voiceless," and is a "missing passion." In the incomplete prayer of the mourners in the eighth verse of "From Amherst to Kashmir"—"There is no god but"—the poet deliberately omits the last word that completes the prayer in *The Koran*, perhaps because he believes that it is useless, and only an ineffectual and unreal logocentric construct meant to serve as the last futile refuge of the helpless. Nor can Shahid ultimately derive any consolation after the death of his mother by clinging on to the logos of the existence of afterlife. He had once said to Amitav Ghosh, "I love to think that I'll meet my mother in the after-life, if there is an after-life" (Imam, 360–361). But, his uncompromising refusal to deceive himself as an intellectual would never allow him to forget that this world is "the *only* world." Thus, Shahid can neither believe in the existence of afterlife, nor can he accept the death of his mother. This explains why the final poem as well as the entire volume is characterized by the expression of a postmodern mental state of aporia and liminality or in-betweenness. *Rooms Are Never Finished* is a collage of elegies that constitute a monumental dirge as a whole, but Shahid reverses the form of elegy by refusing to locate any source of comfort or consolation at the end which marks all traditional elegies. This is because Shahid himself knows that his grief is unbearable and yet inconsolable. This irreconcilable plight of the poet urges him to restlessly and deliriously straddle and experiment with various poetic forms—canzone, prose poem, terza rima, sapphic, ghazal, sestina, quasida, marsiya, shikwa—in order to explore the most effective medium through which he can give vent to his sorrow. That is why all the small requiems in the collection, especially the concluding one, end in "unending conclusions." As Schneiderman perciepiently observes:

> At the end . . . Merrill delivers comfort in the form of the universality of suffering. Shahid should quiet his tears not because his loss serves a celestial plan or because his mother will soon be returned to the earth but because loss is the foundational condition of life. (102)

Poetry, and especially the poetry of mourning, can never be finished; it is, as in Shahid's case, only abandoned. Shahid's lamentation is only "HUSH[ED]" by Merrill, who himself knows that Shahid's mourning for his mother and his motherland, his grief for the loss of love and beauty, will never come to an end. When Eqbal Ahmad, who always moved in his heart "between sad countries," wishes that the story of his own lifelong struggle and sorrow should not end Shahid's grief for loss or estrangement, for the state of exile thrust upon the minority by the majority, we hear Merrill's voice of wisdom: "IT WON'T." In fact, Shahid is enmeshed in the grip of "an ultimate shaking grief," so that now he "senses first responsibility / In a world of possessions" and "He is learning . . . / The epistemology of loss."[27] At this point, the readers can be pertinently reminded of Faust's observation quoted in the first epigraph of this article: "what you never lose, you must forever mourn." In fact, Shahid has lost his mother only clinically or empirically, but psychologically he has never been able to reconcile to her loss, and, therefore, his mourning for her loss will never end. Long after "I Dream I Am at the Ghat of the Only World" comes to an end, Shahid's weeping keeps resonating in the mind of the readers who can almost hear him silently mourn, like Margarete, Faust's beloved, wailing for her dead mother: "She won't beckon or nod, her head is too sore, / She has slept so long, she'll awake no more" (Goethe, 132). And Shahid recalls the philosophical articulation of the boatman Ghulam Mohommad who says: "*To be rowed forever is the last afterlife.*"[28] Gula's words suggest that drifting in a stream of fluidity is the only state that one has to firmly embrace, that to be in a state of continuous exile is the cruelest condition of life that one has to negotiate. It is true that the knowledge that Shahid—who is culturally indoctrinated ever since his entrance into the Lacanian Symbolic Order of reality which marks the beginning of his consciousness—allows Ghulam Mohommad and James Merrill to instill in him will not leave him with any sense of consolatory ease. But, fortified with this knowledge and strengthened by an intellectual courage, he can perceive that from this point his delusory "journey's end will begin" to goad him on to the start of another journey, "to be rowed again,"[29] to move from one state of exile to another, to drift without the dream of anchoring, because there is nowhere to anchor in. Thus, *Rooms Are Never Finished* appeals to the readers as a kind of unending musical mourning and heart-rending lamentation with which even the elemental presences like air, water, and earth empathize. It is a muffled wail that disrupts the apparent poise of the universe, a cry that moves and shakes even the stars, the moon, the sky, and the planets, and thus becomes a unique and unforgettable specimen of what can be described as a cosmic elegy that teaches the world how to mourn and how not to.

Notes

1. Johann Wolfgang von Goethe, *Faust: A Tragedy*, 2nd ed. Trans. Walter Arndt & Cyrus Hamlin. New York: Norton, 2001.

2. Sigmund Freud, "Mourning and Melancholia." *The Complete Psychological Works of Sigmund Freud, Vol. XIV* (London: The Hogarth Press and the Institute of Psychoanalysis, 1917).

3. "Howl" is the title of one of Allen Ginsberg's most popular poems. Shahid was deeply influenced by the poetry of Ginsberg. While Ginsberg's poem, written in four parts in 1955, is a vociferous and angry lamentation of the situation in which he sees "the best minds of [his] generation destroyed" in post–World War II America, Shahid's poems in *The Country without a Post Office* and *Rooms Are Never Finished* lament the annihilation of lives and despoliation of beauties in Kashmir and in the other parts of the globe torn asunder by ethnic conflicts toward the end of the twentieth century. Both Ginsberg and Agha Shahid Ali protest the governmental violence and oppression, though in two different contexts. Only, while Ginsberg's protest is loud, noisy, and uncensored, Shahid's is poetically so controlled and so delicately internalized and muted by self-censorship that it assumes the form of an aesthetically restrained mourning. Allen Ginsberg, *Collected Poems: 1947–1980* (New York: Harper & Row, 1984), 126–134.

4. All quotations from poems in *The Country without a Post Office* are taken from Agha Shahid Ali, *The Country without a Post Office* (New Delhi: Ravi Dayal Publisher and Penguin Books, 2013).

5. See Claire Chambers, "The Last Saffron: Agha Shahid Ali's Kashmir," Contemporary World Literature 7 (May/June 2011), *Literary Non Fiction*, http://contemporaryworldliterature.com/blog/essays

6. Hopkins's sonnet begins thus: "I wake and feel the fell of dark, not day." And Shahid's expression echoes Hopkins's lines from this sonnet: "And my lament / Is cries countless, cries like dead letters sent / To dearest him that lives alas! away." Francis Turner Palgrave, *The Golden Treasury* (Oxford: Oxford University Press, 1964), 396. In fact, Shahid quotes the last one and a half of these lines to provide an epigraph to the title poem of his volume *The Country without a Post Office*. op. cit. 40.

7. Saroja Sundararajan, *Kashmir Crisis: Unholy Anglo-Pak Nexus* (Delhi: Kalpaz Publications, 2010), 30.

8. "Lapidation" in English and "Rajam" in Arabic is one of the most gruesome and barbaric laws of the Christian as well as Arabic/Islamic civilization in which the person judged guilty is killed by stoning.

9. "Kaddish" is an ancient Jewish prayer in Aramaic recited in several forms in the daily ritual of services at the Synagogue, and when mourning the death of a close relative, and "Specif" is a mourner's prayer recited daily at public services during the first eleven months after the death of a parent or other close relative and on subsequent anniversaries of the death. Ginsberg, *Collected Poems*, 209–224.

10. The sound of wailing of the wounded gazelle (a lamb-like animal that is Shahid's Blakean symbol of meekness, humility, tenderness, beauty, and innocence) is heard throughout *Rooms Are Never Finished*. "The cry of a gazelle when it is cornered and foresees its death [contains] something akin to witnessing fear, knowledge, regret, and grief, and then, certainly, love for the vanishing world." Amy Newman, "'Separation's Geography': Agha Shahid Ali's Scholarship of Evanescence," *Mad Heart Be Brave: Essays on the Poetry of Agha Shahid Ali*, ed. Kazim Ali (Ann Arbor: University of Michigan Press, 2017), 73.

11. This reminds one of the French poet Paul Valery's idea of poetry: "A poem is never finished; it's always an accident that puts a stop to it . . ." W. H. Auden, while answering a question in an interview at Swarthmore College, paraphrased Valery's idea thus: "I agree very much with Paul Valery, who said: 'A poem is never finished; it's only abandoned.'" "An hour of questions and answers with Auden, Part two: What a poet can do, political poetry, favorite (and 'unfavorite') poems, corrections and collaborations," November15, 1971. www.swarthmore.edu/library/auden/QandApt2.html

Auden's paraphrase of Valery's words is also quoted in Sedgwick Fred, *Read My Mind: Young Children, Poetry and Learning* (London & New York: Routledge, 1997), 62. Paul Valery's idea to which Auden agrees applies all the more to the poetry of mourning, which can never be finished but can only die down when the flow of the emotion of sorrow tends to dry up in the dreary desert sands of repetitive, unending, and inexhaustible elegiac expression. This chapter will revert back to this point as it draws to a close.

12. The phrase "Eleven Stars" in the title alludes to the story of Prophet Joseph's/Yusuf's dream in which he saw eleven stars and the sun and the moon prostrate themselves before him in obeisance. When Joseph shared his dream with his father, he was warned not to say anything about the dream to his brothers, because, his father feared, they might plot evil against him. This allusion thus points to the stark, brazen reality of fraternal antagonism and forebodes fratricide.

13. Merrill's last book, *A Scattering of Salts* deals with the themes of lost love, memory, passing of time, immortality, endless process of reincarnation of souls, and the ability of the living to communicate with the dead.

14. "An Interview with Agha Shahid Ali." Interview by Christine Benvenuto, *Massachusetts Review*, 43, no. 2: 261–268 (2002), 266.

15. Ibid., 266.

16. The term is associated with the theories of Mikhail Bakhtin. But here it is used to mean "multi-voiced," a plurality of independent voices expressing their feelings, illuminated by a single poetic or authorial consciousness so as to weave a universal pattern and matrix of lamentation that leads the readers into an exploration of the epistemology of mourning.

17. The poetic friendship of Agha Shahid Ali and James Merrill as well as the latter's aesthetic impact on the former is too well known to need to be established with elaborate references. Yet, a few comments on this point may be worth noting. Jason Schneiderman, for example, observes, "Merrill's influence on Ali was profound." Jason Schneiderman, "The Loved One Always Leaves: The Poetic Friendship of Agha Shahid Ali and James Merrill," *Mad Heart Be Brave: Essays on the Poetry of Agha Shahid Ali,* ed. Kazim Ali (Ann Arbor: University of Michigan Press, 2017),100. Amitav Ghosh, a friend and ardent admirer of Shahid, who "Knew" the poet's work "long before [he]met him," remarks that Merrill had "radically alter[ed] the direction of his poetry." Amitav Ghosh, "'The Ghat of the

Only World': Agha Shahid Ali in Brooklyn," *The Imam and the Indian* (New Delhi: Ravi Dayal Publisher, 2002) 341, 345.

18. Amitav Ghosh, *The Shadow Lines* (New Delhi: Ravi Dayal Publisher, 1998), 225.

19. Terry Eagleton, *Literary Theory: An Introduction* (Oxford: Basil Blackwell, 1983), 128.

20. Ibid., 133.

21. This phrase, which has become famous after the publication of Amitav Ghosh's novel on partition and diaspora, exposes the anti-humanist hollowness and absurdity of all logocentric, divisionistic markers, as they have been described by the narrator in Ghosh's book thus: "They had drawn their borders, believing in that pattern, in the enchantment of lines, hoping perhaps that once they had etched their borders upon the map, the two bits of land would sail away from each other like the shifting tectonic plates of the prehistoric Gondwanaland" (op. cit. 233). A little later in the novel, the narrator registers his complaining and angry frustration about the ludicrous futility of the lines of partition thus: ". . . why don't they draw thousands of little lines through the whole subcontinent and give every little place a new name? What would it change? It's a mirage; the whole thing is a mirage" (op. cit. 247).

22. See John C. Hawley, *Amitav Ghosh: An Introduction*; Contemporary Indian Writers in English (New Delhi: Cambridge University Press, 2008).

23. The crux of Amartya Sen's thesis is that "Our shared humanity gets savagely challenged when the manifold divisions in the world are unified into one allegedly dominant system of classification—in terms of religion, or community, or culture, or nation, or civilization . . ." Amartya Sen. *Identity and Violence: The Illusion of Destiny* (London: Penguin Books, 2006), xiii. Sen exposes "the illusion of a singular identity that others must attribute to the person to be demeaned" for "the purpose of denigration (along with descriptive distortions of the ascribed identity)." Ibid., 8. "Violence," according to Sen, "is promoted by the cultivation of a sense of inevitability about some allegedly unique—often belligerent—identity that we are supposed to have and which apparently makes extensive demands on us. . . . The imposition of an allegedly unique identity is often a crucial component of the 'martial art' of fomenting sectarian confrontation." Ibid., xiii. It is this belligerent labeling of an identitarian tag by the majority to a minority individual or community or ethnic group or race or nation which ruins the sense of "the shared membership of the human race." Ibid., 3. "The prospects of peace in the contemporary world," Sen prophetically asserts, "may well lie in the recognition of the plurality of our affiliations and in the use of reasoning as common inhabitants of a wide world, rather than making us into inmates rigidly incarcerated in little containers." Ibid., xvii.

24. In this poem Walcott also gives vent to his sense of psychic impasse issuing out of an inner conflict between the innate pull of his loyalty to his historical and

racial identity (African background) and the irresistible counter-pull of his allegiance to his cultural identity:

> Where shall I turn, divided to the vein?
> I who have cursed
> The drunken officer of British rule, how choose
> Between this Africa and the English tongue I love?
> Betray them both, or give back what they give?
> How can I face such slaughter and be cool?
> How can I turn from Africa and live?

Ajanta Dutt, Ed. *Neruda, Walcott and Atwood: Poets of the Americas* (Delhi: Worldview Publications, 2002), 104–105.

25. The Structuralist view of the "Self" or the subject is that it is primary, integrated, unified, autonomous, and homogeneous. For Post-Structuralism, the "Self" is secondary, fragmentary, volatile, standing in its own shadow, and constructed by language and all sorts of racial, economic, political, and cultural ideologies. The postmodern view of the Self is that it is the "SITE rather than CENTRE or PRESENCE, is where things happen, or that to which things happen, rather than that which makes things happen: extra-individual forces use the subject [or the self] to exert their sway, the subject does not use them (although it thinks that it does . . .)" Jeremy Hawthorn, *A Glossary of Contemporary Literary Theory*, 4th ed. (London: Arnold, 2000), 347.

26. "Simulacra" is the plural form of "simulacrum," which refers to "the copy without an original," and the world of "hyperreality," a notion that Baudrillard shares with Umberto Eco, is a world in which "imitations or 'fakes' take precedence over and usurp the real." Raman Selden, Peter Widdowson, Peter Brooker, *A Reader's Guide to Contemporary Literary Theory*, 5th ed. (New Delhi: Pearson Education, 2006), 211.

27. John Berryman, "The Ball Poem," *The New Poetry* (Harmondsworth: Penguin Books, 1962), 36.

28. This testifies to Shahid's gesture of incorporating in the volume of his mourning not only the "Grand Narratives" or "metanarratives" or "supernarratives" but also the micronarratives or the "mininarratives," to use Lyotard's terms. This observation is also substantiated earlier in *Rooms Are Never Finished* by Shahid's allusions as frequently to the protagonists in the stories of the Christian, Hindu, and Muslim mythologies (such as Hussain, Zainab, Jesus, God, Satan, Ganesha, Radha, and others) as to the common members of humanity (such as the general mourners of Kashmir, the nurse in the Lenox Hill hospital, the air hostess in Barcelona Airport, the exiled Granadian who represents all the exiles in human history), and even to the wailing waters, mourning guitars, and weeping violins.

29. The predominant image of "rowing" in the concluding poem of *Rooms Are Never Finished* is a metaphor of fluidity both in the literal and figurative senses, because it is inextricably associated with water and sailing.

Works Cited

Ali, Agha Shahid. *The Veiled Suite: The Collected Poems*. India: Penguin Books, 2010.
Ali, Agha Shahid. *The Country without a Post Office*. India: Ravi Dayal Publisher and Penguin Books, 2013.
Auden, W. H. "An hour of questions and answers with Auden, Part two: What a poet can do, political poetry, favorite (and 'unfavorite') poems, corrections and collaborations," November 15, 1971. www.swarthmore.edu / library / auden / QandApt2.html
Berryman, John. "The Ball Poem," *The New Poetry*. Harmondsworth: Penguin Books, 1962.
Chambers, Claire. "The Last Saffron: Agha Shahid Ali's Kashmir," Contemporary World Literature 7 (May/June 2011), *Literary Non Fiction*, 5. http://contemporary worldliterature.com/blog/essays
Dutt, Ajanta. Ed. *Neruda, Walcott and Atwood: Poets of the Americas*. Delhi: Worldview Publications, 2002.
Eagleton, Terry. *Literary Theory: An Introduction*. Oxford: Basil Blackwell, 1983.
Freud, Sigmund. "Mourning and Melancholia," *The Complete Psychological Works of Sigmund Freud, Vol. XIV* (London: The Hogarth Press and the Institute of Psychoanalysis, 1917).
Ghosh, Amitav. "'The Ghat of the Only World': Agha Shahid Ali in Brooklyn," *The Imam and the Indian*. New Delhi: Ravi Dayal Publisher, 2002, 340–361.
Ghosh, Amitav. *The Shadow Lines*. New Delhi: Ravi Dayal Publisher, 1998.
Ginsberg, Allen, *Collected Poems: 1947–1980*. New York: Harper & Row, 1984.
Goethe, Johann Wolfgang von. *Faust: A Tragedy*. 2nd ed. Trans. Walter Arndt & Cyrus Hamlin, New York: W. W. Norton, 2001.
Hawley, John C. *Amitav Ghosh: An Introduction*; Contemporary Indian Writers in English. New Delhi: Cambridge University Press, 2008.
Hawthorn, Jeremy. *A Glossary of Contemporary Literary Theory*, 4th ed. London: Arnold, 2000.
Merrill, James. *A Scattering of Salts*. New York: Knopf, 1996.
Newman, Amy. "'Separation's Geography': Agha Shahid Ali's Scholarship of Evanescence," *Mad Heart Be Brave: Essays on the Poetry of Agha Shahid Ali*, ed. Kazim Ali. Ann Arbor: University of Michigan Press, 2017.
Schneiderman, Jason. "The Loved One Always Leaves: The Poetic Friendship of Agha Shahid Ali and James Merrill," *Mad Heart Be Brave: Essays on the Poetry of Agha Shahid Ali*, ed. Kazim Ali. Ann Arbor: University of Michigan Press, 2017.
Sedgwick, Fred. *Read My Mind: Young Children, Poetry and Learning*. London & New York: Routledge, 1997.
Selden, Raman, Peter Widdowson, and Peter Brooker. *A Reader's Guide to Contemporary Literary Theory*, 5th ed. New Delhi: Pearson Education, 2006.

Sen, Amartya. *Identity and Violence: The Illusion of Destiny*. London: Penguin Books, 2006.
Sundararajan, Saroja. *Kashmir Crisis: Unholy Anglo-Pak Nexus*. Delhi: Kalpaz Publications, 2010.

17

Let Your Mirrored Convexities Multiply
On Agha Shahid Ali's "Tonight"

Kazim Ali

The ghazal in America reads differently than it does in its local contexts, perhaps because here it maps not against a classical poetics but rather against a postmodern poetics in its emotional tone that often includes loss and longing, a devotion between human and divine that is more vexed than connective, and a formal disjunction that privileges the fragmenting of perception and surprising moves of meaning-making that juxtaposition can offer in a language in which preposition, conjunction, and verb have a firmer and more expected architectural role in a sentence or poetic line than in Urdu, where the prepositions are *post* positions and the verb (whether of action or inaction) typically comes *after* the object upon which the verb acts. Perhaps it is appropriate that the ghazal had to wait for Agha Shahid Ali to come into English. Like the form, he too was transnational, having spent part of his childhood in America while his father was completing his PhD, and then moving back here while doing his own graduate work. Like the ghazal, Shahid also traveled—from Pennsylvania to Arizona and then back, settling first in the Finger Lakes region, then New England, then Utah and finally in New York City. The form of the ghazal too traveled—from Arabic to Farsi to Urdu, and in each place it took on a new character in the hands of new masters.

As for Agha Shahid Ali, he had aesthetic trajectories as well as geographic ones; he moved from the free verse of his earliest writings into received European forms like the canzone, the villanelle, and the Sapphic stanza, which he particularly enjoyed precisely because of the challenge of writing dactylic-trochaic feet in an English line. "It was *meant* for *Greek!*" he would remind his classes while simultaneously admonishing them to work harder to conform to the form. Somehow, also, he was able to imitate the sound and rhythm of Urdu, as well as its sense of drama and tragic tone, in the poems he was writing in American English. As the forms themselves got more and more complex, his English also veered from the loose colloquial of earlier books into a somewhat more rarefied expression of "literariness" that felt particularly Urdu.

Most poetry audiences understand the rules of the ghazal: that it is made of couplets of varying emotional tones or subjects; they may even have different speakers or range from first to third person. The couplets themselves, though discrete, are united by a formal scheme set up by the first couplet. These formal qualities stem from the fact that the ghazal developed as a form for performance and the strict formal approach allowed the performer/singer to improvise within the scheme and oftentimes invent variant couplets on the spot. Famous ghazals are known as much as songs as they are as recitations or as literary texts. Because of the sometimes improvisatory nature of performance, there can be a somewhat informal relationship to "completeness," in that several couplets can be omitted in performance, lines or couplets can be repeated many times, and couplets (besides the first and last) can even be performed out of order. In fact, there are two differing versions of the ghazal "Tonight." The first and shorter version appeared in *The Country without a Post Office*. A somewhat reordered version with the original two couplets compressed into one and with many additional couplets added appeared in Shahid's posthumous collection *Call Me Ishmael Tonight*; both versions appear in his collected poems *The Veiled Suite*.

That there are several different versions of "Tonight" only connects the poem more with the original tradition, and perhaps even implies that a poet today could engage with this ghazal and invent her or his own couplets in recitation. The recitative style traditionally includes a habitual repetition of the first line of the couplet, as in the American form of the blues stanza; the literary purpose is probably to give a strong emphasis to the first line and set up anticipation for delivery of the rhyme and refrain of the second line. But there is a practical purpose as well: it gives the performer the time and space to invent a second line to follow.

The first variation between the two versions appears in the very first couplet. Whereas in the original version, the couplet read, "Where are you now? Who lies beneath your spell tonight / before you agonize him in farewell tonight?," the second line of the newer version reads, "Whom else from rapture's road will you expel tonight?" Whether the addressed "you" is a woman or God is unknown. As already mentioned, this can even change from couplet to couplet. But here it seems that the allegorical is always present with the immediate quotidian read—it could be an expulsion from Paradise, or it could be a more ordinary paradise of the lover. Besides God or the lover (and in the tradition of the ghazal, one of these often functions as a metaphor for the other), since the poem originally appeared in a book about Kashmir, it could also speak about the expulsion from that homeland.

The formal unity of the couplets gives the reader a constant against which to experience the shifts in perception from couplet to couplet. One is reminded of the drone, which plays such an important aural role in Indian classical music. The other major quality of the ghazal is a sense of referentiality, always leaning on Quranic stories or earlier texts. "Tonight" is no different, and in fact it invokes its postmodernity by relying on a couplet constructed of cuts from an Emily Dickinson poem. While the line of Dickinson reads, "How tell trinket to make me beautiful fabrics of Cashmere," Shahid amends and re-stitches it as, "Those 'fabrics of Cashmere'—'to make Me beautiful—' / 'Trinket'—to gem—'Me to adorn—How—Tell'—tonight?"

In a couplet about God's "vintage loneliness" (presented as a positive and divine attribute) turning to "vinegar" there is a second variation—rather than dwelling on God, it shifts to the reason for His loneliness: "All the archangels—their wings frozen—fell tonight." So the "loneliness" or "oneness" (in Arabic the same word), originally presented as a hallowed concept, here is literally *spoiled*. God has expelled His archangels and is alone. The immediate following couplet points out the stakes when it declares of the idols in the Ka'aba begging not to be destroyed: "Only we can convert the infidel tonight." This couplet shifts from the story of the fallen angels to the much later story of the prophet Muhammad smashing the idols in the Ka'aba, when it implies that it is only the sinner who can save others. One can now realize that only the fallen angels can truly understand God, and understand the torture of separation from God; they have lost more than those still in His kingdom.

There is a lovely couplet next, which is not in the original version of the poem: "Mughul ceilings, let your mirrored convexities / multiply me at once under your spell tonight." This couplet alludes to the cultural syncretism that characterized Indian cultural and political life for many centuries but also, in particular, the development in Islamic cultural expressions that came from its blending with South Asian spiritual and artistic traditions. The poet here declares himself multiple—in a Whitmanesque sense, perhaps—but also alludes to the state of being ensorcelled or enchanted, much like the state of *junoon* (or "madness") associated with Sufi religious ecstasy.

The following couplet speaks of a temple in which all the statues have been smashed, reminding the reader of the previous couplet in which the idols beg not to be smashed, but here there is a priest in saffron, letting the reader know that this is not the masjid of the earlier couplet, but a Hindu temple. There is a "he" in a couplet that follows this one and refers to the priest in saffron, but in the new version that couplet appears earlier and has no antecedent. The priest appears in the couplet *following* this one—so the "He" could refer to any number of figures who appear previously, including God, since the pronoun appears at the beginning of a sentence with initial capitalization.

The smashing of a Hindu temple appearing after the couplet about the idols in the masjid comments on the often reciprocal violence in Kashmir and in other places in India. This mirroring of violence also reminds us that Islam in India was syncretic, *especially* in Kashmir, merging with local Kashmiri Shaivite and Hatha Yoga traditions to create a particular kind of mystical approach to Islam that included devotional music drawn from Hindu traditions (qawali). It is pertinent to mention here, of course, the Mughal prince Dara Sikoh's role in bringing yoga across the Middle East, in reverse direction of the way the ghazal traveled. In fact, many of the earliest illustrations we have of yoga asanas come from the illustrations in Farsi translation that Dara Sikoh commissioned of the ancient yogic texts.

In the midst of this complex and varied meditation on alienation, joining and hybridity of spirit and love, the speaker declares himself perhaps a sinner but *not* an unbeliever, in a new couplet: "God, limit these punishments, there's still Judgment Day— / I'm a mere sinner, I'm no infidel tonight." This is a speaker trying to negotiate space for himself to live in the world, to escape from a system of signs and signals that would seek to impose judgment and sentencing upon him.

Sinners and infidels and fallen archangels are all heroic here and Shahid's playful blasphemy continues with the dramatic appearance of Queen Jezebel, a pagan figure from the Bible, whose husband is King Ahab. In the Biblical story the hero is supposed to be the prophet Elijah, but here Shahid damns Elijah and blesses Jezebel. The drawing in of a Biblical story also serves to heighten the sense of multiplicity in the weave of textual allusions that construct the poem.

"He" is a little self-referential (even before the closing couplet of the ghazal in which the poet ordinarily uses his own name in the text of the poem as a way of claiming authorship of what was essentially an oral work in days before wide print distribution) when he mentions "the wounded gazelle"—as Agha Shahid Ali would often point out at his readings, American audiences typically mispronounced "ghazal" as "gazelle." As Stephanie Burt has written of this couplet, "Is the poet the wounded, dying, captured animal? Or is he the pursuing lover, the hunter [. . .] who may never catch his prey? The hunt ends at dusk, with the last of the Islamic calls to prayer."[1] In any case, the relationship between God and the supplicant, between citizen and citizen, between the lover and the beloved, between the poet and the poem, remains multiple and vexed.

In the closing couplet, Shahid identifies himself not only by his real name, but he assumes an attribute, that of Ishmael: "And I, Shahid, only am escaped to tell thee— / God sobs in my arms. Call me Ishmael tonight." The reference at the end of the couplet is not only to the famous opening of *Moby-Dick*, but also to the Ishmael of scripture—in the Quran, it is Ishmael, not Isaac, who is chosen by his father as a sacrifice. But the couplet is doubly allusive; its opening echoes the book of Job from the Bible. In this case, one is tempted then to read Ishmael (especially coming so soon after Jezebel) as the Biblical Ishmael, who is somewhat different. There, he is the forgotten brother, the illegitimate son of the cast-out first wife, excluded from the father. In fact, there is a triple allusion in the poem—*four*, if you count that Jezebel's husband in the Bible was King Ahab, another sly *Moby-Dick* reference—because the phrase "And I only am escaped to tell thee" is also a quote from the Bible, from the Book of Job, which in fact serves as Melville's epigraph to the epilogue chapter of *Moby-Dick*.

These weaves of intertextuality do remind one of the multiplicity implied by the appearance of the Mughal ceilings earlier in the poem. The architecture of the Mughal empire not only highlights the hybrid nature of what is now being sold as a monolithic "Indianness" (which had never existed in history), but is also an example of the true "classicism" of traditional Islamic arts—besides architecture, one can include calligraphy, poetry, and mathematics—pointing not toward the transcendent singularity of mimesis present in the Western ideal but rather into the notion of pluralism and abstraction.

The diverse and scintillating meanings presented by a ghazal's varying couplets—joined solely by their formal properties—refuse the ordinary transaction of a reading experience: one in which the writer offers "meaning" to the reader. The culture and literary traditions of South Asia have always been polyglot, after all, and drawing from infinite influences. In the contemporary world, it seems these influences are refused and there are efforts, for example, in the Arab world to purge Persian influences from Islam, just as there is in India to return to some sense of Hindu purity—a purity, which like the *wahabi* influences in Islam, is a most modern construction. And in Shahid's ghazal "Tonight," closure is refused. At the end of *Moby-Dick*, after all, Ishmael is left floating in the middle of the ocean. As far as Ishmael from the scriptures, not much is said after he has his narrow escape from his father's knife. He drifts out of the story. Perhaps the ghazal is postmodern after all. A different future, more couplets, may always be written.

Note

1. Burt, Stephanie. "Poem Guide: Agha Shahid Ali's 'Tonight.'" https://www.poetryfoundation.org/articles/69597/agha-shahid-ali-tonight

18

An Interview with Agha Shahid Ali

SUVIR KAUL

Edited transcript of an interview recorded at the Mass Communications Research Center, Jamia Milia Islamia, New Delhi in August 1997.

SK: Would you like to talk about your professional life in the United States? What encourages you to keep writing?

ASA: I am a professor of English and a creative writer at the University of Massachusetts, Amherst, and I am director of the program in creative writing there. These institutions support writers. They reward you for publishing what you would be publishing anyway.

SK: In one of your poems in *A Nostalgist's Map of America* there are a few lines in which you write about coming across an "exit to Calcutta" and thus thinking that India always exists off the turnpikes of America. That's a very interesting conjunction—the conjunction of being in exile. What does it mean to you to be an Indian in America, to be on the turnpikes in America watching out for signposts to Calcutta . . .

ASA: What happened was when I was en route to Ohio and I saw the sign for Calcutta. I did not take the exit for a mundane reason—we were in a hurry. But later when the contrast occurred in the poem, the fact that I didn't take it became important, so that I could turn it into Calcutta, India, even though I have never been to Bengal.

SK: So much of your work is caught up with issues of really finding Calcutta in America—I am using that symbolically—with issues of cultural transformation in one form or the other. How does that work for you?

ASA: This is often a question of textures and landscapes, foods, smells, and of all that can remind us of certain moments in the past. Now like many of us I did not go to America because I was impoverished here, so I am not like people who escape the potato famine in Ireland. Nor was I persecuted; I went there on my own choice. So I became an expatriate rather than an exile. I often use the word "exile" because I like the word. When I went there, I went with a certain amount of cultural baggage, which is already tripartite: it is loosely Hindu, Muslim, and Western. I grew up with them and all these are crystallized by the moment of exile. I always think of how these things live simultaneously together . . . are there contradictions, aren't there contradictions . . . I found that they do not have to be debilitating. As an academic, I can come back to my roots for three months every summer—even if I had lived in India, I could be working in Bangalore, or I could be in Trivandrum. So I would still be away from the places I grew up in. So I do not think that I have lost anything. This departure has become a way of holding on fully for me.

SK: I was struck by the fact that you write ghazals in English. There is an enormous problem of transliteration here, of being able to write across cultures. What are the salient features of the form that you keep in mind when you think about writing the ghazal in English in America?

ASA: Well, first of all I never thought that I would be able to write ghazals in English 'til I came across a ghazal written by an American poet named John Hollander. I was very excited and said, "Oh! my goodness, why haven't I thought of this because here's the tradition I grew up with," particularly as I know that in literary history forms are constantly being taken into other areas and then being domesticated.

SK: What is the kind of ghazal that you keep in mind when you try to write one?

ASA: We have the tendency to see the ghazal in Urdu as a relatively easy form because we know that the refrain is repeated all the time. In the process, we just forget that there is a rhyme that precedes the refrain. Also, anyone who has some decent knowledge of Urdu can claim to know the clichéd storehouse of images and motifs, from the Beloved, to the flame, and so on. Genius is when somebody can take this entire vocabulary and turn it on its head again and again, and that's the exciting thing. Or constantly endow it with all kinds of motifs which it did not have or imbue it with all those meanings simultaneously.

SK: Would you like to read your poem "Ghazal" from your new book *The Country without a Post Office*?

ASA: [reads "Ghazal"]:

> Where are you now? Who lies beneath your spell tonight
> before you agonize him in farewell tonight?
>
> Pale hands that once loved me beside the Shalimar:
> Whom else from rapture's road will you expel tonight?
>
> Those "Fabrics of Cashmere—" "to make Me beautiful—"
> "Trinket"—to gem—Me to adorn—"How—tell"—tonight?
>
> I beg for haven: Prisons, let open your gates—
> A refugee from Belief seeks a cell tonight.
>
> Executioners near the woman at the window.
> Damn you, Elijah, I'll bless Jezebel tonight.

I had been writing this ghazal, and I then came across this TV program on Jezebel and she has always been described as this bad woman, a harlot. But I now realize that she was quite a brave woman—there is this Elijah who's screaming at her like a raving fundamentalist. When they come to kill her, she stands at her window, she makes an incredibly heroic picture. (Continues reading)

> Lord, cried out the idols, Don't let us be broken,
> Only we can convert the infidel tonight.

Has God's vintage loneliness turned to vinegar?
He's poured rust into the Sacred Well tonight.

In the heart's veined temple all statues have been smashed.
No priest in saffron's left to toll its knell tonight.

(And now for the signature couplet:)

And I, Shahid, only am escaped to tell thee—
God sobs in my arms. Call me Ishmael tonight.[1]

SK: Can we rest on the phrase "Call me Ishmael tonight," because it obviously carries within it two traditions: one is of course Ishmael within the Muslim tradition, but also a neomythic American tradition, since *Moby-Dick* opens with "Call me Ishmael." Again we have that same conjunction of cultural traditions.

ASA: I always use these phrases because I like the sound of them. I mean, that imperative "Call me Ishmael" is such a startling way to begin a novel. And of course that fits in with the ending when he says I alone have survived to tell this tale and you find the mythic pattern—one person survives to tell a tale. I am not quite sure when I began thinking of the religious connotation but I found the idea of sacrifice very interesting.

SK: So is Ishmael here the witness or the victim?

ASA: He's also the one who is exiled. He is in exile with his mother. He goes away to Arabia.

SK: We will go on to talk about figures of exile in your poetry, but I thought perhaps we will stay for a little while longer with your experiments. You have written a villanelle, which is a comparatively unusual form. What attracts the poet like you to these forms?

ASA: One that attracts the poet is the fact that it is a challenge. You are always dying to do new things . . . you are constantly on the lookout for that. I was also looking for departures from my earlier work which had largely open forms where you have to create rules for yourself to make sure that you are not just being self-indulgent in a facile way. These tight forms help, especially as you already have examples of past genius. They are a challenge but they also help you remain honest when you are dealing with a difficult subject matter—that is, the shackles are strangely liberating. I do not think you really free yourself *from* a form, you free yourself *through* the form and you experiment. You see when the subject matter is difficult, it is so easy to become sentimental and facile and I would say silly. And therefore, I found these forms have kept me honest.

SK: This is an important lesson for any younger poet to learn, for there is a sense that free verse is its own authority. What you are suggesting is that the only way in which you learn to write with power is if you can learn to write via a fairly structured system, where you can really learn the system, come to terms with it and make it express your own concerns.

ASA: Well, you can of course arrive at a very sophisticated kind of free verse by just writing for a long time. But structured writing also becomes a way of later arriving at free verse if you want. People who write free verse are often not asking themselves enough questions, so it has become a means for a very lack-luster kind of self-expression: "I also have a heart, I have feelings, I can alter them and then chop them into lines." It does not go beyond that. I find that very disappointing—it is not interesting to read.

SK: There is another poem that I like very much—"Dear Shahid"—if only because it refuses our conventional understanding of the difference between poetry and prose, it is a prose poem. For a lot of people who don't read poetry, a prose poem is the fudging of the difference: any piece of prose can masquerade as a poem, can claim to have the rhythmic structure of a poem. What is your way of categorizing the difference between prose and poetry?

ASA: That could be an endless answer but more simply, what I did was realize that in this relatively short space I had to create the same kind of effect that a poem had. But my unit of argument would not be the stanza or the line, it would be the phrase, sentence and the paragraph. But I had to bring the same sort of intensity to it. That was the way I managed to solve it. Partly because the moment we move to prose, there is the desire to tell a story. The way I tell my students about it is, when you reach the end of the page and if you want to know what happened next, then it has not worked as a poem. It should be a complete piece. Sometimes the line between poetry and prose is very blurred, but I think it is meant to be.

SK: Would you like to read it so that we can talk about some of its details? Form apart, the concerns of this poem are in some ways the central concerns of this volume.

ASA: This actually is a combination of various letters I received [and] many I did not receive. I think poetry can tell lies, tell technical lies in order to reveal deeper truths.

SK: Before you begin, I want to remind our listeners that the title of the volume is *The Country without a Post Office*. So the thematic of letters, particularly lost letters, is obviously very central.

ASA: Obviously. That reminds me, I love the ending of Melville's *Bartleby the Scrivener* where when you are wondering what Bartleby is all about you are told that he used to work in the Dead Letter Office. All letters speeding to death . . .

SK: There is also a context nearer home: there is a whole genre of Hindi films in which the lost letter (this includes *Pakeezah*) is an important way of talking about ruptures—people leaving, people not coming back, the transmission of messages being interrupted because of cataclysms of one kind or the other. So the lost letter is obviously a way of describing disruptions in the social fabric that are much larger than those of the individual or the family.

ASA: OK. [he reads "Dear Shahid"]

Dear Shahid,

I am writing to you from your far-off country. Far even from us who live here. Where you no longer are. Everyone carries his address in his pocket so that at least his body will reach home.
    Rumours break on their way to us in the city. But word still reaches us from border towns: Men are forced to stand barefoot in snow waters all night. The women are alone inside. Soldiers smash radios and televisions. With bare hands they tear our houses to pieces.
    You must have heard Rizwan was killed. Rizwan: Guardian of the Gates of Paradise. Only eighteen years old. Yesterday at Hideout Café (everyone there asks about you), a doctor—who

had just treated a sixteen-year-old boy released from an interrogation centre—said: *I want to ask the fortune tellers: Did anything in his line of Fate reveal that the webs of his hands would be cut with a knife?*

This letter, *insh'Allah*, will reach you for my brother goes south tomorrow where he shall post it. Here one can't even manage postage stamps. Today I went to the post office. Across the river. Bags and bags—hundreds of canvas bags—all undelivered mail. By chance, I looked down and there on the floor I saw this letter addressed to you. So I am enclosing it. I hope it's from someone you are longing for news of.

Things here are as usual though we always talk about you. Will you come soon? Waiting for you is like waiting for spring. We are waiting for the almond blossoms. And, if God wills, O! those days of peace when we all were in love and the rain was in our hands wherever we went.

SK: That is lovely. What I was struck by when I read it is that it has the credibility of a letter written by somebody possessed of a sensibility. But it does have certain kinds of motifs, images, repeated rhythms, that suggest the work of a poet. And I was wondering whether in your poetry there is an element of the commonsensical, where the word as it is spoken, as it is used commonly, is of consequence even as much, if not more, than the word in its finished form. Is this perhaps how you think about your poetry—written shall we say with the warp of the spoken language and a woof of the cultivated artistic detail?

ASA: That is the wonderful way to put it!

SK: The volume is scattered with references to places that I know because I know Srinagar: I know Zero Bridge, other localities, Gupkar Road—the book is replete with local references. But the local reference is always contained within a larger set of themes. That is what I meant when I said that perhaps it is a combination of the commonsensical, the everyday, and the contemplative mode, the meditative mode, that marks your writing.

ASA: I do not know what to say to this except that that is what it is. By the commonsensical you mean just ordinary words or that they are suddenly changed?

SK: I mean ordinary words, ordinary usage. One of the great skills of a poet is that the ordinary can be turned into a moment of coruscating brilliance or real illumination. There is usage in your poetry that approximates the patterns and the practices of everyday speech but that is always interleaved with and over-written by much more considered use of language, and that is the play that I like very much. Would you like to read a few stanzas from "A Pastoral"?—I think they effectively combine the element of spoken speech with the element of surprise.

ASA: [reads from "A Pastoral"]

> Will we follow the horned lark, pry
> open the back gate into the poplar groves,
> go past the search post into the cemetery,
> the dust still uneasy on hurried graves
> with no names, like all new ones in the city?
>
> "It's true" (we'll hear our gardener
> again). "That bird is silent all winter.
> Its voice returns in spring, a plaintive cry.
> That's when it saw the mountain falcon
> rip open, in mid-air, the blue magpie,
> then carry it, limp from the talons."
>
> Pluck the blood: My words will echo thus
> at sunset, by the ivy, but to what purpose?
> In the drawer of the cedar stand,
> white in the verandah, we'll find letters:
> When the post offices died, the mailman
> knew we'd return to answer them. Better
>
> if he'd let them speed to death,
> blacked out by Autumn's Press Trust—
> not like this, taking away our breath,
> holding it with love's anonymous
> scripts: "See how your world has cracked.
> Why aren't you here? Where are you? Come back."

SK: I was going to call your attention to the opening of the poem: "We shall meet again, in Srinagar." The location of most of these poems in fact is the Valley and its difficulties for the last decade or so. So many of the images of your poems are derived from your observations of nature, people, cultural practices, but also of violence. The falcon springing upon the blue magpie and carrying it limp from its talons—this is an extraordinarily local and powerful image of violence. What is the relation between such violence and the finished technical quality of this poem? Is there a connection?

ASA: I think it brings us to the earlier point that we were talking about. How do you deal with very painful material which has a certain stature? I think you serve it by being not chaotic in what you create but by being as finished as possible. This is the only way to contain that violence and serve that material. I do not know why that's so. I cannot give a clear answer. But when I started this poem, I was thinking of Mandelstam, the great Russian poet and his poem which begins with "We shall meet again, in Petersburg," written I think at a point when Petersburg no longer existed.

I was reading a book on the birds of the Himalayas, and then this is where luck also came into play: I found that this particular bird, the horned lark, is truly silent in winter and as it warms, its voice starts returning. So it works so well as metaphor and as absolute fact. It needs spring to speak.

SK: I am struck by what you said about the degree of control that attachment to form grants the poet or indeed the writer when he or she is dealing with painful, moving, challenging issues. Steven Spielberg, the maker of extraordinarily mindless popular films, also made *Schindler's List*, and he made it in black and white because he said that he could not make a film on the Holocaust in color. He needed the distance and the precision granted by the tones of black and white in order to be able to deal with the Holocaust.

What you described as the contrast between the subject matter of pain and the aesthetic pleasure that comes from finding a vehicle in which to express that pain can also be exemplified from your poem "Muharram in Srinagar, 1992." Could you read from it please?

ASA: This is a pantoum, and it has that circular quality we sometimes find in the ghazal . . . you are constantly being returned to something. The progressions are not linear in any dull way.

[He reads the poem]

> Death flies in, thin bureaucrat, from the plains—
> a one-way passenger, again. The Monsoon rains

smash their bangles, like widows, against the mountains.
Our hands disappear. He travels first-class, sipping champagne.
One-way passengers again, the monsoon rains
break their hands. Will ours return, ever, to hold a bouquet?
He travels first-class. Our hands disappear. Sipping champagne,
he goes through the morning schedule for Doomsday:

"Break their hands." Will ours return with guns, or a bouquet?
Ice hardens its fat near his heart. We're cut to the brains.
He memorizes, clause by clause, the contract for Doomsday.
We mourn the martyrs of Karbala, our skins torn with chains.

Ice hardens its fat in his heart, and we're cut to the brains.
Near the ramp colonels wait with garlands by a jeep.
(O mourners, Husain bleeds, tear your skins with chains!)
The plane lands. In the Vale the children are dead, or asleep.

He descends. The colonels salute. A captain starts the jeep.
The Mansion by the lake awaits him with roses. He's driven
through streets bereft of children: they are dead, not asleep.
O, when will our hands return, if only broken?

The Mansion is white, lit up with roses. He is driven
through streets in which blood flows like Husain's.
Our hands won't return to us, not even mutilated, when
Death comes—thin bureaucrat—from the plains.

SK: What is extraordinary about this poem is the simplicity of its images. The figure of death, the "thin bureaucrat from the plains" could be a figure out of Tarot, only this is a figure of death in its contemporary variant. There is an Eliotian quality to it, a kind of precision where a single phrase can stand in for a whole set of values, not simply an administrative structure but the structure of values and the ethos, the code, that says it must impose its will, its organization, upon a space or a people. That kind of logic is another theme in a great many of these poems. There is a contrast between local disorder, local systems of organization and something that seeks to impose a larger structure or will upon it. Let me take you to a passage where you write about Habba Khatun. Habba Khatun as we know is of extraordinary importance to the valley of Kashmir. She is venerated by both Hindus and

Muslims—she is a figure of that kind of cultural consolidation. I would like to read some lines and ask you to think about them some more. This is the fourth section.

[SK reads from "The Blesséd Word: A Prologue"]

> Each fall they gather *chinar* leaves, singing what the hills have reechoed for four hundred years, the songs of Habba Khatun, the peasant girl who became the queen. When her husband was exiled from the Valley by the Moghul king Akbar, she went among the people with her sorrow. Her grief, alive to this day, in her own roused the people into frenzied opposition to Moghul rule. And since then Kashmir has never been free . . .

There is another passage [in "*Son et Lumière* at Shalimar Garden"] in which you talk about "the Moghuls' thirst for / terracing the seasons / into symmetry." We all know that these gardens and that form of terracing, that imposition of structure, symmetry and order, was an imperial importation into Srinagar. The play between local disorder, with its fecundity, its richness, and an externally imposed system of order, resonate through all these poems. Is that something you consciously worked into your poetry?

ASA: I don't know how consciously I did it. But now you point it out, I know that it is there. In the Moharram poem, for instance, I was aware of two or three things: first there is the problem of simile. Pablo Neruda once asked if you could have a line which says "the blood of children flowed on the streets?" What is there that can match the blood of children flowing on the streets? This is also an aesthetic problem, and the way he solves it is by writing "And the blood of children flowed on streets like the blood of children flows on the streets." There is no equivalence outside itself. Look how he takes care of the problem of simile there! It is really a brilliant moment. In the experience of Islamic history, the destruction of the Prophet's grandchildren and his family at the battle of Karbala is something that has such intensity that I can in the poem talk about children dying or weeping or whatever and compare it to the blood of Hussain flowing. Because it carries weight.

The other is the idea of the thin bureaucrat from the plains. There is a poem by the great German-Jewish poet Paul Celan called "Death Fuge," which contains the line "death is a master from Germany," and this poem is one of the most powerful ever written on the Holocaust.

SK: There is another moment where you describe the kind of idea that says we will destroy the garden to preserve the heaven, which is an evocative way to talk about the dissonance between administrative and political exigency and the idea of local cultures. In another passage you write of the administrator who dreams of saving nations by destroying its cities—in each case a feature of the whole is excised and yet we are convinced that we are in fact preserving the whole. That seems to be the problem of political logic, which produces its own aesthetic, its own dream world.

ASA: Yes, it does. It absolutely does. It has its own connections with reality.

SK: In your work there is a metaphysical explanation of evil, of pain, of horror, there are moments where you talk about God having turned his face, Bhagwan or Allah having given up on us. There is also a much more detailed, much more passionate account in which the local, the here-and-now is probed for explanations about what has gone wrong. Are there moments at which you stop and say, really the only way to explain a dilemma is to have recourse to a metaphysics?

ASA: I think, to some extent, yes. But as you said, in moving toward the metaphysics, there must be constant acknowledgment of the here-and-now because otherwise it can also become an invitation to sheer irresponsibility.

Note

1. Agha Shahid Ali, *The Country without a Post Office*. New York: Norton, 1997. New Delhi: Ravi Dayal and Penguin, 2013. All the poems or parts of them read out by Agha Shahid Ali and Suvir Kaul in this Interview are from this edition of the book.

Bibliography

Works of Agha Shahid Ali

Books

Bone-Sculpture. Calcutta: Writers Workshop, 1972.
In Memory of Begum Akhtar & Other Poems. Calcutta: Writers Workshop, 1979.
T.S. Eliot as Editor. Ann Arbor: University of Michigan Press, 1986.
A Walk Through the Yellow Pages. Tucson, AZ: Sun/Gemini Press, 1987.
The Half-Inch Himalayas. Middletown, CT: Wesleyan University Press, 1987.
A Nostalgist's Map of America. New York: W. W. Norton, 1991.
The Beloved Witness: Selected Poems. New Delhi, Viking Penguin, 1992.
The Rebel's Silhouette: Selected Poems by Faiz Ahmed Faiz. Salt Lake City, UT: Peregrine Smith, 1992.
The Country without a Post Office. New York: W. W. Norton, 1997.
Ravishing DisUnities: Real Ghazals in English. Middletown, CT: Wesleyan University Press, 2000.
Rooms Are Never Finished. New York: W. W. Norton, 2003.
Call Me Ishmael Tonight. New York: W. W. Norton, 2003.
The Veiled Suite: The Collected Poems. New York: Penguin Books, 2010.

Essays

"*The Satanic Verses*: A Secular Muslim's Response." *Yale Journal of Criticism* 4, no. 1 (1990): 295–300.
"The True Subject: The Poetry of Faiz Ahmed Faiz." *Grand Street* 9, no. 2 (1990): 129–138.
"The Blessed Word." *Field* 45 (1991): 17–21
"*The Rebel's Silhouette*: Translating Faiz Ahmed Faiz." In *Between Languages and Culture and Cross-Cultural Texts*. Edited by Anuradha Dingwaney and Carol Maier. Pittsburgh, PA: University of Pittsburgh Press, 1995.

"A Muslim Snobbery in America: May I?" *Green Mountains Review* 10 (1997): 86–96.

"The Ghazal in America: May I?" In *After New Formalism: Poets on Form, Narrative, and Tradition*. Edited by Annie Finch, pp. 123–132. Ashland, OR: Story Line, 1999.

"Ghazal: To Be Teased into DisUnity." In *An Exaltation of Forms: Contemporary Poets Celebrate the Diversity of their Art*. Edited by Annie Finch and Kathrine Varnes. Ann Arbor: University of Michigan Press, 2002.

INTERVIEWS

"Agha Shahid Ali." Interview by Lawrence Needham. *Verse* 17.2–3/18.1 (2001).

"Agha Shahid Ali." Interview by Christine Benvenuto. *Massachusetts Review* 43, no. 2: (2002): 261–268.

"Agha Shahid Ali: The Lost Interview." Interview by Stacey Chase, March 3–4, 1990. *The Cafe Review* (Spring 2011). https://www.thecafereview.com/spring-2011-interview-agha-shahid-ali-the-lost-interview

"An Interview with Poet Agha Shahid Ali." Interview by Eric Gamalinda, *Poets & Writers* (March/April 2002).

"Calligraphy of Coils. A Conversation with Kashmiri Poet Agha Shahid Ali." Interview by Rehan Ansari and Rajinder S. Pal. *Ravi Magazine* (August 2017). https://www.ravimagazine.com/conversation-kashmiri-poet-agha-shahid-ali

"Waiting for Word in the Paradise That Was Kashmir." Interview by Deborah Klenotic. *UMass Magazine* (Spring 1998). https://www.umass.edu/umassmag/archives/1998/spring_98/spg98_books_ali.html

Secondary Sources

Ali, Kazim. *Mad Heart Be Brave*. Ann Arbor: University of Michigan Press, 2017.

Bhattacharjee, Manas. "Looking for Shahid." *The Hindu*. December 3, 2011.

Chambers, Claire. "The Last Saffron: Agha Shahid Ali's Kashmir." *Contemporary World Literature* 7 (May/June 2011).

Dar, Huma. "A Passport of the Country without a Post Office." *PULSE*. December 8, 2011. http://pulsemedia.org/2011/12/08/a-passport-of-the-country-without-a-post-office

Ghosh, Amitav. "The Ghat of the Only World." *The Imam and the Indian*, pp. 340–361. Delhi: Ravi Dayal, 2002.

Ghosh, Amitav. "The Greatest Sorrow: Times of Joy Recalled in Wretchedness." *The Imam and the Indian*, pp. 305–325. Delhi: Ravi Dayal, 2002.

Hall, Daniel. "Foreword." *The Veiled Suite* by Agha Shahid Ali. Gurgaon: Penguin Books India, 2010.

King, Bruce. "The Diaspora: Agha Shahid Ali's Tricultural Nostalgia," *Modern Indian Poetry in English*. Revised ed., pp. 257–274. New Delhi: OUP, 2001.

Kinshuk, Rudra. "Agha Shahid Ali's The Country without a Post Office: A Contextualized Reading of the Kashmir Tragedy." *Muse India* 72 (March/April 2017).

Mai, Xiwen. "Mapping America, Re-mapping the World: The Cosmopolitanism of Agha Shahid Ali's *A Nostalgist's Map of America*." Graduate English Association New Voices Conference 2007.

Mattoo, Neerja. "Agha Shahid Ali As I Knew Him." *Indian Literature* 207 (2002): 175–179.

Mehrotra, Arvind Krishna. *The Oxford India Anthology of Twelve Modern Indian Poets* (New Delhi: Oxford University Press, 2001.

Mehrotra, Arvind Krishna. "Refusal to Mourn." *The Hindu* (January 2002).

Nelson, Emmanuel. "The Sorrows of a Broken Time." *Reworlding: Writers of the Indian Diaspora*. Westport, CT: Greenwood Press, 1993.

About the Editors

Tapan Kumar Ghosh is an associate professor of English at Tarakeswar Degree College, Burdwan University, West Bengal (India). He has had a distinguished academic career. He obtained his PhD for research on the fiction of Arun Joshi in 1993. He has authored and edited nearly a dozen books, including *Arun Joshi's Fiction: The Labyrinth of Life*, *Midnight's Children: A Reader's Companion*, *The Golden Notebook: A Critical Study*, *The Fiction of Kiran Desai*, *Things Fall Apart: A Critical Study*, *Chetan Bhagat: The Icon of Popular Fiction*, *In Pursuit of Amitav Ghosh: Some Recent Readings*, and *Mapping Out the Rushdie Republic: Some Recent Surveys*. Dr Ghosh has published scholarly articles on Rabindranath Tagore, Nirad C. Chaudhuri, Amitav Ghosh, Arundhati Roy, Mukul Kesavan, Shashi Tharoor, Rukun Advani, Aravind Adiga, and other writers in various anthologies and international journals.

Sisir Kumar Chatterjee received his PhD in 2002 and has taught in the government colleges of West Bengal, India, for over three decades. Currently, he works as an associate professor in the post-graduate department of English at Hooghly Mohsin College, Chinsurah, Hooghly, West Bengal. He has published more than twenty research articles and two books, *Philip Larkin: Poetry that Builds Bridges* (2006) and *The Fire Sermon* (2010). He received an Outstanding Teacher Award-Siksharatna 2017 from the government of West Bengal, India. His areas of interest include Indian English Fiction and post-1950s British poetry.

About the Contributors

Kazim Ali is the author of many books of poetry, fiction, essays, and criticism, including *Sky Ward* (2013) and *Resident Alien: On Border-crossing and the Undocumented Divine* (2015). He is also the editor of *Mad Heart Be Brave: Essays on the Poetry of Agha Shahid Ali* (2017) and *Jean Valentine: This-World Company* and translator of books by Sohrab Sepehri, Marguerite Duras, and Ananda Devi. He is an associate professor of creative writing and comparative literature at Oberlin College.

Peter Balakian is the author of seven books of poems, four books of prose, and two collaborative translations. *Ozone Journal* won the 2016 Pulitzer Prize for poetry, and *Black Dog of Fate* won the 1998 PEN/Martha Albrand Prize for the Art of the Memoir. He is Donald M. and Constance H. Rebar Professor of the Humanities in the Department of English and Director of Creative Writing at Colgate University. His work has been translated into more than a dozen languages.

Vedatrayee Banerjee is an assistant professor in the department of English, Tarakeswar Degree College. She is also a PhD Research Scholar at the department of English Jadavpur University. Her areas of research interest include Partition literature, postcolonial theory, and third space theory.

Abin Chakraborty works as an assistant professor of English at Chandernagore College, Chandernagore, Hooghly, West Bengal, India. He has published papers in several national and international journals and contributed articles at many conferences in India and the United Kingdom. He is co-editor of *Uneven Times: Critical Perspectives in Postcolonialism*.

Claire Chambers is a senior lecturer at the University of York, where she researches and teaches twentieth- and twenty-first-century writing in English from South Asia, the Arab world, and their diasporas. She is the author of *British Muslim Fictions: Interviews with Contemporary Writers* (2011), co-editor of *Imagining Muslims in South Asia and the Diaspora* (2015), and author of *Britain through Muslim Eyes: Literary Representations, 1780–1988* (2015), which is a literary history of Muslim writing in Britain from the late eighteenth century to the eve of Salman Rushdie's publication of *The Satanic Verses*. She is now writing a sequel, *Muslim Representations of Britain, 1988–Present*. Her research has been supported by funding from HEFCE, the British Academy and the Arts, and the Humanities Research Council (AHRC). She has published widely in such journals as *Postcolonial Text* and *Contemporary Women's Writing*. She is co-editor (with Rachael Gilmour at Queen Mary University of London) of the *Journal of Commonwealth Literature*.

Sinchan Chatterjee, a graduate (with Honors in English) of St. Xavier's College, Kolkata, under the University of Calcutta, is pursuing MA in English at Jadavpur University, Kolkata, West Bengal, India. His stories have been published in *The Statesman* as well as in international literary journals. His debut collection of short stories, *In Search of a Story*, was published in 2018. His first book of poems, *Plato in a Metro*, was published by Writers Workshop in 2019 in Kolkata, West Bengal, India. His second collection of poems, *War of the Roses*, was published in 2020 in Mumbai, India. He is the winner of the Penguin Random House India Essay Contest.

Martín Espada was born in Brooklyn, New York, in 1957. He received a BA in history from the University of Wisconsin-Madison and a JD in law from Northeastern University. His latest collection of poems is *Vivas to Those Who Have Failed* (2016). Other books of poems include *The Trouble Ball* (2011), *The Republic of Poetry* (2006), *Alabanza* (2003), *Imagine the Angels of Bread* (1996), and *Rebellion is the Circle of a Lover's Hands* (1990).He has received the Shelley Memorial Award, the Robert Creeley Award, the National Hispanic Cultural Center Literary Award, the PEN/Revson Fellowship, and a Guggenheim Fellowship. *The Republic of Poetry* was a finalist for the Pulitzer Prize. His book of essays, *Zapata's Disciple* (1998), was banned in Tucson as part of the Mexican-American Studies Program outlawed by the state of Arizona, and has been issued in a new edition by Curbstone/Northwestern University Press. A former tenant lawyer in Greater Boston's

Latino community, Espada is a professor of English at the University of Massachusetts-Amherst.

Gayatri Gopinath is an associate professor in the department of Social and Cultural Analysis, and the director of the Center for the Study of Gender and Sexuality at New York University. She works at the intersection of transnational feminist and queer studies, postcolonial studies, and diaspora studies, and is the author of two monographs: *Impossible Desires: Queer Diasporas and South Asian Public Cultures* (2005) and *Unruly Visions: The Aesthetic Practices of Queer Diaspora* (2018). She has published numerous essays on gender, sexuality, and queer diasporic cultural production in journals such as *Journal of Middle East Women's Studies, GLQ, Social Text*, and *positions*.

Amzed Hossein is currently a professor in the department of English, Aliah University, Kolkata. He did his PhD on the poetry of Ted Hughes at IIT, Kharagpur. His areas of interest are contemporary British Poetry, Utopian Literature, Indian Writing in English, and Dalit and Marginal Literature. He writes both in English and Bangla. He has published books and research papers on Ted Hughes, Sylvia Plath, H. L. V. Derozio, Girish Karnad, Rokeya Sakhawat Hossain, Delawarr Hosaen Ahmed Meerza, Jibanananda Das, and translated short stories of Bangla Dalit and Muslim women authors. His interview with Ted Hughes can be read online at http://ann.skea.com/AsiaFestivalInterview.html.

Suvir Kaul is A.M. Rosenthal Professor of English at the University of Pennsylvania. He received his BA, MA, and M Phil degrees from the University of Delhi and his PhD from Cornell University. His first job was at the SGTB Khalsa College in Delhi; since then, he has taught at the University of Illinois at Urbana-Champaign, Stanford University, and the Jamia Milia Islamia as a visiting professor. He has also held post-doctoral fellowships at the University of Canterbury at Kent and at the Society for the Humanities at Cornell University. He teaches courses in eighteenth-century British literature, contemporary South Asian writing in English, and in literary and critical Theory. He has published four books—*Of Gardens and Graves: Essays on Kashmir; Poems in Translation* (2015), *Eighteenth-century British Literature and Postcolonial Studies* (2009), *Poems of Nation, Anthems of Empire: English Verse in the Long Eighteenth Century* (2000), and *Thomas Gray and Literary Authority: Ideology and Poetics in Eighteenth-Century England* (1992)—and edited a collection of essays entitled *The Partitions of Memory: The Afterlife* *of the Division of India* (2001). He co-edited (with Ania Loomba, Antoinette Burton, Matti Bunzl, and Jed Esty) an interdisciplinary volume entitled *Postcolonial Studies and Beyond* (2005). At Penn, he has served as the director of the South Asia Center (2005–2007) and as Chair of the English Department (2007–2010).

Christine Kitano is the author of two collections of poetry, *Sky Country* and *Birds of Paradise*. She is an assistant professor at Ithaca College in Ithaca, New York, where she teaches courses in creative writing, poetry, and Asian American Literature.

Amy Newman is the author of five collections of poetry, most recently *On This Day in Poetry History*. Her poems and essays have appeared in journals including *Poetry, The Kenyon Review, The Missouri Review,* and *Hotel Amerika*, and in anthologies including *The Iowa Anthology of New American Poetries, The Rose Metal Press Field Guide to Prose Poetry, An Introduction to the Prose Poem,* and *The Hide-and-Seek Muse*. She won a fellowship to the MacDowell Arts Colony as well as state arts grants in Ohio and Illinois. She was recently awarded the Friends of Literature Prize from *Poetry* for her poem "Howl." She is a Board of Trustees Professor in the Department of English at Northern Illinois University.

Maureen Nolan is a former journalist and currently a senior writer with the *Hamilton Alumni Review*.

Fatima Noori is a guest lecturer and a senior research fellow in the department of English & Modern European Languages, University of Allahabad. She completed a BA in English literature and psychology and an MA in English literature from the University of Allahabad. She teaches Shakespeare, modern drama, and poetry to undergraduate students. She was a Fulbright Doctoral Fellow, researching at the Agha Shahid Ali Digital Archives at Hamilton College, Clinton, New York, during the year 2015–2016. She has made international presentations and published several papers on the poetic works of Agha Shahid Ali. Besides poetry, Fatima also enjoys Bollywood music, cooking, and hosting.

Jason A. Schneiderman is the author of *Primary Source* (2016), *Striking Surface* (2010), and *Sublimation Point* (2004), as well as editor of *Queer: A Reader for Writers* (2016). He received a PhD in literature from the graduate center of the City University of New York; an MFA in poetry from NYU;

and a BA in English from the University of Maryland. He writes about poetry, poetics, queer theory, and queer literature. He is an associate professor of English at the Borough of Manhattan Community College, CUNY.

Deeptesh Sen is a PhD student in the department of English at Jadavpur University. His areas of research interest include European modernism, T. S. Eliot, and Lacanian psychoanalysis.

Sagaree Sengupta is a writer, translator, and teacher who lives in Cumberland, Maine. She has published translations of poems, short stories, and novels from Hindi, Urdu, and Bengali. Her ghazal appeared in *Ravishing DisUnities: Real Ghazals in English* (2000), edited by Agha Shahid Ali. Other poems and a short story have appeared in literary journals. She is interested in the wider literary and artistic traditions of South Asia and has published research articles on the path-breaking nineteenth-century Hindi/Brajbhasha writer Bharatendu Harishchandra, as well as on later Indian and Pakistani authors. Her translation of Krishna Baldev Vaid's *The Diary of a Maidservant* was supported by a National Endowment for the Arts Grant in 2002. She has served in the faculty at the University of Texas-Austin, the University of Wisconsin-Madison, and Bates College. Currently, she is a full-time English teacher at Maine Girls' Academy in Portland and facilitates adult reading discussions around the state for the Maine Humanities Council. She is an avid textile artist who makes original quilts and art-to-wear, mixing new and repurposed fabrics. She holds a PhD in Asian Studies from the University of Pennsylvania, an MA in South Asian Studies from the University of Wisconsin, and a BA in English from Cornell University. For more of her writing, see her blog, "Minor News from Inland Maine."

Dara Wier has recently completed her thirteenth book, *In the Still of the Night*, a collection of thirteen poems, which was named a best book of the year by Publisher's Weekly. Her work has been supported by the Guggenheim Foundation and the U.S. National Endowment for the Arts and has appeared in *Granta, American Poetry Review, The Harvard Review, The Nation, The New Republic, Fence,* and *Washington Square,* among others. She is executive editor of the literary magazine *jubilat*, and publisher and editor of Factory Hollow Press. She teaches in the MFA for Poets and Writers at the University of Massachusetts Amherst and co-directs The Juniper Summer Institute and Workshops, as well as the Juniper Initiative for Literary Arts and Action.

Index

"Abani Bari Acho?"/"Abani, are you home?," 142, 147
"About Me," 68
"Above the Cities," 194
Abraham, 197
absolutism/absolutist, 107, 210
a capella, 170
Ackerman, Diane, 97
Adam, 178, 203
Adey, Peter, 180, 185
Adorno, Theodor, 80
"Advertisement (Found Poem)," 100
advertisement(s), 9, 143, 145, 148
Aerial Life: Spaces, Mobilities, Affects, 185
A/aesthetic(s)/(ally), 27–28, 30, 96, 106, 111–13, 117, 119, 144, 148, 173, 213–14, 220, 233, 235–36, 245
A/affect(s), 100, 111, 142, 146, 185
"After Seeing Kozintsev's *King Lear* in Delhi," 8
"After Seeing the Film *Who's Afraid of Virginia Woolf?*," 124
"After the August Wedding in Lahore, Pakistan," 20, 76, 80, 106, 177, 190
afterlife, 85, 206, 211–12, 245
"Agha Shahid Ali and the Ghazals in English," 89–98

"Agha Shahid Ali: Calligraphy of Coils," 86, 120, 184, 186, 238
"Agha Shahid Ali: Notes and Anecdotes on the Growth of the Poet," 51–69
"Agha Shahid Ali's Canzones and the Forms of Exile," 109
Agha Shahid Ali's Gay Nation, 29, 63, 69
"Agha Shahid Ali: The Lost Interview," 29, 159, 238
agonize(d)/agonizing, 175, 187, 189, 192, 207, 221, 227
Ahab, 222, 223
Ahmad, Aijaz, 97
Ahmad, Eqbal, 23, 84, 205, 207, 211
Ahmed Faiz, Faiz, 2, 4, 6, 7, 21, 24, 40, 56, 57, 61, 62, 69, 73, 76, 85, 127, 129, 136, 193, 208, 237
Ahmed, Sara, 116, 119
Ahmedabad, 6
Airport, 9, 21, 79, 169, 170, 195, 199, 216
Akbar, 14, 235
Akhtar, Begum, 2, 5, 6, 15, 21, 23, 36, 38, 52, 56, 62, 65, 76, 79, 82, 84, 91, 103, 117, 121, 126–28, 131, 136, 142, 161, 169–70, 193–94, 196, 205, 207–208, 237

"a last image," 124
aletheia, 153
Al-Faran, 17
Ali, Agha Shahid, 1, 3, 5, 10, 13–14, 17–18, 22, 24, 26, 28–31, 33, 37, 43, 46, 51, 63, 68, 69, 71, 85–90, 94, 97–99, 109, 111–12, 114, 120–21, 126, 131, 133, 139, 141, 143, 145, 147–49, 154, 158–61, 171, 173, 177–78, 184–86, 188, 207, 209, 213–15, 217, 219–20, 223–25, 236–39, 243, 246–47
Ali, Kazim, 89, 213–14, 217, 219–24, 238, 243
Ali, Tariq, 30, 183–86
alien/alienation, 2, 28, 84, 121–22, 124, 128, 150, 158, 209, 222, 243
Alighieri, Dante, 76, 85, 104
Allah, 22, 31, 36, 67, 231, 236
allegorical, 221
America(n-ness), 4, 5, 7, 9–10, 12, 17, 24–28, 34–35, 39, 43–46, 53–54, 56–58, 60–62, 71, 89, 96–97, 99, 101, 113, 117, 119, 137, 139, 155, 157–59, 164, 170–71, 173–74, 178, 208, 220, 223, 226, 228, 244, 246
Amherst, 3, 15, 20–22, 34, 39, 41, 44–45, 56, 66, 68–69, 82–83, 85, 106, 141, 174, 179–80, 192, 197, 205, 210, 225, 245, 247
Amitav Ghosh: An Introduction, 215, 217
anacoluthon, 79
"Ancestors," 131
Andalusia(n), 20, 23, 202–204, 209–10
Andaman, 83
"An hour of questions and answers with Auden, Part two: What a poet can do, political poetry, favorite (and 'unfavorite') poems, corrections and collaborations," 214, 217

"Another Death," 125
apocalypse, 152
aporia, 211
Appiah, 36
Arab/Arabic, 1, 22–23, 35, 38, 44, 67–68, 72, 74, 81, 105, 107–109, 170, 202, 204, 207, 209–10, 213, 219, 221, 224, 228
Arabia(n), 12, 25, 44, 72, 202, 228
archetype, 203
architectural, 219
"Archiving Absences: Charting Chronotopes in Agha Shahid Ali's Cartography of Desire," 149–60
Arizona, 2, 3, 9, 11–12, 27, 52–54, 59, 78, 112, 115–16, 120, 133, 155–57, 174, 219, 244
Armenia(n), 16, 33–34, 36–37
Art of Criticism, The, 60, 69
Article, 24, 49, 71, 82, 85, 159, 160, 183, 184, 186, 212, 224, 241, 243, 247
Ashraf Ali, Agha, 1
Ashraf, Sufia, 61
Asia(n), 1, 28, 93–94, 96–97, 116, 119, 149, 155, 171, 178, 183, 222, 224, 244–47
"At Jama Masjid, Delhi," 130–31
"At the Museum," 48
Auden, W. H., 4–5, 61, 122, 214, 217
Aulia, Nizamuddin, 6, 130–31
"Autumn in Srinagar," 124
Award, 24, 45, 67, 101, 241, 244, 246
Azadi, 14, 16, 20, 29, 175, 183

Bai, Rasoolan, 6, 128
Bakhtin, Mikhail, 151, 160, 214
Balakian, Peter, 33–38, 243
"Ball Poem, The," 216–17
Banerjee, Vedatrayee, 141–48, 243
Bangladesh War, 79, 169

"Barcelona Airport," 199, 216
Bartleby the Scrivener, 230
Baudrillard, 210, 216
Beatles, 164
"Beginnings: A Journey with Micronarratives," 121–32
"Begum Akhtar," 128
Behn, Robin, 90, 98
"Bell Telephone Hours," 9, 148
"Beloved Witness, Beloved Friend," 43–49
Beloved Witness, The: Selected Poems, 13, 161, 163, 165, 170–71, 237
Belsen, 10
Bendall, Molly, 97
Bengal(i), 8, 122, 142, 147, 155, 226, 241, 243–44, 247
Benjamin, Walter, 144, 151, 159
Benvenuto, Christine, 4, 24, 29, 73, 85, 207, 214, 238
Berbers, 202
Berryman, John, 216–17
"Beyond English," 26, 68, 108
"Beyond the Ash Rains," 11
Bhagwan, 236
Bhairavi, 127
bhajan, 193–94
Bhakti, 27
Bildungsroman, 182
binaries, 106
biriyanize(d), 99
Bisbee, 54–55, 156
Bishop, Elizabeth, 25, 40
"Bitter Chill of Winter," 184–85
Blakean, 213
Blasphemy, 147, 222
"Blessed Word, The: A Prologue," 14, 36, 235, 237
Bloom, Harold, 62, 69
blues, 220
Bodies That Matter: On the Discursive Limits of 'Sex', 185–86

Bombay film/Bollywood cinema, 37, 65, 195, 246
Bone-Sculpture, 2, 4, 5, 52, 74, 121–24, 126, 131, 161–62, 237
"Bones," 5, 122–23, 162–63
Book of Gold Leaves, 182, 185
Bose, Sumantra, 184, 186
Bosnia, 16–17, 27, 56, 102, 178, 180, 188, 209
Boston, 171, 194, 244
Bouldrey, Brian, 68
"Braiding Disparate Strands: Tracing the Arcs of Agha Shahid Ali's *The Half-Inch Himalayas*," 133–39
brain cancer, 3, 20–21, 36, 45, 82, 112, 174, 189
British rule, 8, 216
Buatta, Mario, 84
Buddha, 191, 208
Buddhist, 96
Burt, Stephanie, 223–24
"Butcher, A," 55, 129, 135
Butler, Judith, 181, 185–86
"By the Waters of the Sind," 197, 199

Cafe Review, The, 29, 238
Calcutta, 2, 5, 11, 12, 35, 38, 52, 79, 115–16, 121, 131, 155–56, 181, 225–26, 237, 244
California, 12, 155
Call me Ishmael Tonight, 24, 25, 62, 66, 131, 220, 228, 237
C/calligraphy, 41, 86, 120, 184, 186, 223, 238
"Can Poetry Console a Grieving Public?," 159–60
"Can't get through to you please Mr. Postman," 145
Canaday, John, 97
canonical, 4, 150, 162
canzone(s), 10, 21, 44, 76, 82, 99, 101, 105–106, 109, 141, 211, 220

capitalist, 146
carnival, 146
carpe diem, 152
cartography, 12, 100, 117, 149, 151, 154, 158
Catholic, 3, 4, 52, 54, 121, 173
Cavafy, 135–37
Celan, Paul, 235
Chakraborty, Abin, 99–108, 243
Chakraborty, Dipesh, 156, 159
Chambers, Claire, 13, 173–86, 213, 244
Chandra, G. S. Sharat, 97
"Changing Light at Sandover," 23
Chase, Stacey, 4, 29, 155, 159, 238
Chatterjee, Sinchan, 24, 187–218, 244
Chattopadhyay, Shakti, 142, 147
Chechnya, 16, 27, 79, 178, 188, 209
Chile, 27, 79, 188, 209
China, 28, 146
Christian Ostro, Hans, 17, 29, 59
Christian(ity), 4, 17, 20, 22, 29, 59, 108, 173–74, 177–78, 188, 192, 200, 202–203, 213, 216
Christmas, 143, 147
"Christmas, 1980s," 147
chronotope/chronotopic, 149, 151, 158
cinematic, 188
"City of Daughters, The," 16
civilization, 26, 58, 71, 123, 162, 192, 202, 208, 213, 215
classical, 10, 62, 65, 94, 126–27, 219, 221
Clotho, 175
Coles, Katharine, 97
Collaborator, The, 30, 182–83, 185–86
colloquial(ity), 104, 220
colonial(ism)/colonializaion, 8, 67, 83, 111, 113, 116, 120, 155, 157–58, 164, 179, 185–86
Colorado, 39
communication, 9, 13, 19–20, 80, 120, 141–46, 179–80, 204, 225

consolation/consolatory, 18, 23, 130, 178, 194, 211–12
consumerist, 146
Contemporary World Literature, 184, 213, 217, 238
"Conversations with Agha Shahid Ali," 85
cook, 33, 34, 39, 40, 43
"Correspondent, The," 17, 180, 183
cosmic, 105, 124, 126, 188–89, 198, 203–204, 207, 212
cosmopolitan(ism), 4, 17, 56, 66, 151, 159–60, 173, 239
counter-insurgency, 101
Country without a Post Office, The, 4, 13, 15, 18, 27, 29, 35, 44, 56, 59–60, 72, 74, 76, 79–80, 85, 101–102, 128, 145, 147–48, 160, 173–76, 178, 180–81, 185, 189, 191, 213, 217, 220, 227, 230, 236–37
"Country without a Post Office, The," 13, 16, 18, 35, 47, 55, 68, 80, 178–79, 182, 238, 239
couplet(s), 13, 25, 26, 56, 65, 72, 73, 79, 90–97, 103, 107, 109, 117, 121, 124, 127, 129–31, 135–37, 153, 166, 177, 220–24, 228
"Cracked Portraits," 8, 135
"Cremation," 5
crucifixion, 22, 54, 201
"Crucifixion," 11, 54
culinary (skills), 3
Curfewed Night, 30, 182, 185–86

Dacca, 8, 34, 37, 55
"Dacca Gauzes, The," 34
dactylic, 220
dadras, 126
Dal Lake, 105, 177
Damascus, 21, 194
Dargah, 6, 130–31

Daruwalla, Keki, 97
Darwish, Mahmoud, 20, 23, 202
Das, Kamala, 62
De Quincy, Thomas, 34
"Dear Editor," 2, 122
"Dear Shahid," 15, 59, 80, 145, 147, 179–80, 229–30
death, 20–22, 27, 45, 61–62, 66, 72, 74, 76, 78, 81–82, 84, 94, 102–105, 108, 114–17, 121–28, 131, 135–39, 141–42, 145–47, 150, 153–54, 163, 165, 173, 176, 180, 191–98, 200–202, 205–207, 210–11, 213, 230, 232–35
"Death Fuge," 235
deconstruct(s)/deconstruction/deconstructivist, 199, 208–10
Dedalus, Stephen, 151
Deir Yassein, 16, 27, 108, 188, 209
Delhi (New)/(Old), 1, 2, 5, 7, 8, 15–17, 29, 34, 44, 52, 55, 57, 59, 67, 69, 74, 79, 85, 109, 112, 121–22, 130–32, 134–35, 149–50, 169, 171, 173, 179, 180, 182, 186, 190, 194–95, 213, 215–18, 225, 236–39, 245
Derrida, Jacques, 160
desert, 5, 11–13, 27, 47, 54–55, 65, 79, 116, 138, 151–53, 155–56, 168, 170, 193–94, 197, 207, 214
desire, 36, 39, 43, 68, 75, 82, 83, 94, 111–13, 116, 118, 123, 125, 137, 139, 149, 151–53, 158, 162, 201, 203, 229, 245
destiny, 126, 170, 215, 218
de-territorialization, 2, 158
devotional, 193, 222
Dhaka, 181
"Dialing a Joke: Agha Shahid Ali's Long-distance Calls to Lands without a Post Office," 141–48

Dialogic Imagination, The: Four Essays by M.M., 160
diaspora/diasporic, 34, 111–13, 118–19, 149, 203, 215, 239, 244–45
Dickinson, Emily, 4, 11–12, 15, 36, 76, 78, 117, 141, 221
Dinsman, Melissa, 144, 148
disillusionment, 126
displacement, 112, 116, 133–34, 138–39, 188
dispossession, 72, 79, 81, 117
Divina commedia/Divine Comedy, The, 104
"Diwali, 1971," 125
Dogra dynasty, 177
Doomsday, 9, 194, 197, 207, 234
doppelgangers, 136
double(s)/doubling/doubleness, 65, 76, 119, 136, 138, 180–81
"Dream of Glass Bangles, A," 7, 124
dream/dreamscape, 6, 7, 15, 23, 27, 29, 35, 40, 56, 63, 76, 79, 83–85, 103, 123–26, 128, 135, 138, 168, 180, 183, 191–92, 205–207, 212, 214, 236
drone, 221
duality, 133
Duschinski, Haley, 30

Eagleton, Terry, 209, 215
"Earth," 200
East(ern), 17, 62, 71, 85, 133, 170, 222, 245
"Easter, 1916," 179, 184, 186
Eco, Umberto, 216
"Editor Revisited, The," 122
ekphrastic, 135
elegy/elegies/elegiac, 6, 21–23, 56, 61, 106, 115–16, 120, 126, 128, 149–50, 153, 158, 187, 192–93, 202–203, 205, 208, 211–12, 214

element(s)/elemental, 22, 117, 189, 198, 204, 207, 212, 231–32
elephant(s), 38, 82, 191–93, 201, 207–208, 210
"Eleven Stars over Andalusia," 20, 23, 202, 204, 209, 210
Elijah, 223, 227
Eliot(ian) (T. S.), 2, 4–5, 27, 52, 62, 101, 122, 153, 161–63, 165, 171, 174, 188, 199, 207, 234, 237, 247
Empire: A Very Short Introduction, 184, 186
Empire Writes Back, The, 179, 186
Encyclopedia of Poetry and Poetics, 87
England, 8, 39, 219, 245
"English in Tri-cultural Moment," 121, 132
English, 21–22, 24–29, 36, 43–44, 47, 52–53, 57–59, 61–62, 68–69, 71, 73, 85, 89–91, 93–96, 112–14, 121, 138, 149–50, 155–56, 161, 163, 165–71, 176, 188, 191, 200–204, 207–12, 216, 225–26, 228, 235
enjambment, 101, 104
enlightenment, 204
entropic, 144
"Ephemera as Evidence: Introductory Notes to Queer Acts," 118, 120
epigraph(s), 10–12, 15, 19, 54, 64, 76, 84, 95, 104, 117, 179, 182, 189, 191, 195, 199, 212–13, 223
epilogue, 223
"Epistemology of Mourning: A Reading of *Rooms are Never Finished*," 24, 187–218
Eros, 147
Espada, Martín, 31–32, 244
Mad Heart Be Brave: Essays on the Poetry of Agha Shahid Ali, 47, 148, 213–14, 217, 238, 243
essentialist, 210

ethnic(ity), 103, 150, 199, 202, 213, 215
Europe(an), 23, 25, 27, 105, 159–60, 163–64, 179, 220, 246–47
Eurocentric, 162
"Eurydice," 10, 55
E/evanescence, 4–6, 11–112, 34–35, 53, 71, 76–79, 115, 117–18, 153, 156, 204, 210, 213, 217
Eve, 178
exile(d)/exilic, 4–7, 9–10, 13, 21, 29, 34, 59–60, 71–76, 81, 83–85, 87, 105–107, 109, 112–14, 121, 138, 149–50, 155–56, 161, 163, 165–71, 176, 188, 191, 200–204, 207–12, 216, 225–26, 228, 235
exodus, 14, 17, 23, 27, 176, 204
expatriate, 59, 149, 226
experiment(s), 10, 13, 56, 100–101, 121, 211, 228–29
Ezekiel, Nissim, 53, 62

"Far Cry from Africa, A," 209
fairy tales, 10, 143
Fakir, 66, 130
"Farewell," 14, 16, 29, 44, 65, 102, 176, 178, 181, 189
Farooqi, Mehr Afshan, 132
Farsi, 1, 219, 222
"Fate's Brief Memoir, A," 76, 104, 175
Faust: A Tragedy, 212, 217
Fellowship, 24, 67–69, 244–46
"Film Bhajan Found on a 78 RPM," 195
Finch, Annie, 97, 238
"First Day of Spring," 17, 104
Fischer, Michael, 71, 85
flaneur, 143
flashback(s), 155, 169
fliers, 100
"Flight from Houston in January," 65

"Floating Post Office, The," 81, 104
fluidity, 204, 212, 216
flux, 169, 203–204
Forbidden Sex/Texts, 29, 69
form(s), 10, 13, 21–22, 27, 44, 54, 56, 61–62, 72, 74, 76, 80–81, 99–102, 105, 109, 114–18, 127, 131, 136–37, 141, 150, 191, 211, 213, 220, 226, 228–29, 238
"For You," 65
"Fourth Day, The," 197
fracture, 78, 91, 167
"Fragments," 125
Frankfurt, 194
free verse, 24–25, 56, 99–101, 131, 165, 220, 229
freedom, 14, 20, 30, 37, 59–60, 73, 107, 147, 179, 185–86, 193, 204
Freud, Sigmund, 212, 217
friendship(s), 11, 45, 56, 101, 113–15, 117, 154, 214, 217
"From Amherst to Kashmir," 20–22, 82–83, 192, 197, 210
"From Another Desert," 12, 153
"From the Start," 65
Frost, 62
fundamentalist, 227
funeral(s), 28

Gabriel, 208
Gamalinda, Eric, 79, 85–86, 238
Ganesh, Chitra, 119
Ganesha, 216
gay (ness), 3, 29, 63, 67–69, 113, 115–16, 119, 136–37
gazelle, 21, 73–75, 82–84, 194, 207–208, 213, 223
generic, 40
genocide, 34, 36–37, 116, 157
geographical, 4, 28, 181, 209–10
geophilosophical, 2, 28, 171

geo-political, 203, 210
German(y), 55, 235
Ghalib, Mirza, 6, 21–22, 55, 62, 65, 68, 93, 95–98, 127, 129, 132, 136, 153, 207–208
Ghalib's Ghazal, 196
gharana, 126
"'Ghat of the Only World, The': Agha Shahid Ali in Brooklyn," 28–30, 69, 87, 114, 159, 217, 238
"Ghazal for Open Hands," 31–32
"Ghazal on Ghazals," 94
ghazal/ghazalified, 6, 13, 21–26, 36, 38, 41, 44, 46–47, 55, 61–65, 67, 72–74, 76, 80, 82–83, 90–97, 99, 101, 105, 107–109, 117, 121–22, 124, 126–28, 130–31, 136, 138–39, 141–42, 173, 175, 188, 193–94, 207–208, 210–11, 219–24, 226–27, 233, 247
"Ghazal," 1, 15, 81, 170, 201, 227
Ghazals of Ghalib, 97, 98
"Ghazal: The Charms of a Considered Disunity," 90, 98
Ghosh, Amitav, 3, 10, 18, 27–28, 52, 56, 82, 87, 106, 114, 120, 154, 159, 174, 178, 179, 181, 184, 186, 209, 211, 214, 215, 217, 241
Gide, 137
Ginsberg, Allen, 213, 217
Ginsberg, Naomi, 192
global, 26, 79, 179, 188
Glossary of Contemporary Literary Theory, A, 216–17
God/god(s), 9, 17, 20, 22, 26, 31, 48, 62, 79, 95, 102, 104, 107, 128, 146–47, 193–98, 200–201, 207–10, 216, 221–23, 228, 231, 236
"God," 196
Goethe, Johann Wolfgang von, 187, 212, 217

Gondwanaland, 215
Goodyear, Sara Suleri, 24, 25, 184–85
Gopinath, Gayatri, 3, 111–20, 245
Granada/Granadian, 188, 202–204, 208–10, 216
grand narratives, 121, 158, 216
grandmother, 1, 8, 15, 51, 55, 128–29, 135, 164, 180
grave(s)/graveyard, 27, 30–32, 41, 54, 122–24, 126–27, 166, 170, 183, 185, 187, 196–97, 206, 232, 245
Greek, 4, 220
grief, 8, 20, 27, 36, 65, 73–74, 76–77, 81–82, 127–28, 150, 178, 188–89, 191–94, 197–98, 200–201, 206–208, 211, 213, 235
guerrilla warfare, 176
Gula, 205–206, 212
Gupkar Road, 231
Gypsies, 202

Hacker, Marlyn, 61, 97
Hafiz of Shiraz: *Thirty Poems*, 97, 98
Halberstam, Jack, 119
Halberstam, Judith, 119
Half-Inch Himalayas, The, 7, 27, 43, 52, 55, 75, 99–100, 113, 127–29, 133, 138–39, 147, 161, 165–67, 237

Hall, Daniel, 48, 56, 63, 66, 69
Hallam, Arthur, 153
Hamilton Alumni Review, 49, 246
Hamilton College, 21, 33, 44–45, 54, 60, 69, 246
"Hans Christian Ostro," 29, 59
"Hansel and Gretel," 55
Hardy, 164
Harrison, James, 24, 73
Hatha Yoga, 222
hauntology, 158
Hawley, John C., 209, 215, 217

Hawthorn, Jeremy, 216
Hazratbal, 174
Heaney, Seamus, 101, 150
Heath-Stubbs, John, 98
"Heaven," 200
Heckt, Anthony, 61
hegemonic, 156, 199
Heideggerian, 153
Hejinian, Lyn, 150
hell, 10, 21, 55, 104, 107, 194, 200, 206
"Hell," 200
Hemphill, 137
hermaphrodites, 122
Herring, Scott, 116, 119
heteroglossic, 102
heterosexuality, 116, 119, 136
Himalmag, 78, 86, 184, 186
Hindi films, 230
Hindu College, 2, 52, 122, 150
Hindu Kush, 78, 115
Hindu Rulers, Muslim Subjects, 30
Hindu, The, 30, 238–39
Hindustani, 126
Hollander, John, 24, 61, 81, 83, 86–87, 94, 98, 226
Hollins Critic, The, 85
H/holocaust, 18, 27, 195, 207, 233, 235
"Homage to Faiz Ahmed Faiz," 127, 136
home(less-lessness), 9, 10, 34, 44–45, 57, 60, 62, 71–72, 74–77, 82–84, 86, 92, 95, 98, 108, 113–14, 124, 127, 134, 141–43, 150–51, 155, 161, 165–70, 179, 181, 188–90, 194–95, 201, 207, 230
homoerotic, 113
homonormative, 111, 116, 118
homophobic, 119
homophone, 137
homosexual(ity), 3, 63, 67, 113, 115, 137

Hope, Lawrence, 95, 98
Hopkins, G(erard). M(anley)., 4, 19–20, 190, 213
hospitality, 3
Hossein, Amzed, 121–32, 245
"Houses," 167
"How can I write above the clouds?," 203
Howe, Stephen, 184, 186
"Howl," 213, 246
Hughes, Ted, 101, 245
human (rights), 12, 25, 47, 71–72, 76, 79–80, 93, 123, 125, 144, 146, 188–90, 192, 199, 202–203, 207, 215–16, 219
hummingbird(s), 77–78, 80
humour, 5, 9, 44, 63–65, 143, 199
Hun, 191
Hussain, Imam, 21, 22, 61, 82, 192–94, 197, 207, 216, 235
hybrid(ity), 99–100, 109, 139, 222–23
hyperreal(ity), 210, 216

"I am one of the kings of the end," 203
"I Go Back to May 1937," 134
"I Dream I Am at the Ghat of the Only World," 23, 29, 56, 76, 84–85, 205, 212
"I Dream I Am the Only Passenger on Flight 423 to Srinagar," 76, 103, 128, 180
"I Dream It Is Afternoon When I Return to Delhi," 138
"I See Kashmir from New Delhi at Midnight," 15–17, 59, 179–80, 182, 190
"I wake and feel the fell of dark not day," 19, 213
"'I will open the waves': Examining the Hybrid Forms in Agha Shahid Ali's Poetry," 99–109

Iblis, 201, 207
iconography, 135
Identity and Violence: The Illusion of Destiny, 215, 218
identity, 3, 14, 27, 60–61, 97, 100, 102, 112, 119, 123, 126, 136, 138, 150–51, 173–74, 176, 181, 191, 203, 209, 215–16, 218
idiom, 7, 9, 10, 27, 58, 62, 67, 118
illusion, 22, 124, 215, 218
image(s)/imagery, 5, 6, 10–11, 13, 16, 20, 58, 61–62, 65–66, 74–75, 96, 101, 103, 106, 107, 123–24, 126, 129, 131, 133–35, 138, 142, 144, 151, 166, 168, 170, 173–74, 176–78, 180–81, 190, 197, 216, 227, 231, 233–34
imaginary homeland, 4, 7, 36
Imam and the Indian, The, 29, 30, 184, 186, 215, 217, 238
impressionism, 188
"In Arabic," 67–68
In Memory of Begum Akhtar & Other Poems, 2, 5, 52, 121, 126, 131, 161, 163, 237
"In Memory of Begum Akhtar," 65, 128
"In Search of Evanescence," 11–12, 34, 53, 76, 78, 115, 117
"In the exodus I love you more," 204
in-betweenness, 211
India(n), 1–2, 6–9, 12–13, 15, 19, 27–30, 33, 35, 44, 46, 52–53, 57–59, 61–62, 65, 67–69, 71, 74, 83, 85, 90, 93, 105, 113, 116, 122, 127–29, 131–32, 134–35, 143, 149–50, 155–56, 158, 161, 170–71, 173–76, 179–86, 189–90, 215, 217, 221–26, 238–39, 241, 243–47
Indian army/Indian security force(s), 15, 29, 30, 57, 176, 181, 183, 189, 190

Indiana, 1–2, 52, 69, 121, 173
Indo-Muslim Cultures in Transitions, 132
insurgency, 13, 18, 101, 175, 178, 182, 190
intercultural, 93, 95, 108
interethnic, 176
international(ism), 4, 16, 46, 58, 60, 79, 160, 178–79, 189, 241, 243–44, 246
interreligious, 176–77
intertextual(ity), 4, 117, 223
Interview with Agha Shahid Ali, An, 29–30, 214, 225–36
Intimate Enemy, The: Loss and Recovery of Self Under Colonialism, 185–86
"Introducing," 163
Iqbal Ali, Agha, 25, 51, 65–66, 68–69
Iqbal, Allama, 177
Ireland, 179, 226
Isaac, 223
Ishmael, 26, 66, 107–108, 223–24, 228
Islam(ic), 4, 6, 16, 20–23, 26, 31, 58, 61, 66, 108, 121, 128–29, 174, 179, 188, 192, 200, 213, 222–24, 235
Islamophobia, 108, 199
Israel, David Raphael, 96
"'It Is This': Agha Shahid Ali's Representation of Kashmir," 13, 173–86
Italian, 33, 61, 64, 83, 198

Jahanara, 130
Jamia Milia Islamia, 225, 245
Jammu, 35, 57, 179
Jay Lifton, Robert, 36
Jehangir, 177
Jenkins, Paul, 93–94
Jerusalem, 193
Jesus, 4, 22, 66, 193, 197, 201, 208, 216

Jew(s)/(ish), 17, 20, 104, 177, 202, 213, 235
Jezebel, 222–23, 227
Jhelum, 23, 79, 113, 205
Job, 108, 223
"Jogger on Riverside Drive, 5:00 A.M., The," 137
Joseph, 23, 214
journey(s), 9, 12, 21–23, 27, 51, 54, 72, 75, 78, 83–85, 116, 119, 121, 125, 130, 134, 144, 153, 180, 194, 196, 204, 206, 212
Joyce, 151, 159
Judaism, 108
Judgment Day, 222
junoon, 222

Ka'aba, 221
Kabir, 27
Kabir, Ananya Jahanara, 184, 186
Kaddish, 192, 213
kairos, 154
Kalapani, 83
Karakoram, 78, 115
Karbala, 20–22, 61, 192–94, 197, 207, 234–35
"Karbala: A History of the 'House of Sorrow,'" 21, 27, 192
Kashghar, 28, 51
Kashmir Crisis: Unholy Anglo-Pak Nexus, 213, 218
Kashmir Monitor, 184, 186
Kashmir, 1–4, 7, 13–23, 27–31, 34–35, 44–46, 51–53, 56–63, 66–67, 74–75, 79–84, 95, 99–107, 109, 112–14, 119–21, 131, 133–35, 138, 141–46, 149–50, 162, 164–66, 173–98, 200, 205–10, 213, 216–18, 221–22, 234–35, 238–39, 245
Kashmir: Roots of Conflict, Paths to Peace, 184, 186

Kashmir: The Case for Freedom, 30, 185–86
Kashmir —The Untold Story, 30
"Kashmiri Song," 95, 98
Katyal, Akhil, 69
Kaul, Suvir, 30, 225–36, 245
Keats, 43, 164–65
"Keeper of the Dead Hotel, The," 12, 54
Khatun, Habba, 14, 234–35
Khusro, 129–30
King Lear, 8, 104, 125
Kipling, Rudyard, 145
Kitano, Christine, 161–70, 246
Kolatkar, 53
Koran, the, 135, 196, 211
Krishna, 4, 66, 193–95, 207–208
Kufa, 194

Lacanian, 212, 247
Lacavaro, Anthony, 45
Laila, 12
Lal, P., 2
lament(s)/(ed)/(ing)/(ation), 7, 17–23, 29, 61, 82, 94, 96, 102, 105, 107, 181, 187–98, 201–14
landscape(s), 5, 53, 71, 74–75, 78–83, 112–18, 135, 138, 151–58, 169, 177, 226
"Language Games," 144
lapidation, 192, 213
"Last Saffron, The," 16, 63, 102–103, 147, 177–78, 180
"Last Saffron, The,: Agha Shahid Ali's Kashmir," 213, 217, 238
"Learning Urdu," 129
"Leaving the City," 137
legend(s)/(ary), 5, 8, 12, 14, 26, 61, 68, 130–31, 181, 188, 194, 200, 202
"Legends of Kashmir," 131
leitmotif, 21, 178, 181

"Lenox Hill," 21, 61, 76, 82, 191–92
Leonard, Karen, 128, 132
Lethe, 153
letter(s), 13–14, 18–20, 27, 46–47, 52–53, 56, 60, 63, 65–69, 80–81, 104–105, 129, 132, 137, 141–42, 145, 168, 176, 179–80, 184, 189–90, 213, 230–32
"'Let Your Mirrored Convexities Multiply: On Agha Shahid Ali's 'Tonight,'" 219–24
liminal(ity), 152, 180, 211
Line of Control, 175, 182
"Listeners, The," 142
Literary Theory: An Introduction, 215, 217
"Little Red Riding Hood," 144
logocentric(ism), 203–204, 209–11, 215
logos(es), 210–11
loneliness, 5, 55, 107, 122–24, 137, 145, 202, 221, 228
"Looking for Shahid," 30, 238
loss(es), 4–8, 12–13, 18, 20, 23, 27, 29, 36, 41, 44, 56, 62, 72, 74–79, 81–85, 95–96, 101, 105, 109, 113, 117, 121, 124, 126, 128, 137–38, 143, 149–55, 170–71, 178, 185–88, 191, 194, 196–98, 201–204, 207–208, 211–12, 219
"Lost Memory of Delhi, A," 7, 134
Lowell, Robert, 62
"Lunerscape," 124
"Lycidas," 127
Lyotard, 216
lyric(s)/(al)/(ism), 5, 12, 24, 35, 94, 101, 114, 118, 128, 131, 137, 148, 198, 202–204, 209–10

MacArthur, Douglas, 183
Mad Woman, 89
Madhubala, 164

Magdalene (Mary), 201
magic realism, 152
Mahapatra, Jayanta, 53
Mahjoor, 164–65
Mai, Xiwen, 155, 159–60, 239
mail(s)/(box)/(man), 7, 60, 75, 77, 99, 113, 134, 141–42, 145, 154, 165–66, 179–80, 231–32
majlis, 82, 193
Majnoon, 12, 153
majoritarian, 199
majuscules, 85
Mandelstam (Osip), 4, 14, 20, 36, 233
Manhattan, 191, 247
map(s)/(ping), 4–5, 11, 18, 22, 35, 75, 77–78, 80, 117, 119, 151, 153–60, 209, 215, 219, 241
"Mapping America, Re-mapping the World: The Cosmopolitanism of Agha Shahid Ali's *A Nostalgist's Map of America*," 159–60, 239
Mare, Walter de la, 142
marsiya, 61, 192, 211
Marx(ist-s), 122, 128, 159–60
Mary, Virgin, 201
matla, 72–73
Matthews (William), 91–93
McCallum (Shara), 89, 97–98
"Medusa," 55
Meena Kumari, 164
Megha Malhar, 127
Mehrotra, A. K., 52, 69, 99, 239
Melville, 223, 230
memory, 5, 7, 9–10, 21, 25, 31, 44–45, 59, 61, 65, 75, 77, 79, 102–103, 106, 108, 113–14, 121, 123, 127–28, 130–31, 134, 136, 139, 141, 149, 151–54, 158, 162, 166–68, 170, 178, 190–91, 193–94, 198, 203–205, 208, 214
"Memory," 21, 194
mentor(s), 10, 19, 101, 113, 115
menus, 100
Merchant (Hoshang), 3, 29, 63, 67–69
Merrill, James, 4, 10, 19, 23–24, 40, 46–47, 52, 56–57, 84–85, 101, 113, 205–206, 208, 212, 214, 217
metanarratives, 216
metaphor(s)/(ic)/(ical)/(ically), 8–9, 13, 20, 58, 62, 77, 79, 95, 102, 151, 168, 180, 216, 221, 233
metaphysics/metaphysical, 236
metonym(ic), 134, 190
metronormative/metronormativity, 112, 116, 119
micronarratives, 121, 124–25, 130–31, 216
Middle East Report, 71, 85
migration, 119, 134, 204
Mihiragula, 82, 191, 210
militant(s), 17, 19, 27, 59, 68, 104, 182–83, 189
Milton(ic), 127, 178
mininarratives, 216
Ministry of Utmost Happiness, The, 30
Mir, 6, 65, 68, 93, 96, 127, 129, 136
mirror(s/ed/ing), 12, 65, 72, 81, 106–107, 126, 138, 144, 157, 165, 180–81, 199–200, 219, 221–22
Moby-Dick, 26, 223–24, 228
Modern Indian Poetry in English, 29, 85, 132, 239
modern(ity)/(ism)/(ist-s), 5, 27, 55, 94, 105, 108, 111, 121, 128, 131, 134, 142–43, 149–51, 156, 158, 188, 200, 224, 246–47
Modernism at the Microphone: Radio, Propaganda and Literary Aesthetics during World War II, 144, 148
Mohommad, Ghulam, 205, 207–208, 212
Monette, 137
monolithic, 156, 223
monostitch, 102

"Monsoon Note on Old Age, A," 135
Moraes, Dom, 53
mosque, 6, 13, 17, 55, 65, 82, 103, 128, 130, 135
mother, 1, 3, 6–9, 20–24, 36, 38, 41, 45, 55–56, 61–63, 66–67, 72, 74–75, 81–84, 105, 128, 135, 138, 150, 166–67, 174, 181, 183, 188–202, 205–209, 211–12, 228
motherland, 105, 188, 202, 211
motif(s), 12, 18, 21, 62, 93–94, 176, 178, 181, 227, 231
mourn(s)/(ed)/(ing)/(ful)/(er-s), 5, 16, 21–24, 27, 29, 61, 82, 93, 123, 127, 137, 150–51, 155, 158, 162–63, 187–88, 191–93, 196–99, 201, 203–204, 207–16, 234
"Mourning and Melancholia," 212, 217
"Mouwashah," 202
muezzin, 6, 19, 208
Mughal(s)/Mughul(s), 5–6, 8, 14, 65, 130, 177, 221–22
Mughal-e-Azam, 65
Muhammad, 130, 193, 221
Muhammad Shah II, 130
"Muharram in Srinagar, 1992," 233
Muharram/Mohorrum/Moharram, 5, 21, 123, 162, 194, 235
Muldoon, Paul, 97
multicultural(ist), 9, 26, 67, 150, 199, 202, 208
multiethnic, 9
multiplicity/multiplicities, 105, 167, 198, 208, 223
Muñoz, José Esteban, 117, 119–20
music(al)/(ian-s), 3, 27, 29, 34, 44, 126–28, 130, 142, 182, 208, 212, 221–22, 246
Muslim(s), 1, 3–4, 13–14, 17, 19–20, 22–23, 28–29, 37, 44, 51, 58, 62, 66, 104, 128, 130, 135, 164, 173–77, 179, 181, 189–90, 199, 202–203, 207, 210, 216, 226, 228, 237, 244–45
mystic(s)/(al), 92, 94, 96, 130, 222
myth(s)/(ic-al)/(ology)/(ologies)/ (ological)/(ologize-s), 4, 5, 10–12, 35–36, 54–55, 78, 115, 134, 166, 169, 174–75, 177, 188, 191–92, 200, 202–203, 208, 216, 228

Nadir Shah, 6, 130
Nandy, Ashis, 181, 185–86
narrative(s) structure(s), 5, 9, 10–11, 13–14, 18, 20, 61, 72, 75, 90, 94, 112, 121, 123, 135, 158, 169, 178, 188, 190, 205
nation(s)/(al-ist-s)/(ality)/(alism-s), 2, 9, 23, 27, 59, 69, 107, 111–13, 116–18, 121, 130, 150–51, 154, 158, 170, 173, 175, 179, 181, 183, 199, 202, 209, 215, 236, 241, 243
nature, 53, 77–78, 117, 127, 149, 164, 181, 220, 223, 233
"Nature of Temporal Order, The," 201
Nazi, 10, 55
Nehru, Jawaharlal, 176
neomythic, 228
Neruda, Pablo, 216–17, 235
Neruda, Walcott and Atwood: Poets of the Americas, 216–17
"New Delhi Airport," 195
New York (City), 2, 33, 36–37, 44, 49, 53–54, 57, 59, 69, 74, 80, 85–86, 97–98, 112, 116, 119, 159–60, 168, 171, 174, 185, 212–14, 217, 219, 236–37, 244–46
New York Times Sunday Magazine, 80, 86
Newman, Amy, 71–86, 213, 217, 246
Newman, Will, 47
Nietzsche, 22
Nolan, Maureen, 43–48, 246

Noori, Fatima, 51–68, 246
Nooruddin Wali, Sheikh, 13
"Nostalgist's Map of America, A," 11, 77, 117
Nostalgist's Map of America, A, 10, 27, 43, 53–54, 56, 72, 75–76, 79, 100, 115–16, 150–51, 153, 155, 158–61, 168, 225, 237, 239
"Note Autobiographical–1," 128
"Note Autobiographical–2," 128
"Notes for the Unabandoned Stranger," 123, 126
Novus, Angelus, 151

objective/objectivity, 19, 24, 62, 76, 166, 199, 205
"Of it All," 63
"O water, be a string to my guitar," 203
O'Keeffe, Georgia, 12, 79
O'Neill, Patricia, 43–47, 61, 66, 69
"On our last evening on this land," 202
ontological, 5, 158, 210
ode(s), 20, 23, 164
oeuvre, 29, 72, 76, 143
Of Gardens and Graves: Kashmir, Poetry, Politics, 30, 245
Ohio, 11–12, 35, 115, 155–56, 225, 246
Old, Sharon, 134
"One day I will sit on the pavement," 203
Orient(al-ist), 3, 34, 145, 174
"Oriental Rug, The," 34
Orientalizing America: Beginning and Middle Passages, 85
originary, 210
Orlando, Philip Paul/Phil, 115, 151
Orpheus, 10
"Out of Focus: Agha Shahid Ali's Queer Optics," 111–20

Oxford India Anthology of Modern Urdu Literature, The: Poetry and Prose Miscellany, 132
Oxford India Ghalib, The: Life, Letters and Ghazals, 132

paisley(s), 16, 19, 37, 99, 178
Pakeezah, 230
Pakhtun, 175
Pakistan(i), 19–20, 34–35, 44, 57, 74, 76, 80, 106, 113, 129, 134, 170, 174–75, 177, 180, 182–83, 190, 247
Palestine, 16, 23, 27, 60, 100, 178, 188, 209
palimpsestic(ally), 117–18
Pandit(s), 14, 17, 29, 57, 175–76, 189
pantoum(s), 74, 76, 80, 233
Paradise Lost, 178
paradise, 14–16, 18, 21, 59, 72, 75, 79, 80–82, 84–85, 101, 103–104, 176–78, 181–82, 190, 194, 203, 221, 230, 238, 246
paradoxical(ities), 208–10
partition(s/ed), 6, 9, 71, 128–29, 134, 149, 175, 179, 209, 215, 243, 245
Paschen, Elyse, 34, 97
past(s), 5, 7, 12, 20, 22, 34, 74–76, 106–107, 111, 114, 120, 123–24, 131, 135, 149, 151–53, 155–59, 168–71, 181, 192–94, 197–98, 204, 207, 210, 226, 229
pastoral, 13
"Pastoral, A," 16, 18, 95, 232
Pather Panchali, 6
Peer, Basharat, 30, 182–83, 185–86
Pennsylvania State University, 2, 52, 174
Perfume, 146, 148
Persian, 1, 6, 24, 35–36, 38, 61, 67, 74, 89, 92–94, 97–98, 105, 107–109, 170, 224

Petersburg, 14, 36, 233
Philadelphia, 11, 155, 171
"Philadelphia, 2:00 A.M.," 137
phoenix, 181
Picture of Dorian Gray, The, 8
Pinksy, Robert, 36
Pir Panjal Range/Pass, 191, 193, 207
Plath, Sylvia, 28, 62, 207, 245
Plato, 135
pluralistic, 202
"Poem Guide: Agha Shahid Ali's 'Tonight,'" 224
"Poems Are Never Finished," 85–86
Poets and Writers, 79, 85, 247
"Poets on Bathroom Walls," 10, 63, 148
Poet's Work, Poet's Play, 162, 164, 171
polyglot, 224
polyphonic, 208
polysemic, 109
post office(s), 18–19, 27, 60, 75, 81, 141–42, 179–80, 184, 231–32
"Postcard from Kashmir," 7, 75, 77, 113–14, 133, 165–66
postcard(s), 7, 65, 75, 77, 80, 114, 133–34, 141, 166
Postcolonial Poetry in English, 109
Postcolonial Studies, 82, 87, 120, 245–46
postcolonial, 2, 65, 71, 99, 100, 105, 108–109, 113, 120, 150, 243, 245
postmodern(ist-s/ity), 27, 67, 123, 166, 200, 208, 210, 216, 219, 221, 224
post-structuralist, 208
"Prayer Rug," 55
prayer(s), 6, 19–20, 22–23, 31–32, 37, 48, 96, 124–25, 129–30, 135, 196, 198, 210–11, 213, 223
present, 8, 12, 20, 22, 57, 74, 77, 80, 106–107, 114, 147, 168–69, 171, 178, 192–93, 196–97, 208, 221, 224
Presley, Elvis, 164

"Previous Occupant, The," 136–37
proem, 133, 135
prophetic(ally), 35, 215
prosody, 25, 136
Provincializing Europe: Postcolonial Thought and Historical Difference, 159–60
psychoanalysis, 181, 212, 217, 247
pun, 92, 108, 137
"Purse-Seiner Atlantis, The," 22, 201, 209

"Qawwali at Nizamuddin Aulia's Dargah," 6, 130–31
quasida, 20, 211
"Quasida," 202
quatrain(s), 13, 16, 80, 95, 103, 130, 136
"Queer Disorientations, States of Suspension," 118
queer(ness/dom), 3, 111–20, 137, 245–47
Quraishi, Humra, 30
Quran(ic), The, 23, 66, 189, 202, 208, 223

racial, 111, 116
Radha, 193–95, 207–208, 216
radif, 72–73, 76, 90, 105, 121
"Radio Kashmir," 138
radio(s), 89, 141–42, 145, 190, 230
"Raga Jogia," 21, 193
raga(s), 21, 62, 82, 100, 127, 193
Rai, Mridu, 30
R/rajam, 192, 213
Ramanujan, A. K., 53
Ramazani, Jahan, 105, 108–109, 149–50, 159–60
Rauscher, Judith, 157, 159
Ravishing DisUnities: Real Ghazals in English, 25, 36, 69, 73, 85, 89, 91, 98, 131, 184–85, 237, 247

Ray, Satyajit, 6
Read My Mind: Young Children, Poetry and Learning, 214, 217
Reader's Guide to Contemporary Literary Theory, A, 216–17
reality, 9, 12, 22, 94, 114, 122, 134, 162, 166, 188–89, 206, 210, 212, 214, 236
Rebel's Silhouette, The (:Selected Poems by Faiz Ahmed Faiz), 2, 7, 12, 15, 21, 24, 57, 61–62, 69, 73, 85–86, 237
Reconquista, 203
redundancy, 144
Reflections on Exile, 72, 85, 87
refrain, 18, 25, 64, 72–73, 94, 105, 121, 153, 220, 227
"Rehearsal of Loss, A," 11
relationality, 112, 115, 117–18
renaissance, 72
repression, 18, 178, 190
Resisting Occupation in Kashmir, 30
"Resume," 55
re-territorialization, 2, 158
"Return to Harmony," 59
return(s/ed), 2, 14–16, 18–19, 21, 33–34, 52, 56, 59, 73, 75–76, 79, 81, 113–14, 125, 134, 137–38, 153, 166–68, 170, 174, 176, 178, 194, 196, 204–205, 211, 224, 232–34
rhyming couplets, 13
Rhyme's Reason, 86–87, 98
Rich, Adrienne, 24, 62, 73
"Riots, Rumours, and Relics: Amitav Ghosh's *The Shadow Lines*" 184, 186
Rizwan, 15–16, 141, 176, 180–82, 190, 230
R/romantic(s), 25, 124, 151, 163–65
"Rooms Are Never Finished," 22, 83
Rooms Are Never Finished, 4, 13, 15, 20–22, 24, 27, 29, 45, 61, 64, 72, 75–76, 81, 105, 187–89, 191, 198–99, 202, 205, 207–208, 210–13, 216, 237
root(s)/(ed)/(less)/(lessness), 2, 4, 22, 59, 61–62, 74–75, 82, 92, 122, 150, 156, 161–62, 184, 186, 188, 191, 201, 209, 226
Rose, Jacqueline, 120
Rosenbergs, 80
"Route of Evanescence, A," 11, 76
Roy, Arundhati, 30, 241
Rumi, 27
Rushdie (Salman), 46, 53, 182, 185–86, 244
Russian, 14, 233

Sabra-Shatila, 27, 188, 209
saffron, 16, 26, 63, 102, 107, 178, 180, 191, 222, 228
Said, Edward, 46, 60, 69, 72, 83, 85
Saigal, K. L., 6, 128
salvation, 48, 72, 200
Samarkand, 28, 51
San Francisco, 116, 119
Santiago, 79
Sarajevo, 16–17, 27, 180, 188, 209
Satan, 48, 200–201, 207–208, 216
Scattering of Salts, A, 205, 214, 217
Schneiderman, Jason A., 133–38, 211, 214, 217, 246
scholarship, 45, 71, 77, 112–13, 119, 150
scripture(s), 188, 195, 223–24
"Secular Comedy, A," 22, 200
Selden, Raman, 216–17
self-reflexivity, 103
Sen, Amartya, 209, 215, 218
Sen, Deeptesh, 149–60, 247
Sengupta, Sagaree, 89–98, 247
Sen, Suchitra, 164

"'Separation's Geography': Agha Shahid Ali's Scholarship of Evanescence," 71–87
sestets, 13
sestina(s), 10, 13, 25, 56, 73–74, 80–81, 99, 101, 104–105, 211
sex(ual-ity/ities), 3, 63, 67–68, 111–14, 136–37, 209, 245
Shadow Lines, The, 109, 174, 181, 184, 186, 215, 217
Shah, Nadir, 6, 130
Shahid, 1–10, 12–30, 32–41, 43–47, 51–57, 59–69, 71–86, 89–91, 93, 95–96, 99–109, 112–20, 122, 127–29, 131, 133–39, 141–47, 149–56, 158, 161–71, 173–74, 176–84, 188–201, 204–14, 216, 219–24, 228–30
"Shahid: Some Memories," 33–38
Shahjahan, 130
Shaivite, 222
Shakespeare(an) (William), 8, 122, 152, 159, 164, 182, 246
Shalimar Gardens, 177
Shalimar the Clown, 182, 185–86
Shammas (Anton), 80, 86, 108
Shamsie, Kamila, 44
Shankar, Lavina Dhingra, 119
Shelley, 43, 52, 163–65, 244
Shia, 1, 51, 62, 173
shikwa, 22, 196, 211
signifier(s), 128, 137, 199
Sikoh, Dara, 222
"Silk Road," 37
simulacrum/simulacra, 7, 210, 216
Singh, Hari, 175, 177
Smith, Bruce, 35
Smith, Patricia, 89
"Snow on the Desert," 12–13, 47, 79, 168, 170
"Snowmen," 8, 28, 51, 55

"Somewhere without Me My Life Begins," 39–41
"Some Vision of the World Cashmere," 15, 147, 180
"Son et Lumière at Shalimar Garden," 235
sonnet(s), 21, 25, 73, 134, 150, 159, 190, 213
Sonoran, 11
"Sorrow," 89, 98
"Sound of Silence, The," 146
South Asia(n), 28, 89, 93–94, 96–97, 116, 119, 149, 155, 171, 178, 183, 222, 224, 244–47
space(s), 22, 29, 63, 75, 83, 102, 106, 111–12, 114–15, 117–19, 123–24, 128, 130, 136, 151–52, 154–55, 167–71, 180, 185–86, 196, 199, 204, 220, 222, 229, 234, 243
Spain, 20, 23, 202
specif, 192, 213
Spectres of Marx: The State of Debt, the Work of Mourning & the New International, 160
Spielberg, Steven, 233
spiritual vision, 200
Srikanth, Rajini, 119, 170–71
"Srinagar Airport," 195
Srinagar, 1–3, 7, 14–17, 20, 29, 36, 52, 59, 76, 103, 124, 128, 173, 175–77, 180, 182, 195, 231–33, 235
Stanley Taylor, Jamie, 3, 53
"Stationery," 55, 137
Stein, Gertrude, 150
Steiner, George, 71
"Story of a Silence," 56, 135
"Story of Saffron, A," 184, 186
Structuralist, 216
Styron, Rose, 36
subaltern, 129

subnational, 111, 116
Sufi(s)/(ism), 27, 30, 174, 188, 222
"Summers of Translation," 21–22, 193
Sundararajan, Saroja, 213, 218
supernarratives, 216
supranational, 111, 116
surreal(ism/ist-ic), 5, 10, 59, 123, 125–26, 138, 166–68, 188
"Survivor," 138, 166–68
symbol(s)/(lic)/(ism), 6, 26, 178, 188, 204, 212–13
Synagogue, 213
syncretic/syncretism, 103, 108, 174, 221–22
synecdochal, 16, 199

T. S. Eliot as Editor, 2, 52, 237
Tacitus, 179
Tate, James, 40–41
Tate, Jim, 34
technique(s), 7, 14, 150, 188
telegrams, 142
telephone(s), 46, 64, 75, 77, 141–47, 180
television(s), 142–43, 145, 190, 230
temperament, 28, 65, 67, 128
temple(s), 4, 17, 26, 55, 65–66, 103, 107, 122, 195, 210, 222, 228
Tennyson, 153
tercets, 56, 103, 136
"terrible sonnets," 19, 190
territorialize/territorialization, 108, 158
terrorist(s), 14, 48, 176, 190, 199
terza rima(s), 13–14, 22, 74, 76, 80, 84–85, 101, 104, 190, 211
Thanatos, 147
Tharoor, Shashi, 182, 185–86, 241
"The Greatest Sorrow: Times of Joy Recalled in Wretchedness," 18, 30, 178, 184, 186, 238
"The Lives They Lived: Looking for Some Place to Call Home," 86

" 'The Loved One Always Leaves': The Poetic Friendship of Agha Shahid Ali and James Merrill," 214, 217
The Practice of Poetry: Writing Exercises from Poets Who Teach, 90, 98
"The Refrains of Kashmir: Agha Shahid Ali's Canzones and the Forms of Exile," 105, 109
"There is a sky beyond the sky for me," 23, 203
"Theses on the Philosophy of History," 151, 159–60
"Things," 63
thumri(s), 6, 9, 126
Till I End My Song: A Gathering of Last Poems, 62, 69
T/time(s), 4, 6, 7, 12–14, 18–20, 22, 25, 34, 36–37, 39–41, 45, 47–48, 53–54, 57, 59, 64, 66, 73, 75–76, 78–81, 91, 96–97, 107, 114–15, 118, 123, 125–27, 130–31, 136, 138–39, 142–44, 147, 150–55, 157, 159, 163, 169–71, 176–78, 180–81, 184, 189, 193–94, 197, 200, 202–207, 214, 220, 227, 229
"To Autumn," 165
"Tonight," 25, 55, 65, 95, 219–21, 224
trace(s), 11, 93, 118, 121, 131, 133, 152–53, 156, 158, 208–209
"Tradition, Home, and Exile in Agha Shahid Ali's *The Beloved Witness*," 161–71
T/tragedy, 8, 12, 16, 22, 80, 129, 136, 212, 217, 239
transcultural, 4, 22, 151
Transethnic, 159
transgeographic, 4
T/translation(s), 2, 21, 57, 61, 69, 89, 97, 147, 202, 222, 243, 247
Transnational Poetics, A, 109, 159–60

transnational(ist)/(ism), 22, 27, 105, 109, 150, 158, 160, 173, 199, 208–209, 219, 245
trauma(tic)/traumatizing, 107, 113, 188, 191, 201–202
trochaic, 220
trope(s), 9, 18, 61, 75, 120, 136–37, 166, 178, 181
"Truth has two faces and the snow is black," 203
T/truth(s), 47, 77, 93–94, 123–24, 145, 153, 163, 207, 210, 230
Tucson, 79, 148, 169, 237, 244
Turkish, 36
Twichell (Chase), 90, 97–98
Twyker, Tom, 146, 148

Ulysses, 151, 159
University of Arizona, 2, 52, 133
Unruly Visions: the Aesthetic Practices of Queer Diaspora, 111, 118–19, 245
Urdu, 1–3, 6–7, 22, 24, 27, 35, 38, 56–57, 61–62, 65, 67–69, 90, 92–97, 105, 107–108, 117, 122, 128–30, 132, 164–65, 182, 192, 219–20, 227, 247
USA, 146
U/utopia(n), 18, 59, 117, 119, 178, 245
Uzbek, 28, 51

"Vacating an Apartment," 9, 136–37, 147
Valery, Paul, 214
Veiled Suite, The (:Collected Poems), 49, 56, 62, 69, 86–87, 98, 109, 127, 131, 189, 217, 220, 237, 238
"Veiled Suite, The," 45, 61, 65
ventriloquistic, 208
Verdenal, Jean, 153
vers-libre, 165
Vietnam, 165

villanelle(s), 13, 74, 76, 80, 99, 141, 220, 228
"Villanelle, A," 16, 59
violence, 3, 37, 44, 76, 101, 104, 106–107, 116, 129, 136, 155, 157, 166, 175–78, 180, 182, 191, 200, 209, 213, 222, 233
"Violins," 204
violins, 207–208, 216
vocal music, 126

Wadsworth, Bill, 34
wahabi, 224
Waheed (Mirza), 30, 182–86
Walcott (Derek), 179, 209, 215–17
Walk Through the Yellow Pages, A, 7, 9, 75, 100, 143–46, 148, 161, 237
"Walled City, The: 7 Poems on Delhi," 130
Waste Land, The, 5, 153, 162–63, 165, 171
West(ern), 17, 24, 27, 39, 57–58, 60, 62, 121, 133–34, 138, 162–64, 170, 174, 178, 224, 226, 241, 243–44
"What The Brook Saw: A Need for Pathetic Fallacy," 185–86
White House, 147
Whitman(esque), 62, 222
"Who am I after the night of the estranged?," 203
Wideman, John Edgar, 97
Wier, Dara, 34, 39–40, 247
Wilde, Oscar, 8
Wilner, Eleanor, 96
"Wireless," 145
"Wolf's Postscript," 55
"Wolf's Postscript to Little Red Riding Hood, The," 148
World Next Door, The: South Asian American Literature and the Idea of America, 171

worldview, 4, 17, 202, 209
World War I, 162, 165
World War II, 144, 148, 213
Wrestling with the Angel, 68
Writer's Almanac, The, 89, 98
Writers Workshop, 2, 5, 52, 121, 131, 237, 244

Xinjiang, 28, 51

Yarana: *Gay Writing from India*, 68

Yeats (W. B.), 4–5, 79, 101, 107, 179, 184, 186
"You," 125
Yusuf, 214

Zafar Ahmad, Hena, 25
Zafar, Bahadur Shah, 8
Zainab, 21–22, 82, 193–95, 201, 207–208, 216
"Zainab's Lament in Damuscus," 21
Zero Bridge, 16, 231

www.ingramcontent.com/pod-product-compliance
Lightning Source LLC
Chambersburg PA
CBHW020642230426
43665CB00008B/279